SERVICES
AND
CIRCUSES

SERVICES AND CIRCUSES

Community and the Welfare State

by Frédéric Lesemann

Translated by Lorne Huston and Margaret Heap

BLACK ROSE BOOKS

Montréal

Black Rose Books No. M81
Hardcover ISBN 0-920057-06-3
Paperback ISBN 0-920057-05-5

Canadian Cataloguing in Publication Data

Lesemann, Frédéric, 1942-
    Services and Circuses

Translation of: Du Pain et des services
Includes bibliographical references

ISBN 0-920057-06-3 (bound).   ISBN 0-920057-05-5 (pbk.).

1. Public welfare administration — Québec (Province).
2. Health services administration — Québec (Province).
3. Québec (Province) — Social policy.
I. Title.

RA395.CL47   1984   361'.9714   C84-090090-2

Cover design: J.W. Stewart

BLACK ROSE BOOKS
3981 boul. St-Laurent
Montréal, Québec H2W 1Y5

Printed and bound in Québec, Canada

Table of Contents

Foreword

Increasingly more and more people come into contact, on a daily basis, with welfare state organizations. Whether it be hospitals, schools, services for the elderly, income or jobs providing these services, it is difficult to escape the grasp of these state institutions. The welfare state, a creature of advanced capitalism, grew out of the struggles of the working class and of women of all classes for a better way of life.

The services produced *appear* to have two sides. They seem to meet certain needs that cannot be met through unbridled market capitalism; yet in form and content they are integrated into the social relations of bureaucratic capitalism. Further, welfare state programmes are experienced as alienating for those who work in them, and for those who are on their receiving end. Services are planned from the top of monstrous bureaucracies extending their tentacles of control into all aspects of daily life. The "human face" of the state with a momentum of its own is governed by the logic of centralization and the same bureaucratic relations of modern industry.

Frédéric Lesemann's study of the social and health services in Québec provides an insightful discussion of the debates and ideologies surrounding their development. Out of the turbulence of the 1960's, and the so-called "Quiet Revolution," quickly emerged a series of reform efforts designed to build a modern state apparatus. Social and health service reform was a major plank. Claude Castonguay provided the leadership, as a principal author of a report on these services. Then, as minister of social affairs, he launched and piloted one of the most comprehensive reforms of health and social services ever witnessed in North America. This book analyzes the underlying ideologies, conflicts, and power relations implicit in these reforms. Lesemann focuses on the rise of a "new middle class" who took over these services from traditional elements linked to the Church, while within this new class, a number committed to centralizing power and using "modern" methods of technocratic planning took control. Social and health services planning and implementation quickly came into the hands of a relatively small group of technocratic planners usurping any power both from those who were responsible for providing services and from those receiving them. The rapidity of this change, and related debates, provide an excellent example of the dynamics of state power, the process of social reform and how welfare state development occurs.

The strength of this volume is not only in its rich detail that addresses these issues, but its implicit attack on the assumptions of social democratic or "progressive" welfare state reform. These reforms had two major goals: 1) to assure universal access to health and social services, and 2) to rationally plan their distribution. Although mouthing a commitment to decentralization and some local control, centralization was the reality. The promises to attack social problems such as poverty and ill health were quickly abandoned as it became clear that the underpinning forms of domination that keep people sick and poor could not be eradicated by traditional services delivered through larger, more rational institutions. The social democratic hope clearly implied a centralization of resources in the hands of technocrats, who would plan and administer the welfare state for "the people." But, as Lesemann shows, administering services *for* the people implies a clearly defined relation of power and control *over* the people. The new administrative stratum developed its own interest and power base, as it marched off to "solve" unsolvable social contradictions by integrating and moulding the poor, the underclass, women and deviants into productive, efficient workers and consumers. Lesemann's book presents a critique not only of the end product—the welfare state—but more importantly, the new technocratic machine and its managers that emerged in this period. The Québec reforms show that these methods do not unlock social progress, but rather, impose new cages, as the state, in the name of equality and reform, imprisons more and more aspects of daily life with these new solutions.

From the 1960's, welfare state services grew rapidly in Québec and elsewhere. The economic assumptions underlying this growth were that economic prosperity would continue, and if necessary through the state's manipulation of expenditures, debt, and interest rates. With the present economic recession, the expansion of these state activities has been stopped and cut back. We are not, however, witnessing the disappearance of the welfare state. In Québec, the services have been cut, but more important is the tightening of bureaucratic control for both employees and recipients. The period can be described as a "restructuring" of state welfare. If services are understood as a relationship between the working class and women on one side, and the market and the state on the other side, then this relationship has been redefined in the process. For example, the discipline imposed on the unemployed, women, and youth has been increased. The humane face of welfare provision has been clouded as bureaucracies tighten their hold. Social work services are increasingly tied to legal definition. Welfare recipients are subject to greater scrutiny by a larger army of inspectors. These changes or reduced expenditures, and tighter control, would be made more difficult if large-scale bureaucratic organization and managerial systems were not in place.

By exploring the management of changing social relations through welfare services, Lesemann's book increases our understanding. He describes the technocratic approach as a process that cannot be separated from the services themselves. In the case of Québec, the social processes leading to the bureaucratization of services and the concentration of power in the ministry of social affairs were dramatic. Social life, particularly of those most dependent on state social services,

11

became increasingly defined by these changes. The present period of redefinition of services has subjected the most powerless members of society to increasing control of their daily activities. Those employed in the agencies have lost control of their own labour processes as managerial control is tightened along with cutbacks. In the process of secularization and increased governmental control described by Lesemann, two strata of the new middle class emerge: that of the liberal professional and of the technocratic. This new class usurped control of welfare services from the Church; the liberal professionals valued professional autonomy and control of the services on a regional basis; the technocrats wanted the centralization of planning of services and control by "modern" economic management. The latter group won out in this debate, giving us the present centralized services.

This aspect of the study should be of interest outside Québec, because its critique encompasses the whole scientific-technocratic approach to the planning and management of social services. The outcome in Québec was not automatic but was a complex debate on how to manage the social relations of advanced capitalism without interfering with the basic processes of capital accumulation. Although the technocratic approach and its centralization further consolidated by the Parti Québécois is more developed in Québec, with its "modern" and scientific methods of control, than in other provinces, this study is instructive to everyone who works directly in the state and should be understood in order to resist forms of social domination.

Recent left critiques of the welfare state [1] have clarified the nature of state social services, the relation of these services to market capitalism, the limits of social reform, and the forms of power, particularly class and patriarchal power, implicit in these services. Lesemann's work makes an important contribution to that discussion, particularly in its critique of technocratic power and its study of social processes. At the same time, Lesemann's analysis falls short. His theory of the state is not developed systematically or consistently. Sometimes he describes the state as "functionalist," meaning that it safeguards continuing economic development by establishing certain institutions that are necessary to manage social

12

relations. In this study, as Québec became more industrialized, and tied into advanced monopoly capitalism, it required more social welfare and health services in order to meet changing social conditions. State services replaced the more traditional parish structure to meet problems like poor health of workers, poverty in society, and the negative consequences of urbanization. The left variant[2] of this argument is that these services play two functions in society. They legitimate class rule and they are necessary for the physical reproduction of workers. This highly deterministic argument tends to be ahistorical in the sense that the struggles of the working class, the unemployed, and women do not play a role in the outcome.

At other times, however, Lesemann is less deterministic. Although his description acknowledges a general drift toward the technocratic in almost all societies, he maintains that the debate does not have a predetermined outcome. He neglects, however, to complete his analysis of the social forces that determine the development of certain institutions with a detailed historical examination of the period in which the reforms take place. Although the debates within the middle stratum of Québec society are addressed in the book, social forces such as the roles of the traditional and international bourgeoisie and the struggles of the working class in their workplaces and their neighbourhoods are not developed as important factors. The processes of class role limited the kind and the extent of services made available, while the struggles of the working class to protect their standard of living pushed those limits.

During the 1960's and 1970's, many broadly based social struggles emerged in Québec[3] which had an important impact on health and social services. Rapid unionization and militancy in the public sector was accompanied by a leftward shift in the trade union movement. In neighbourhoods, citizens' committees, organized welfare rights groups, and popular clinics challenged traditional definitions of health and medical control of services. Other neighbourhood activities included the establishment of day care centres, coops, and new radical political groupings. Strong pressures from below raised demands for basic social change which challenged assumptions

13

of capitalist society. Lesemann shows us that the new social and health services were not neutral products of a bureaucracy, but instead established a visible governmental presence in neighbourhoods, imposing new forms of control on everyday life. For example, several local community health and social service centres (CLSCs) grew out of popularly controlled community clinics, at times coopting onto their boards token representation of that community. These institutions imposed a curative and individualistic preventive medical model rather than one that defined health and illness in their wider political, economic and social contexts, which challenged dominant assumptions. CLSCs imposed a traditional division of labour, eliminating more radical forms of collective control and sharing of tasks. Not all CLSCs came out of these counter-organizations, but in many districts this transformation profoundly demobilized the more radical elements of the popular movement. As Stephen Yeo points out in another context, this process of the state taking over locally controlled institutions is a process of deskilling the working class. [4]

The debates within the middle stratum took place in a context of social unrest and popular struggles, as this stratum searched for a strategy to maintain social order most effectively. Lesemann contributes to our understanding of how such strategies of domination take shape and are implemented. The establishment of social services represents one response of the state to the activity of the working class, the poor, and women. In Québec, during this period, it was complemented by the implementation of the War Measures Act as direct repression, and by the cooptive effect of numerous provincial and federal grants. Reform in capitalism needs to be situated within the dynamic of social struggles, and the response by the ruling authorities to these struggles. Lesemann's discussion of the development of the social and health services shows how that debate took place within a period of social tension.

During the period analyzed in this book, a new middle stratum became increasingly influential in defining the Québec welfare state. This group, or as Lesemann refers to them—the new petite-bourgeoisie—took control of social welfare institutions away from the traditional petite-bourgeoisie allied to Church structures. His analysis is important because it deals

14

with the ideologies and relations established by both these groups. However, several theoretical questions should be raised in order to broaden the discussion. How do these groups emerge? What are their class interests? Do they possess an internal unity of class interest? What is their relationship to the traditional ruling class and to the working class?[5] Lesemann assumes that this new petite-bourgeoisie constitutes a class with an independent class interest, but he does not explore his assumptions. Class is viewed as a *position* in the social structure, rather than as relations that are formed and reconstituted through an historical process and specific conflicts. As E.P. Thompson points out:

> "By class I understand an historical phenomenon, unifying a number of disparate and seemingly unconnected events, both in the raw material of experience and in consciousness....I do not see class as a 'structure,' nor even as a 'category,' but as something which in fact happens... in human relationships.
>
> ...we cannot understand class unless we see it as a social and cultural formation arising from processes which can only be studied as they work themselves out over a considerable historical period."[6]

The historical period of this study is one in which class relations in Québec were redefined. As the state began to play an active role in channelling protest and discontent into its bureaucracies, the rising petite-bourgeoisie played an important role. They tried to shape the ideologies of the working class, promising that state initiated reforms would provide concrete solutions to social inequalities and that workers would have some say in their management. Similar strategies were employed in labour relations in an attempt—only partly successful—to defuse and to demobilize class conflict. This role of the new petite-bourgeoisie and the reforms it implemented provided a new definition of class rule. This process, in which human agency forms initiatives "from below," is an active one. It is a process of reaction, conflict, proposals, and counter-proposals in which the inevitable social antagonisms are played out. During this period, the state, using "progressive" social programmes, was able to redefine the demands and struggles of neighbourhood groups and trade unions, drawing these groups increasingly into state structures and bureaucratic relations. The new petite-bourgeoisie, as described by Lesemann, played a key role in this process, drawing support from the more moderate community leaders, often using nationalist rhetoric presenting the state as the people. As this middle stratum consolidated its power base it began to share a common interest and perspective on managing the affairs of others through the state. This process is not new, as one early British reformer stated in 1910:

"We have got to be better capitalists than the capitalists are. When we—that is, the administrative classes—have more will, more relentlessness, more austerity, more organizing ability, more class consciousness than they (the employees) have, we shall crumple them in our hands... from day to day my dream shall be of a new model army, of vigilant administrators supplanting property inch by inch, steadily and slowly—with a jovial carouse to loosen the muscles now and again."[7]

The actions of the technocrats in Québec led to their taking over a newly created bureaucratic structure, consolidating their power base in it, and using the programme of social reform to legitimate themselves.

Bureaucratizing social relations created conditions in which new struggles emerged, redefining class relations. The role played by social workers provides a good example of this redefinition,[8] showing again that class formation and definition are active social processes. Social workers, with the reforms, were employed directly in state bureaucracies, which cost them their job autonomy characteristic of university trained professionals. Work loads, job descriptions, interventions became increasingly defined from the top. Social workers, mainly women, execute the orders and policies of state managers, usually men. Their job description became "deskilled" as tasks were more narrowly defined, specified, subdivided, and as techniques of scientific management were brought into social work bureaucracies. Worker discretion, initiative, and skill requirements were diminished. Social workers have unionized as a response to this process; ambivalently, they have joined the working class movement. Their relationship to the process of production is similar to that of other workers with orders coming from the top. As a consequence, social workers behave like other trade unionists, protecting their conditions of work. The inherent antagonism between what social workers do — the control relation they have with those on the bottom of the social structure — and the way they do it — as workers in a state bureaucracy, coupled with traditional training and aspiration, has left social workers in an unclear position. However, as social and political struggles unfold, as clients become increasingly victimized by the economic recession, social workers' consciousness of the class nature of our society and its forms of domination may change. Social workers may become less ambivalent about the tension between their positions as workers and their training and aspirations as professionals. The subjective element and human action is crucial to understanding the dynamics and formation of class. Class relations were redefined in Québec in the late 1960's and early 1970's as state employment grew rapidly. Because the new middle stratum is a large and complex group, affected by both objective and subjective factors, specific analyses of each group within the state bureaucracy are required. An all-encompassing "objective" definition does not strengthen but clouds the complexity of the class question.

The welfare state as described in Lesemann's study becomes an important manager of social relations. But although these institutions *attempt* to play the role of social managers, it is *not*, in my opinion, accurate to analyze them *as* managers. Even though rulers try to keep the ruled passive through "bread and circuses" and the underlying threat of repression, they do not necessarily succeed. Conflict and resistance does not disappear, and at times attempts at social management generate more intense social conflict and resistance. The containment of social conflict is an ongoing process. Although tensions, conflicts and contradictions become redefined by social programmes, they do not disappear. As Paul Cardan (Castoriadas) points out:

"The bureaucracy would like to present itself as rationality incarnate, but this rationality is a phantasm. The bureaucracy assigns itself an inherently impossible task: to organize the life and activity of men (and women) from the outside and against their own interests. Thereby it not only deprives itself of their

17

aid—which it is as the same time compelled to solicit—but it ensures their active opposition."[9]

Thus, the notion that the state *can* manage social relations is inadequate.

Concretely, the welfare state has not brought more order, but is both bureaucratically incoherent, irrational, and produces conflict and disobedience. Tighter controls are continually required to maintain worker discipline and control over clients. As the economic recession unfolds, as money is tighter, these bureaucracies resort to more direct forms of control. For example, output measures and scientific management have attempted to direct the activity of social workers. Yet, workers in these institutions, such as social workers, behave like any other workers engaged in industrial sabotage,[10] including ignoring forms, by-passing rules and regulations and manipulating benefits for clients. Trade unions limit management prerogatives. Alienated workers increasingly question their role. The state creates alienated obedience and passivity, and occasional rebellion rather than loyalty. Similarly, the tensions of mounting unemployment demand more spending but tighter social monitoring, and attempts to channel youth into state sponsored structures and activities.

The Québec government's recent proposals to tie social benefits to job training show the state's redefined responses to the contradictions and conflicts of modern capitalism. Not only do these actions not guarantee the population's passivity nor a disappearance of social tensions, but they illuminate the impossibility of total management of social relations. People continue to organize, to resist encroachment on social life, and to protest. State institutions, although forming and defining daily life, never totally control it.

Services and Circuses' critique of social and health services, particularly their technocratic forms of control, is powerful and convincing. Yet, for those who work for the state and for those defined by these services, the book leaves us dissatisfied. The strength of the argument is that large-scale, centralized services although providing benefits on a universal scale, through rational planning,

18

lead to powerlessness and alienation of those who provide and receive the benefits. What, if anything, can be done? How can those directly affected by these forms of social management resist it, in order to regain some control over daily life? I shall discuss the position of social workers as an example of a group profoundly affected by the changes which Lesemann describes.

Social workers can and have pushed in two directions in opposing the technocratic definition. The first is a retreat to pre-Castonguay forms of organization. In this model, social workers defined as autonomous professionals with more control over the labour process could practise according to a tradition of professional intervention. Bureaucratized social services have removed this autonomy in the workplace. Although many in the profession would dearly love to return to the "good old days" of social work professionalism, it is unlikely, even if it were desirable, given the tendencies described in this volume. Thus social workers are caught in a bind: either they can become bureaucratic agents, and work according to technocratically defined rules and regulations, or they resist these conditions, and build oppositional strategies and related alternatives. In the former case, social workers will suffer from increased frustration and shortly become alienated bureaucratic agents with little or no commitment to even the modest liberal ideals of that profession. Increasingly, seduced by high salaries, social workers have opted more and more for this reality. Larger case loads, computerized records, legally defined interventions, and decreased control are the logical consequences of the reforms. In effect, with few protests, social workers have been compliant in this process with little to offer as an alternative.

If, on the other hand, resistance and alternatives make sense, several points of attack are required. Bureaucracies, although collectivizing labour, tend to individualize and fragment production, leaving workers performing their tasks in isolation. Social work training conforms to this model by emphasizing individual work and skills over any kind of collective process. The impact of these two factors mitigates against organizing in the workplace.

To change this situation, however, the first task is for workers to begin to discuss work-related issues together, without which further action is impossible. These groups do *not* have to be within union structures. Because social work unions, although effective in protecting economic issues, tend to mirror the bureaucratic state structure, independent groups discussing issues related to client needs and social work practice are a better basis on which to develop opposition. One task of such independent groups would be to push for union recognition of issues related to social work practice in order to raise them in collective bargaining. As women's caucuses have done with some success, such demands can help form the basis for an opposition within the union, the nature of which is more important than returning to more traditional therapeutic social work. The single most important ongoing concern should be the fulfillment of client needs. People come to social workers as victims of social processes, currently worsened by the economic crisis. Meeting fundamental needs thus becomes a priority. Clients too are as isolated as social workers by the bureaucratic processes. The tasks then are to help people understand the social nature of many personal problems, and to bring clients together to seek collective solutions. It is inadequate to deal with issues such as youth unemployment, violence against women, and the lack of resources through individualized solutions. Because these questions are profoundly social in origin, victims of the problems should begin to take common action in order to at least break down the imposed isolation. In order to pursue this goal, social workers should not only bring clients together, but also make contact with outside social movements and groups such as groups of unemployed workers who can help clients concretely in securing at least the relatively minimal social entitlements guaranteed in our society and break down the internalized personal failure that goes with these problems. The goal of these efforts would be to construct an environment of popular opposition in the agencies. Posters, newspapers, announcements of meetings, and worker initiated speakers from outside groups can help build solidarity between workers, clients, and social movements. Although not overcoming the problem of technocratic control, this approach does bring the broader social struggles closer to clients and social workers, with the effect of breaking down a false consensus between social workers and management, demonstrating that personal problems are social, and supporting demands raised to further client and work interests.

The British document *In and Against the State*[11] further elaborates this position, in which the authors point out:

"Because the state is a form of relations, its workers and clients, if they do not struggle against it, help to perpetuate it. We are implicated in the imposition of capital's social relations. Without oppositional action, we actively perpetuate and recreate a capitalist and sexist and unequal society, not merely by default but through all that we do."[12]

Following from building oppositional groups or counter-organizations in the state, they see one goal as

"...creating new social relations to replace the deforming one through which the state contains class struggle. Counter-organization challenges the traditional boundaries between 'clients' and workers. The forms of organization... involve ways of relating to each other which are anti-capitalist and at the same time, in a partial and temporary way, also socialist and feminist: moves towards collective rather than hierarchical ways of working..."[13]

Resistance developed in the workplace is here defined as going beyond the prepackaged limits imposed by the state, and integrating forms of social practice that challenge class and sexual domination. Some of the recommendations made in this pamphlet include linking demands and needs of clients with the struggles of workers, overcoming the individualization of clients, defining problems that reflect real conditions of capitalist society, and refusing official procedure. These tactics reflect an oppositional attitude, take into account the needs of clients, break down the barriers between workers and clients, and build new organizational forms. The importance of this argument is that it links oppositional strategies with alternative, non-hierarchical forms of organization.

21

The argument is limited in some respects by how far one could go from within the state. Although occasional occupations or work-ins in state organizations reflect sporadic opposition, on the whole workers and clients have accepted the conditions they face. There are several reasons for this. Usually well paid, workers, especially social workers, are essentially no different from anyone else requiring a salary. Management, although limited to some extent by union action, retains its prerogative to fire and to suspend. In recent months, social and health services management has used these powers against workers who have stepped outside of the narrowing definition of work.[14] Clients have little choice, needing as they do the services to ameliorate very desperate personal situations, or as is sometimes the case, being required by law to use social services.[15] In general, the relations of the state are relations of power. They are not neutral technocratic relations established in a vacuum by ideologically neutral managers. They are profoundly class-based and patriarchal, expressed through state programmes and bureaucracies. When social and health services are challenged by their workers and their consumers, the fundamental relations and therefore the stability of the society are implicitly and sometimes explicitly confronted. Further, underpinning the service-giving and cooptive features are the repressive aspects of the state. Bureaucratic power has a tendency to reproduce itself, and once created, its dismantling via parliamentary process is at best unlikely. However, within this basic limit, the building of oppositional groups, linking workers, clients, and outside groups, provides resistance to state power and can contribute to a wider social movement, at least in the short term.

A longer term vision must go beyond the state. As we have seen, a seminal point of Lesemann's study is that more than providing services, the state uses these services to manage and control daily life. A movement of opposition that aims to transform society must have a strategy that links present needs, with a concept of alternative forms, including the questioning of power relations. Building alternative, neighbourhood-controlled social and health

22

services is the direction to go if we want to move beyond the present trends of centralization and domination. Building alternative institutions implies taking back power and control into neighbourhoods and daily life. This does not mean that the state and other relations of power should be ignored, but that these alternatives are part of the struggle against them. The state will not wither away, nor can its institutions be taken over and administered by managers representing the working class. In the first case, the state as a relation of power will perpetuate itself, while in the second, a change in who the state represents does not necessarily change its structures and lead to popular control of institutions.

However, building alternatives is not adequate by itself; it is simply an orientation to social transformation. Isolated alternative social and health service projects, although perhaps providing less alienating services, cannot progress beyond that unless they are linked in a federated network with other similar projects and social movements. Both a critical understanding of the role that a network of alternative structures can play in challenging power, and the concrete practice that they bring, can mobilize many to that cause, and pose genuine alternatives.

These projects may seem utopic; however, if we look back over the historical development of welfare institutions, many projects on a large scale came into conflict with state institutions. Early in the development of the British welfare state, workingmen's societies, known as "Friendly Societies" provided sickness and other benefits to several million workers. They were voluntary, organized and controlled by workers themselves.[16] The development of the welfare state terminated these institutions. As mentioned earlier, popular clinics that developed out of the political and counter-culture movements of the 1960's came into direct conflict with government goals of centralized planning, universal accessibility and formally professionalized services. At the present time, many women's collectives that have established refuges for battered women and rape crisis centres face problems because funding is linked to state control. The state, in the

23

name of better funding, universal accessibility, rationality, and professionalism, attempts to remove local and worker control of services. The conflict is between "society" and the "state." As the state gains control, it eliminates approaches that question the social order, and limits the range and organizational possibilities. The lever that the state uses to take control is funding. Since it is almost impossible as things stand for groups to find adequate funding, they turn to government, charity organizations (United Way, Centraide), or donations, each of which imposes different criteria for funding. Alternative forms of funding are desperately required, such as worker and popular "charities" for which neighbourhoods and unions could be canvassed for funding. Pension funds might be another source. Although limited, any independent base of funding would be a major step forward. Groups engaged in alternative perspectives and services need to come to grips with the problem of funding. Demanding state funding without controls, negotiated collectively, might be an interim approach. The present economic crisis with its related high unemployment creates contradictory opportunities. On the one hand, those who are unemployed, seeking something to do, may join community projects as volunteers. On the other hand, the governments, both Canadian and Québec, are attempting to keep a lid on a potentially explosive situation. They have funded many job creation projects which can be used to a limited extent because they are not linked to more centralized control of longer term funded projects, and therefore can be used in the short run to fill the gaps in community projects.

We face a difficult practical problem. Until substantial funding can be developed, community-based projects are doomed to walk a tight rope, balancing the principles of local control with the safety net of state financing, a net which is both security and a trap. In the short term, groups must learn to strategically manipulate these funds to present militant demands for local control, to adopt principles of volunterism, and to build a longer term orientation that will include independent community funding.

24

Services and Circuses is a warning. It demonstrates how the state, through technocratic management, in the name of social progress, redefines and attempts to take control of daily life. These services meet needs and are preferable to the disaster of provision through the market and profit motives — witness the U.S. health system. However, the impact of social and health service organizations as means of domination and demobilization of popular initiatives cannot be underestimated. The struggle must be against them, not from the point of view of cutting the services that people need but by recapturing them and building viable community options in the context of a wider social movement for social transformation.

Eric Shragge
School of Social Work
McGill University
Montréal, February 1984

Footnotes

1. See Allan Moscovitch and Glenn Drover (eds.), *Inequality: Essays on the Political Economy of Social Welfare*, University of Toronto, 1981; A.W. Djao, *Inequality and Social Policy: The Sociology of Welfare*, John Wiley and Sons, Toronto, 1983; and Ian Gough, *The Political Economy of the Welfare State*, Macmillan, 1978, for traditional left analyses; and Frank Harrison, *The Modern State*, Black Rose Books, Montréal, 1983; and Eric Shragge, "A Libertarian Response to the Welfare State," *Our Generation*, Vol. 15, No. 4, 1983, for a left-libertarian viewpoint.
2. See Gough, *ibid.*, for an elaboration.
3. See Dimitrios Roussopoulos, "Introduction: from then to now," in *The City and Radical Social Change*, Dimitrios Roussopoulos (ed.) Black Rose Books, Montréal, 1982; and Marielle Désy, Marc Ferland, Benoît Lévesque and Yves Vaillancourt, *La Conjoncture au Québec au début des années 80: les enjeux pour le mouvement ouvrier et populaire*, Édition: La Librairie socialiste de l'est du Québec, 1980, Chapters III, IV, V, for a more detailed discussion of this period.

4. Yeo, Stephen, "Working Class Association, private capital, welfare and the state in late nineteenth and early twentieth centuries" in *Social Work, Welfare and the State*, edited by Noel Parry, Michael Rustin, and Carole Satyamurti, Edward Arnold, London, 1979.

5. For an elaboration of this discussion, Pat Walker (ed.) *Between Capital and Labour—The Professional Managerial Class*, Black Rose Books, Montréal, 1978.

6. Thompson, E.P., *The Making of the English Working Class*, Penguin, Harmondsworth, 1968, pp. 9 and 12.

7. Cited in Yeo, *op. cit.*, p. 65.

8. See Lucia Kowaluk, "Working in a Social Agency" in *Working in Canada*, Walter Johnson (ed.) Black Rose Books, Montréal, 1975, Gilbert Renaud, *L'éclatement de la profession en service social*, les éditions coopératives Albert St-Martin, 1978, and Eric Shragge, "Social Workers, Social Services and the State," *Intervention*, Autumn 1977, No. 50, for further discussion.

9. Cardan, Paul, *Modern Capitalism and Revolution*, a Solidarity pamphlet, 2nd Edition, London, 1974.

10. For one study see Geoffrey Pearson, "Making Social Workers: Bad Promises and Good Omens" in *Radical Social Work*, by Roy Bailey and Mike Brake, Pantheon, New York, 1975.

11. London Edinburgh Weekend Return Group—*In and Against the State Discussion Notes for Socialists*, 1979—for a summary and discussion of this document see Eric Shragge "In and Against the State" (book review), *Our Generation*, Vol. 14, No. 1.

12. *Ibid.*, p. 48.

13. *Ibid.*, p. 50.

14. Jürgen Dankwort, a graduate student at McGill, is researching this topic—his MSW thesis will be available in June 1984.

15. For a study of the increasing legal definition of social services in Québec, see Frédéric Lesemann and Gilbert Renaud, "Loi 24 et transformation des pratiques professionnelles en service social," *Intervention*, Summer 1980, No. 58.

16. See Yeo, *op. cit.*

Preface

Bread and services... *panem et circenses*. There was a time when the imperial powers of Rome offered bread and games to the populace. Today, "bread"—a certain income security policy—and services—health, education and welfare—are offered by a technocratic state. In the course of my argument here, I shall suggest that this response to the "needs of clients" is, in fact, a means through which political and social control of Québec society is reorganized.

Over the last twenty years, the fields of health and welfare have been fundamentally restructured by massive state intervention, in particular through the introduction of universal health insurance schemes.

This book seeks to analyze the work of the main government inquiries undertaken by both the federal and provincial (Québec) governments which has stimulated state action on two levels: there has been a complete reorganization of existing services and institutions; at the same time, a whole new system of services has been established. The results can be understood only within the context of an integrated policy of income security.

Who were the actors behind these reforms? What philosophy, what ideology guided them? What was the role of

27

the state and the technocratic élite in the reform process? These are some of the questions that I shall attempt to clarify in the following pages.

Although I shall be constantly referring to the main events that have shaped the field of health and welfare as well as the powers and play of interests behind them, this book is neither an exhaustive study of, nor a textbook on, "social affairs," nor even a critical evaluation of the reforms instituted over the last twenty years.

The main thrust of my argument is that, above and beyond the good intentions of the reformers and the magnanimity of certain technocrats who would like the whole society to have access to well-run state services, there exist class interests which shape the social and political future of health care. In this sense, it is important to realize that to propose unlimited access to health and welfare services is also to create social relations of dependency, whether in relation to the professionals who provide the services, the institutions that organize them, or the politico-administrative powers that manage them.

It is in this light that the new network of Local Community Service Centres (LCSC)* established in Québec during the seventies is particularly interesting. The final chapter seeks to illustrate in some detail how this question of dependency can be understood within an institutionalized system of health services.

Bread and circuses? Bread and services? The spectacular manifestations of state action often disguise class interests. Let us now turn to the analysis of these interests in the field of health and welfare in Québec.

---

* The English acronym is never used, even by Anglophones. For this reason, the French "CLSC" will be used throughout this book.

28

Introduction

"It is not a question of accepting or rejecting a society but rather of analyzing it: of separating what seems to be tied together, of demonstrating the social character of that which seems obvious or even natural, of identifying how the cultural orientation of social power works through this situation and how the forms of social organization reproduce the established order."

Alain Touraine[1]

In most advanced capitalist societies, that is, societies in which the process of economic concentration and monopolization is most developed, there is also a process of centralization of social and economic planning in both the private and public sectors. The states of the Western world, especially since the beginning of the sixties, have greatly increased their role in the socialization of the costs of economic production, whether it be through educational and manpower training reforms, development of communication and transport networks, housing, urban renewal, cultural policy, or, in the case which interests us here, universal access to health and welfare services. The phenomenal growth of state budgets over the last twenty years and their increasing relative importance in the Gross National Product (GNP) has led the state to play a leading role in the economic, political and social orientations of society.

Through its economic activities, through the extensive development of social policy and social planning, and through the growing numbers of state employees and their influence on wage scales and working conditions, the state has become, in advanced (monopolist) capitalist society, the driving force behind a new social and political reality.

The interventions of the state in the areas of health and welfare in Québec and Canada can be seen on three complementary levels: on the level of social policy in the broad sense of the term; on the level of organization and administrative integration of these areas along the lines of industrial production; and finally, on the level of direct ideological management of the population, particularly the poor and economically marginal. These three levels are, of course, interdependent and fulfill specific but complementary functions.

A) In recent years, the state has undertaken a major overhaul of its social policies with a view towards integrating the various *ad hoc* measures into a series of coherent programmes designed to support individual consumption of goods and services. Whether it be through the establishment or extension of health insurance schemes, pension programmes and unemployment insurance, or through the rationalization of welfare and financial support measures such as family allowances and manpower training and mobility programmes, all this points to the organization of an integrated system of social security, or, more precisely, a system of *income security* (as it is called today). This shift in terminology is not insignificant. It expresses the change from a collective sharing of social risks, designed to permit individuals to deal with unfortunate events that they may encounter in their lifetime, to an economic strategy of regulation of individual consumption. Whereas social security was previously conceived of as a form of collective solidarity, it has now become a measure of economic planning[2] in that it constitutes an important instrument in the hands of the state which can help regulate economic activity and collective buying power. This use of social policy for economic objectives enables the state to exercise a stabilizing effect on economic fluctuations and thereby improves its planning capacities. Income security measures are a relatively sophisticated and effective means of stimulating global demand. The state is thus no longer confined to a purely passive role in the economy. The new instruments of income security enable it to intervene strategically and to take initiatives concerning the development and the orientation of the society. Dr. Leonard C. Marsh, an important architect of Keynesian economic policy in Canada, stated as early as 1943:

> "In the widest sense, we must have a policy for economic security as well as for welfare security, which is what 'social security' usually implies, for the two security programmes can be built to buttress each other."[3]

Control of social security is thus crucial to the development of contemporary capitalism. It enables the state to stabilize global demand through countercyclical action, while at the same time curbing potential social unrest. In this light, it is not surprising that since the Second World War, control of social security has progressively shifted from the local to the national level; from the parish or town council to the provincial government and — increasingly in recent years — to the federal level. This shift contradicts the definition of powers in the Canadian constitution which places the responsibility for social security in the hands of the provincial governments, and it is not surprising that this trend towards centralization has created acute tensions between the two levels of government, particularly in the case of Québec.

B) This tendency towards integration of policies concerning education, manpower and health and welfare is paralleled by a rationalization of the organizations that administer these programmes. This later process can be understood only within the context of a new state hegemony over the more traditional forms of organization, production and distribution of services. In fact, there is scarcely an aspect of these programmes that has not been completely reorganized in recent years, whether it be research priorities, or funding procedures, daily operations, training programmes for the personnel, or client education. Even the various professional associations have been profoundly restructured.

The state acts as a "rationalizing" agent and tends to subordinate the traditional forms of organization of these services. The hospitals and social agencies which operated on a relatively independent basis, the classical liberal model of medicine run by independent practitioners, social assistance programmes financed by private charities—are all submitted to a process of integration, systematization and planification that transforms not only the organization structures, but also the roles and functions of the various component parts of the service organizations.

It is in the name of economic efficiency and productivity that the state has conducted this massive effort of rationalization. The fields of health and welfare have been restructured along the lines of advanced industrial management theory. Needs and resources have been inventoried, management models that can produce the optimal utilization of resources have been defined, and a hierarchy of complementary programmes has been designed with a view to functional efficiency. The chaotic and unequal distribution of resources in the hands of health professionals has gradually given way to an integrated system run by bright young social engineers who legitimize their power in the name of the financial and political "responsibilities" of the state in its use of public funds.

Resistance from the traditional élites in the field of health and welfare is perceived by these new managers as a manifestation of narrow corporatist interests seeking to preserve personal privileges. Passionately defending the public interest, and especially the needs of the most disadvantaged sectors of the population, these new reformers argue that progress can be rationally pursued only within the context of organizational reform. In fact, of course, the underlying rationale lies in the inevitable need for state intervention in the areas of human resource management for those sectors of the population affected by the structural transformation of the economy over recent years. The economic crisis that advanced capitalist societies are presently experiencing will, in all likelihood, accelerate this process of reorganization and redistribution of resources. From the point of view of the reformers, this is probably one of the positive aspects of the international economic crisis.[4]

Indeed, it is important to note that within dominant economic rationality, this crisis does have a long-term beneficial effect. While it is true that economic concentration tends to precipitate a crisis, the overall effect of this crisis is, paradoxically, to reinforce the trend toward economic concentration, since it tends to eliminate or marginalize the weaker or more traditional modes of production and the actors involved in these areas. This is true for the production of goods as well as services, in the public sector as much as the private sector. In the field of health and welfare, the crisis takes the form of a new hierarchy of units and agents of production. This process of concentration and centralization of financial control, planning, programming and research by the state is accompanied by a tendency towards administrative decentralization for the intermediate and lower levels of management. The growth of these organizations leads to an increasingly pronounced social and technical division of labour which in turn tends to create proliferation of middle and lower management jobs, breakdown of the traditional professional associations, and growth in the unionization of employees.

C) The third level of state intervention is concerned with ideological hegemony. In particular, it should be noted that the management of the health sector is directly related to the issue of *social* control, particularly of those sectors of the population most threatened by the growing financial and industrial concentration of economic life. These sectors of the population have either been temporarily or permanently excluded from the sphere of production, or else have suffered serious reductions in income due to inflation. The role of the state in compensating for the disastrous effects of chaotic and unequal capitalist development is not, of course, a new one, and yet state action in this area has developed and modernized considerably in recent years. The social services which probably constitute the most refined instruments of population management have been progressively rationalized and integrated into the state organization. The very nature of their existence has been profoundly transformed. Whereas the social services were originally concerned with the administration of charities and the distribution of relief benefits, this work has been gradually taken over by a system of state-run social assistance programmes. More recently, social services have become increasingly involved in shaping the individual or collective behaviour of those categories of the population who have become—or are likely to become—victims of one form or another of marginalization. In technocratic jargon, these categories of the population are somewhat euphemistically called "high-risk categories."

This study, then, proposes a socio-political analysis, in terms of social relations, of the transformations that have occurred in the fields of health and welfare in Québec since 1960. I shall argue that these transformations can be understood only in the context of a progressive penetration of new state functions into health and welfare institutions. More importantly, I shall attempt to show how these changes have brought a new ruling class to power which has completely reorganized the social relations of domination in these fields. Consequently, I shall also discuss the changes that have occurred in the mechanisms of domination and the ideological systems which legitimate them.

Rather than attempting to describe the health and welfare reforms in Québec as such, I shall examine how the action of a particular class which sought to modify the previous complex of class relations in this area was able to modernize and redefine the organizational, political and cultural stakes involved. The objective, therefore, is to attempt to explain the social significance of the reformist ideology of universal access to health and welfare services. At the same time, it will be necessary to look at the management models, the administrative regulations and the types of resistance, tension and struggles that they have engendered.

A major reform such as the one examined here is not as "neutral" nor as purely "technical" as it may seem. A ruling class can never completely conceal its interests behind the laws and the social organizations that it creates.[5] Behind the image of rationality and order lie the conflicts, struggles and debates which reveal the shape and significance of new forms of domination.

The reorganization of health and welfare services by the state began in the early sixties in Québec with the introduction of a universal programme of hospital insurance

34

which, ten years later, after several commissions of inquiry, was transformed into a complete programme of health insurance. This programme profoundly modified not only the production and distribution of services, but also the status of the actors involved.

The reform was closely associated with the work of the Commission of Inquiry on Health and Social Welfare (CIHSW) — commonly known as the Castonguay-Nepveu Commission — created in 1966, which was as remarkable for the scope of its investigations as for the sweeping changes it suggested. A new model of health and welfare services was outlined, advocating a global and integrated approach: priority of prevention over curative measures; horizontal and vertical integration of health and welfare services; decentralization and regionalization of services; multidisciplinary work; participation by the population in the definition of its particular needs and the management of the various institutions. A community action programme was designed to help the population organize in order to express its particular and collective needs in terms of requests for additional services. Last, but not least, was the proposed reform of the various health and welfare professions.

Furthermore — a rare event in political history — the most important figures in this Commission were to find themselves, four years later, at the head of the governmental departments responsible for implementing these recommendations. They were thus able to translate the main political and organizational orientations defined in their research into legislation and various *ad hoc* administrative measures. However, the elaboration of policy is one thing; its translation into reality is often quite another. In this case, the difference between the two can be understood only by analyzing the specific nature of conflictual class interests in the health and welfare field.

The reform had an impact on the social and political scene of Québec quite beyond the field of health and welfare services. It was perceived quite correctly as one of the most important efforts of the state over the last decade. The innovative aspects which it proposed took place within a specific historical context which profoundly affected its political importance and impact. We must begin with an

35

analysis of this period if we wish to understand the new organizational models, the relevant legislation, the class interests that presided over these reforms, and the types of political power that applied them.

Historically, the liberal state, characteristic of competitive capitalism, sought simply to guarantee the free flow of goods, and recognized that each institution (for our purposes, the various professions and organizations concerned with health and welfare) was free to define its role and manage its affairs as it saw fit. The problem of social inequality was left to the free interplay of social groups within the community. Under advanced capitalism, however, the state seeks to submit all spheres of society to the implacable logic of economic rationality. In the field of health and welfare, the state is confronted with two main sources of economic irrationality: (1) the nature of the organization of health and welfare services as such, and (2) the non-productive nature of expenditures necessary to support those sectors of the population that are excluded from productive activity. The management of these sectors of the population can be effectively pursued only through a unified and integrated approach which combines health and welfare services with an appropriate income security policy.

Productivity in health and welfare organizations is dependent not only on the implementation of a new organizational rationale, but also on a new ideological approach to health and welfare problems. The organizational reform has been inspired by the technical, functional and systematic rationality characteristic of modern management techniques in private enterprise. The key concepts here are: scientific organization of labour, coordination and integration of the various units of production, division of labour, hierarchical scaling of roles and functions, centralization of planning and financing combined with a policy of decentralization of administrative functions. The new health and welfare organizational complex thus becomes another institution in which the products (health care, social services, research) are evaluated in terms of costs and benefits, while input/output analysis provides the basis for planning in accordance with the PPBS model (Public Programming Budgeting System).

36

This programme of rationalization is not, of course, without effect on the service and management personnel of the new organizational system. The former independent status of these personnel is abolished in favour of a functional definition of their role within the general framework of the organization.

"Innovative" measures in organizational reform are accompanied by the production of a new health and welfare ideology designed to reinforce the tendency to improved productivity. Thus, we see a new ideology of *health* as opposed to the traditional medical influence on pathology. The "health ideology" emphasizes prevention, continuous health care, and rehabilitation. It implies a critique of "traditional" medical practice which emphasizes a curative, specialized and technological approach. This traditional model is criticized as being *costly* because it necessitates sophisticated equipment, *irrational* because it deals with effects rather than causes, *inefficient* because it isolates the pathology from the patient as a social human being, *élitist* because it is, for all practical purposes, inaccessible to the poorer classes. It is clear that when the state takes over responsibility for medical services, it is economically unthinkable to assume the costs of such an approach for the entire population. In this sense, it becomes imperative to shift the control of the health sector from the hands of the "specialists of illness"—that is, doctors and private interests connected to the medical industry (pharmaceutical companies, laboratories and hospitals)—to the hands of "health economists" and technocratic managers of a new monopolistic health and welfare complex. In other words, the control must be wrested from the corporatist grasp of the illness sector and firmly placed under the auspices of the state-controlled health sector.

This new health model proclaims its innovative nature through the pursuit of five principal objectives:

(1) *Decentralization and regionalization.* Intermediate levels of management are created and are responsible for the financial and technical administration of services. (2) *Participation and community action.* "Consumer responsibility" is encouraged through the integration of community representatives within the service system. Furthermore, the ideology of participation tends to prevent costly and time-consuming

37

confrontations (or "social dysfunctions," as they are called) within the system. (3) *Multidisciplinary team work* is encouraged in order to increase the flexibility and productivity of the personnel. The objective is to break down professional barriers and to delegate and share responsibilities so as to make optimal use of available human resources. (4) *De-institutionalization*. In order to minimize the costs of hospitalization and institutional care, the emphasis is on keeping eventual clients in their home environment. (5) *Prevention*. Public hygiene measures, pre-natal programmes, improved diet education, physical exercise, and so forth, are encouraged with a view to improving the general state of health of the population.

The new health ideology is operationalized in the reform by a new type of establishment which seeks to incarnate the essence of the policies pursued. Set up on a local or community level, working in close contact with existing community resources, this new health institution encourages citizen participation, provides "front line" services that are accessible, continuous and preventive, and psychological and social services by a multidisciplinary team of professionals. In Québec, this idea took the form of the Local Community Service Centres, commonly known by their French acronym, CLSC. Inaugurated by the Québec government in 1971, the CLSC grew directly out of the recommendations of the CIHSW Report.

This process of reorganization and the new ideology that accompanied it were, of course, presented as a purely technical response to health and welfare problems in a world devoid of class relations. In fact, however, this reform can best be understood as the product of a management strategy of social relationships. A new technocratic class, legitimizing its power through its claim to non-partisan competence and financial responsibility, came to the forefront in order to administer the new areas of state intervention.

Developments in the field of social welfare paralleled those taking place in the health sector. Monopoly capitalism has created new forms of temporary or permanent exclusion from the spheres of productive activity which must be dealt with by the state. The traditional organization of social assistance which relied on local bodies (parish and town

38

councils) or on social work agencies has been rendered largely obsolete by the new type of state intervention. Financial assistance was integrated into a more general programme of income security which had as its first objective to encourage the beneficiaries to return to the labour market. The organization of social services underwent the same process of rationalization as the health sector: integration of the various existing institutions, vertical and horizontal restructuration of services, division of labour, and so forth. Here again, the objectives were stated in terms of an ideology of prevention, psychological help, participation and social integration, as well as reliance on community resources. Assistance was to be simple, "human" and practical rather than specialized and clinical. Long-term therapeutic treatment was to be avoided wherever possible. Traditional professional practice was criticized as being too costly and largely ineffective.

As the number and importance of "target groups" of social management grew, the state sought to maintain the social cohesiveness of the collectivity through reorganization and rationalization of services with a view towards increasing their productivity. The reform strategy of the state called for a direct alliance with the *poor*, and in this way it sought to bypass and undercut the power of the various existing social work agencies and the professionals traditionally attached to them, in much the same way that the call for a health strategy undercut the traditional role of pathology-oriented medical authorities. More precisely, the ruling technocratic class tried to make an alliance with these new paraprofessionals in order to make firm its relationship to the lower classes. The main characteristic of these new groups within the welfare administration scene is that they are less qualified—if not completely devoid of professional qualifications. This is in line with the new policy of deprofessionalization. The definition of professional responsibilities must be replaced by a definition of the functional relationships necessary within the new process of production of services. Thus, nurses have been called upon to carry out many of the tasks traditionally performed by general practitioners, while the latter have taken over a good part of the responsibilities of the specialists. The process is similar in the field of social work, where social-aid technicians

39

have replaced social workers and where community organizers call upon the poor to assume responsibility for the improvement of their own situation.

The question of *poverty* in the North American context of the sixties provides an excellent example of the technocratic offensive in the area of social management. The "affluent society" and the "war on poverty" are two interdependent themes developed by the dominant ideology in its attempt to promote technocratic rationality.

The former enabled the new élite to come to power on the crest of the wave of economic growth during the sixties and to consolidate a vast social consensus concerning the imperatives of a consumer society. In Québec in particular, the theme of the affluent society tended to mask the structural weaknesses of the economy, which could only be aggravated by the development of a consumer society.

The latter symbolizes, in the eyes of the new technocrats, a test of the validity of the socio-economic system which they advocate. Since they see themselves as critics of traditional liberal society, the problem of poverty is a fundamental challenge for them. What is at stake is the public recognition of the legitimacy of their power. To solve the problem of poverty is to prove the effectiveness and desirability of their whole system.

In this sense, the intentional dramatization of the problem of poverty sought not only to rally support for dealing with the problems of the poor, but more especially to stimulate public confidence in the capacity of the system to resolve its contradictions. The image of the affluent society, through its proclaimed capacity to generate an overall increase in the standard of living while at the same time allowing for a certain redistribution of income, sought to legitimate the hope for a solution to the problem of poverty without threatening the essential class relationships of domination. The themes of affluence and "war on poverty" were thus used to reinforce social cohesion during a period when social stability was threatened by massive structural transformations. At the same time, these themes were designed to consolidate public support for technocratic management of social relations as a solution to social problems.

The use of the term "war," in and of itself, suggests a strategy of transformation of social relations, a transformation which can come about through the destruction and reconstruction of one mode of organization and production in favour of another. In the present case, the war on poverty can properly be seen as a full-fledged attack on the traditional organizations and professions of liberal capitalism dealing with the poor. The professionalism and specialization of the social professions were severely criticized during the sixties and the vehemence of this critique was in direct relationship to the growing role of the state in the field of social welfare. Non-professionals and community workers were called in to shunt aside the old guard and their antiquated institutions that had become too costly and, in a word, dysfunctional. At the same time, the individual, clinical approach lost ground to a community approach to social problems. This "war" was pursued within an overall framework of social planning, together with a programme of activities defined by the new representatives of the technocratic organization of social services.

The new class in power used the theme of poverty, both symbolically and practically, as a manifestation of its capacity to exercise its new power. The significance of the oft-repeated call to open the gates of the affluent society to the poor makes sense only if the goal of social integration in advanced capitalist society is seen in terms of greater access to a consumer society. In this context, the themes of the "affluent society" and the "war on poverty" complement each other perfectly.

Poverty has always represented a potential threat to the dominant classes. The new technocratic class chose to focus on this problem in an attempt not only to exorcise the threat but also to convince the population of the rationality of the state and to instill confidence in its planning and programming capabilities, in its objectivity as a neutral body independent of class relations and, finally, in the democratic nature of its justice. The legitimation of technocracy requires it to appear as a disinterested élite. It is not an owner but a manager. Rather than protecting particular interests, it seeks to portray as selfish those interests which oppose its rational action.

41

It is the task of analysis, however, to show how management is not only a question of organization but also of domination; not simply a study of social functions, but also of hegemony.[6]

Footnotes

1. Touraine, Alain, in preface to Bronfenbrenner, Urie, *Enfants russes, enfants américains*, Paris, Fleurus, 1972, p. 14.
2. See Pelletier, Michel, *Le Revenu minimum garanti: une stratégie de bien-être social ou un instrument de politique économique?*, Université de Montréal, July 1975, 45 pp., unpublished manuscript.
3. Marsh, L.C. *Report on Social Security in Canada*, Ottawa, 1943, pp. 40, quoted in Pelletier, Michel, *op. cit.*, p. 5.
4. Meister, Albert, *L'Inflation créatrice*, Paris, PUF, 1975.
5. Touraine, Alain, *Production de la société*, Paris, Seuil, 1973, p. 155.
6. *Ibid.*, p. 155.

CHAPTER 1
The Organizational Reform of Health and Welfare in Québec (1960-1970)

The Commission of Inquiry on Health and Social Welfare (CIHSW, also known as the Castonguay-Nepveu Commission), which began its work in 1966, portrayed the health and welfare system of Québec as not only woefully inadequate and outdated but also completely controlled and mismanaged by corporatist professional and institutional interests. This picture of the situation contains a good deal of truth, especially as regards the period before 1960. It does not, however, take into consideration the developments that occurred during the sixties. While it is probably fair to say that up until 1960, the health and welfare field was the bastion of the traditional élites, several important laws were passed after this date which set in motion a process of fundamental change. One of the differences between this process and the approach suggested by the Commission and effectively adopted during the authoritarian reorganization imposed during the seventies, was that change was sought and brought about from within the traditional system. The existing professional associations and various health and welfare establishments recognized that change was inevitable and sought to come to terms with the new situation within the traditional institutional settings. In this sense, their efforts were quite different from those of the new technocratic class, who were "outsiders" and who sought power by opposing the traditional élites.

Petit-bourgeois and clerical domination in the pre-1960 period

On the whole, it can be said that the health and welfare system of Québec before 1960 was the preserve of the traditional "petite-bourgeoisie" and the Church, in particular the religious orders. The latter controlled the vast majority of the institutions: hospitals, hospices, orphanages, juvenile delinquent centres, and so forth, as well as social work agencies and community centres. They were also responsible for the training and hiring of social work and paramedical personnel. Through charity drives and direct parish contributions, they contributed a crucial part of the financial resources necessary to maintain the health and welfare system. In fact, the Church even played an important role in the first government financing policies in this area.

The doctors constituted another important locus of power and, generally speaking, their class interests were closely linked to those of the Church. Finally, the provincial government, which supported the political interests of the alliance between the traditional petite-bourgeoisie and the clergy, intervened in a strictly auxiliary fashion by providing either subsidies for certain institutions or else financial assistance to specific categories of the population. The government did run certain public health programmes, but for the most part it delegated its responsibilities to the religious orders and professional corporations. In 1949, for example, only 8.9% of Québec hospital revenues came from the provincial government. In 1958, government contributions had dropped to 1.1%, while during the same period the proportion paid by patients rose from 67.8% in 1949 to 91.5% in 1958. The rest was contributed by the local government or by charitable organizations.[1]

Whereas important measures had been taken by the

federal government in the area of social policy in general and health policy in particular since the end of the Second World War with the aim of encouraging the provinces to modernize their health and welfare services, the Québec government, which along with all other provincial governments has exclusive jurisdiction in the area of health and welfare, remained almost completely passive. This posture, of course, simply reflected the configuration of social relations within the alliance in power and its interests in the field of health and welfare.

This ultra-conservative role all but precluded government intervention in health and welfare policy, which was left in the hands of the municipalities and parishes. In the health sector, the government did build a few hospitals, mainly in rural areas, but such decisions were more often than not influenced by political considerations or in response to pressure from local élites rather than as a result of any coherent health policy.

Under the banner of intransigent nationalism, the provincial government systematically opposed all attempts at reform undertaken by its federal counterpart. Thus, Québec refused participation in certain federally financed health and welfare programmes, and this had the effect of widening the gap between the level of economic development and the underdevelopment of its health, education and welfare services. The main concern of the provincial government in the pre-1960 period seems to have been to resist all forms of intrusion by the federal government into the areas of provincial jurisdiction.

Similarly, the main concern of the conservative provincial élite was to defend the institutional basis of its power and privileges and therefore to oppose the initiatives of the federal government. Increased state intervention in the financing and management of health and welfare services provoked the most vehement opposition. Given this state of affairs, it is easy to understand why these sectors were a particularly acute source of conflict between the two levels of government, especially considering that social policy in the hands of the state was to play an increasingly strategic role in the determination of economic policy. Within Québec, the recommendations of two provincial commissions of inquiry—the Commission on Social Insurance (Montpetit Commission, 1933) and the Provincial Commission of Inquiry on Hospitals (1943) which suggested a health insurance scheme—were ignored. In fact, the situation in the field of health and welfare was characteristic of the political situation of Québec in general. The sclerosis of the political system, brought about by its defensive orientation within a dependent society, prevented it from adapting to the demands of a changing economic structure. It is this context, then, that enabled the provincial petite-bourgeoisie to continue to exercise its political and ideological hegemony.[2]

The contradiction between the class interests of the petite-bourgeoisie and the clergy on the one hand and the health care needs and poverty of the lower classes on the other was particularly flagrant. From the beginning of the period of industrialization, the working classes constituted an abundant source of cheap surplus labour for foreign enterprises in Québec and were subject to particularly intensive forms of exploitation. Consequently, the state of health of the population was one of the poorest in Canada:

"The average state of health of Québec's population is inferior, on the whole, to that of residents of other provinces... Sons of poor families had to leave school at the age of 13 or 14 to do hard work on the farm, in lumber camps or in factories, thereby ruining their health after a few years. So we find a very large number of persons unfit for certain types of work. Others are totally disabled... [Thus in 1961, the Province of Québec, which accounts for 28.8% of the total population of Canada] had 35.4% of the old-age assistance recipients, 34.1% of the blind recipients, 47.4% of the disabled recipients and 33.9% of unemployed recipients."[3]

Furthermore, in 1958, only 36.3%, and in 1964, 43.1% of the population was covered by a private health insurance plan; these levels were among the lowest in Canada. In comparison, the levels for Ontario at the same dates were 54.2% and 70.9%, respectively. Worse, in Québec, more than 60% of those insured had only partial coverage, the worst record in Canada.[4]

The role of the state was limited to two areas: (1) direct financial assistance to private institutions looking after the indigent, and (2) public health through government regulation of public hygiene, food quality control and vaccinations.

46

The Public Assistance Act of 1921 provided, for the first time, statutory measures for government financing of private charitable institutions. No provision was made for direct assistance to the indigent. The provincial government assumed responsibility for one-third of the costs of accommodation of the indigent in hospices. The municipalities and charitable organizations each paid another third. This law thus constituted a form of state support for religious communities which was to prove crucial for their survival during the Depression years. In spite of the extremely limited role of the state in this law, there was nevertheless strong opposition from certain sectors of the traditional élites, who saw it as fostering state control, secularism and socialism.

The main effect of this law, however, was to reinforce the existing social order and the position of the traditional élites and clergy:

"At the practical level, the law extended the system in use in traditional society. The family and the parish continued to exercise their traditional function of mutual aid, but charitable institutions, such as hostels, hospitals, crèches, sanitoria, refuges and orphanages, without modifying their traditional supportive role, received the financial support of the government and of the municipal organization. Furthermore, the state, by virtue of the law, could help them in the manner it deemed appropriate. It could thus, for example, grant them subsidies to ensure the debt service on loans contracted by institutions for purposes of public assistance. In the years following adoption of the law, a number of dioceses set up institutions and improved those already in existence."[5]

It was only in the health sector that the state directly financed operations. During the 1930's this sector had undergone a series of important changes. In 1922, the provincial government created a Public Hygiene Service. Dispensaries, financed in part by the Rockefeller Foundation, were set up in certain counties by 1926. Seven years later, they were operating throughout the province. A department of health, directly responsible for operation of the dispensaries, was created in 1936. This was to be the situation until 1966, at which time 71% of the personnel was directly involved in public health activities. During the thirties, the dispensaries had attracted a good number of young doctors specializing in public health and epidemiology, although interest soon waned as more prestigious sectors of highly specialized medicine opened up. Recruit-

47

ment of competent personnel for the dispensaries thus became increasingly difficult.

The overall picture of state intervention during this period is essentially characterized by its supportive role. It helped bear the financial burden of economically non-profitable activities (institutional care of the indigent and public health), while leaving intact the absolute hegemony of the Church over the health and welfare sectors. The famous Roman Catholic Bishop's Law of 1950 officially ratified this state of affairs.

By this time, however, two new trends had made the Church particularly anxious to have its traditional prerogatives in these areas clearly recognized: (1) The growth of a new faction of the petite-bourgeoisie. This group of highly educated individuals was linked to the more modern sectors of industrial society and was coming into increasing conflict with the traditional élites composed mainly of the clergy and the liberal professions. (2) The federal government was increasing the pressure on the provinces to modernize their health and welfare policies.

State legislative action: 1960-1970

It was this pressure from the federal government that led to the first important changes in the organization of the health and welfare field. These measures will be discussed in greater detail in the following chapter, but two decisions which were to have a major impact in Québec must be mentioned at this point.

The Canadian Parliament adopted a law concerning hospital insurance in 1957, in spite of Québec's claim that the law constituted an intrusion into a field of exclusively provincial jurisdiction. This law introduced the principle of free hospital care and provided for federal-provincial cost-sharing agreements. It was clear, however, that financing hospitals in this way would inevitably lead to state intervention in the administration and management of hospitals, since the law also stipulated that there was to be supervision of the way in which the money was spent. Such a procedure presupposes, of course, some kind of evaluation of productivity.

The religious communities and the traditional petite-bourgeoisie were thus directly threatened by this new form of state intervention. For three years, they succeeded in preventing the application of the federal law in Québec in spite of pressure from the trade unions and public opinion in general. However, this obstructive attitude was an important factor in their rapid loss of influence on the political scene after 1960. Inversely, the reformist and social-democratic image of the new ruling class which came to power in 1960 was largely due to its immediate and unconditional application of the law. As of January 1, 1961, hospital care became entirely free in Québec—or more exactly, it was paid entirely by the state.

However, the application of the law revealed the woeful inadequacy of the state's administrative machinery. Up until this time, the department of health had been run by doctors and had contented itself with an essentially passive or supportive role of the principal actors: religious communities, doctors, pharmaceutical and health equipment companies.[6] Furthermore, application of the law revealed the administrative incompetency of the hospitals. For example, it was discovered that in 1961, 80% of the hospitals—including the most important teaching hospitals linked to the universities— did not have a financial budget. The government was thus forced to rationalize the overall administration of the hospital system as well as the department of health itself, while at the same time establishing a system of accounting and basic budgeting procedures. The Hospital Act of 1962 had the effect of expropriating the role of the religious communities within the hospitals. Medical bureaus were created to define and control the quality of professional practice; hospital management was turned over to personnel trained in administration. The Church's role in the education of paramedical personnel was gradually phased out during the sixties.

Another law that had an important effect on the organization of health services concerned a limited form of public health insurance. Passed in 1966, this law was a response to the decision taken by the federal government to establish a universal health insurance programme. In Québec,

49

the new law was presented as a pilot project and covered only welfare recipients. Nevertheless, the arduous negotiations, in particular with the doctors, indicated that all parties were aware of the stakes involved. This law marked the final step to state supremacy in the health field. The role of the municipalities and charitable organizations had become negligible, while the religious communities were effectively shunted aside. At the same time, the government fixed the levels of doctors' fees and provided a legal definition of medical acts.[7]

The social service sector evolved along parallel lines. In 1957, in a context of severe economic recession, the Canadian Parliament passed an Unemployment Insurance Act which, again, was not applied in Québec until 1960 due to opposition from the traditional élites. The high level of unemployment in Québec (8.8% in 1958; 7.9% in 1959; 9.1% in 1960; and 9.3% in 1961) sent state expenditures spiralling when the law came into effect. During the first year (1961), $56.5 million was paid out in benefits. By 1965, this figure had risen to $90 million. Up until this point, the state had played an essentially auxiliary role in the field of social assistance, contenting itself with supplementing the budgets of private welfare organizations and leaving the responsibility of direct care for the indigent in the hands of the Church and the municipalities. The application of the Unemployment Insurance Act, however, forced the provincial government to realize the extent and seriousness of the problem of poverty in Québec. The system of individual assistance administered by the municipalities and parishes had kept the social visibility of the poor to a minimum, but the new situation revealed the existence of vast pockets of poverty, particularly in certain rural areas. The massive demand for unemployment insurance benefits forced the state to rely on the social agencies of the dioceses and municipal offices, since it had no administrative infrastructure of its own.

Here again, state intervention revealed the total inadequacy of the administration of social welfare services. The spectacular increase in benefits being paid out, accusations of mismanagement and misuse of benefits led to the creation of a Study Committee on Public Assistance in 1961 (known as the Boucher Committee). This committee was mandated to study

50

the scale of allowance rates according to economic regions, the methods to be used to determine the level of benefits, the various means of collaboration between private and public welfare services, and finally, the measures of prevention and rehabilitation which could be taken to reduce social dependency.[8]

In its report in 1963, the Boucher Committee clearly stated the importance of social security as a key instrument of economic policy for the Québec government. In this sense, the report provided arguments for Québec's new ruling class in its continuing constitutional struggle with the federal government. The report emphasized the fact that the high cost of public welfare in Québec was directly related to the weakness of its economy and to the poor state of health of its population.[9] Furthermore, it proclaimed the necessity for Québec to adopt an *integrated economic and social policy*. Such a policy, it was stressed, could be successfully pursued only through coordination and cooperation of government departments with a view towards establishing a unified strategy in the fields of manpower, education, health and welfare.[10]

The report marked a turning point in the orientation of the Québec government. Not only was it the first time that an effort was made to define an integrated economic and social strategy of development for Québec, but it also stressed the importance of winning back the initiative in certain fields of jurisdiction from the federal government. In this sense, it was clearly in line with the nationalist orientation of the new ruling class in Québec as it attempted to transform the functions of the traditional liberal state. The Committee noted, furthermore, that the Canadian constitution provides Québec with the powers necessary to pursue an autonomous policy of development (in which the field of social security must play a strategic role) if the Québec government chose to fully exercise its prerogatives. The report, in sum, called upon the new technocratic class to take the initiative in its relations with the federal government. This orientation was in complete contrast to the conservative and defensive posture traditionally adopted by previous Québec governments.

Concerning the role of the state within Québec, the Boucher Committee sought to justify expenditures on social assistance, recommended that aid should be recognized as a right and provided on the basis of need, independently of cause, and, finally, encouraged the development of prevention and rehabilitation programmes.

The state, it was suggested, should abandon its traditional supportive role and gradually take charge of the administration of public funds in the welfare sector. It should no longer use social agencies as intermediaries in the application of its policies. The agencies should have the more specific role of looking after prevention and rehabilitation. The state should recognize the interdependent relationship between socio-economic development and "financial assistance to welfare organizations devoted to social prevention and rehabilitation measures."[11] The services provided by the agencies should be made more generally effective and extended to those on welfare. Thus by financing the agencies, the state could establish effective control while at the same time avoid the costly procedure of setting up its own network of services.[12]

These were to be the guiding principles of the process of restructuration of social security and social work programmes during the sixties. Although the issue of social security was an important bone of contention between the federal and the provincial ruling classes, they nevertheless shared a common ideological viewpoint concerning the role of the monopolist state and the functions of social policy. Furthermore, by encouraging the state to play a more active role in the elaboration and application of social policy, the Committee was in fact advocating a change in the relationship between the private and public sectors, that is, between the power base of the traditional élites and the new power base of the technocratic class. The struggle between the former dominant class and the new ruling class, then, was centred around the question of the role of the state in Québec society.

The fundamental restructuring of power in the field of social policy that occurred during the sixties also had important ideological repercussions. The Committee suggested that the "inadmissable concept of public charity"[13] be replaced by the objective of "social justice," which precludes partiality in the distribution of welfare benefits. This change was in keeping with the claim that welfare is a *right,*independently of the reasons which make it necessary. Welfare policies must contribute to the collective development of the society and should not be the sole prerogative of any one institution.

The Committee summarized the changes that occurred in the administration of social services:

"In 1960, both parties [private and public sectors] were faced with spiralling costs and a clientele numerous beyond expectations, and their positions changed sufficiently to undermine the common front of the private agencies and to make the alarmed public sector aware of the new function it would have to assume."[14]

From this point on, the state progressively moved in to take over responsibility for all social services. The Canadian Public Assistance Act of 1966 opened the path to joint financing of social services which set the stage for a period of rapid development.

Organizational change and mutations in the workplace

The situation of the various categories of service personnel was closely related to changes in the institutional conditions of work. The growing tendency towards specialization, to the division of labour, the ways in which groups were formed to defend their interests—all these developments were basically determined by the struggle of the traditional petite-bourgeoisie to maintain its dominant ideological position while at the same time adapting to the new demands of technocratic management.

In the health sector, physicians were faced with a process of increasing specialization as medical research developed. This process, in part a consequence of the law concerning hospital insurance, favoured the position of specialists not only within the overall hospital administration but in relation to the medical profession in general. An indication of this exaggerated tendency towards specialization can be found in the fact that in 1966, specialists accounted for 62% of all doctors in Québec as opposed to 53% for Canada as a whole. It was the specialists who were to profit the most from the growing division of labour and who could best control its technical and social consequences. In contrast, the role of the general practitioners, who had no access to teaching hospitals, was in the process of relative decline. Furthermore, as the winds of reform grew during the sixties, general practitioners were increasingly threatened with the possibility of being incorporated within the civil service as salaried employees.

The first union of doctors was formed in 1962 when the general practitioners founded the FMOQ (Fédération des médecins omnipraticiens du Québec) in response to the deterioration of their social status and financial situation by the hospital insurance law.[15] This union declared its support for the principle of a public and universal scheme of health insurance on the condition that GP's could have access to teaching hospitals, and secondly that a *single* fee schedule be applicable to all medical consultations whether performed by specialists or GP's. This latter demand went against the recommendations of the more traditional and corporatist College of Physicians and Surgeons. This organization, responsible for maintaining standards of professional practice as well as defending doctors' interests in general, was in fact controlled by the specialists, at a time when the relative strength of the GP's had been gradually weakening under the impact of structural changes in the health field and federal government initiatives. The strategy of the general practitioners was to ally themselves with the new technocratic class in power. They supported the policies in favour of state-run organizational reform of the health sector—this was during the period of increasing access to health services—and opposed the traditional petite-bourgeoisie represented by specialists whose power had been reinforced by the health insurance law. These positions brought them into outright opposition to the College of Physicians and Surgeons itself. This alliance between the GP's and the technocratic class in power, however, was strictly tactical. Through their use of group pressure they were able to win the right for anyone who so desired to opt out of the health insurance scheme.

During this time, the specialists decided to unionize in much the same manner as their colleagues. They sought to constitute their own united front against attempts to impose state control over their incomes, their modes of payment and their modes of organization of services. This separation between the two unions undoubtedly made the government's efforts to institute a public health insurance plan somewhat easier, but the way in which the two groups of doctors were able to work together after this initial period enabled them to successfully block all attempts by the technocratic class to incorporate doctors within the civil service. This will become obvious when we turn to look at their strategies as early as 1971 concerning the CLSC (see Chapter Five).

The technocratic class saw the general practitioners as a strategic element within the medical profession because their position of relative domination made them particularly receptive to the proposals for organizational reform in the health sector.

Growing state intervention had created a new function in the health field: that of planning the organization of services; and a new actor: the health economist. The health economists emphasized the necessity of creating a new model of social and community health and sought to win general practitioners as potential allies for their project. The GP's were undoubtedly the most likely candidates for the technocratic model since they can play an important role in reducing costs of medical services and in increasing their social effectiveness. The objective was to reduce to a minimum the two main causes of inefficiency: (1) social and/or geographic barriers to entry in the medical system, and (2) the "reactive," "after the fact" nature of medical intervention as opposed to an "active" policy of prevention and rehabilitation.

As we shall see, these principles of health management run through all government inquiries of the period, both federal and provincial. In Québec, at the same time that the CIHSW was undertaking its investigations, a particularly important pilot project was being developed in the Sherbrooke region under the direction of a health economist named Thomas J. Boudreau. If we mention this figure by name, it is because it is hard to underestimate the strategic role he played in state health reforms, both on the federal and provincial level. Boudreau symbolizes one of the two major tendencies of reform in Québec. He was the chief representative of what we can call the "technoprofessional" tendency which sought to build reform on the basis of "modernized" institutions and professions. Claude Castonguay, president of the CIHSW, and later minister of social affairs, represented the other tendency—the purely technocratic option. It was, of course, Claude Castonguay, as minister, who was later to proceed with the authoritarian imposition of a technocratic and centralizing reform programme. I will come back to this question later.

The University of Sherbrooke and its teaching hospital had opened in 1966 and was thus the most promising location for a new programme of social medicine. Thomas Boudreau was named assistant director.

The training programme for medical students included biology, sociology and economics as the main courses during the first years, instead of anatomy. The new doctors who were being trained were meant to be more than simple practitioners whose main task was to make diagnoses. Rather, this new breed of doctors were meant to be social scientists, professionals capable of undertaking such varied tasks as research on the social epidemiology of particular sicknesses, "optimalizing" the efficiency of a given group of medical staff, administering health programmes, or simply participating in programmes of health education, preventive medicine or public health. [16]

In addition, the strategy in favour of the progressive implementation of a new medical model was, in the eyes of Boudreau, to be worked out in close collaboration with the FMOQ. Several economists wrote regularly in the association's journal, Le Médecin du Québec, and articles explaining one aspect or another of the model appeared regularly. This collaboration was so intense that during the period 1967-1971, the supporters of the new medical model, most of whom were not doctors, provided the bulk of articles for the journal.

The journal did not hesitate to publish articles vehemently critical of the medical profession. The general practitioners, or at least their leaders, had clearly chosen, during these years of the late sixties, to become the most radical and dynamic wing of the medical profession. They fought against the traditional sectors of the profession and sought change by

56

supporting the efforts of the technocratic reformers. Medical unionism contested the old forms of medical practice defended by the College of Physicians and Surgeons and participated actively in the process of reform. For a time, general practitioners and health technocrats were allies. The Sherbrooke project was seen as a chance to proclaim the necessity of abolishing the old, archaic and irrational medical structures which had proven themselves incapable of ensuring "public health." Through their alliance with the technocrats, the general practitioners hoped to escape from the process of domination exercised by the specialists while at the same time avoiding the process of dequalification which would sooner or later affect the specialists who remained blindly attached to the outmoded forms of definition of their interests.

The articles of the journal concerning the new medical model were based on the premises of technocratic management of medicine under the auspices of the state and often included violent critiques of the existing medical practice. The following examples are typical of the comments of the health economists in the journal. They denounce the organizational irrationality:

"This jungle, hidden behind the tightly-closed shutters of the medical profession, is thick with conflicts of interest, of examples of poor allocation of material and human resources.... The rights of efficiency and rationality [must] be defended."[17]

They criticized the overspecialization of medical practice, the mode of remuneration according to the number of medical acts performed, and the model of liberal medicine in general, as excessively costly.

The right to health was proclaimed as a revolutionary right because it legitimized the process of state rationalization:

"The welfare state is finished and a new political form of society has begun: the 'Service State'.... The State is beginning to be perceived no longer as a philanthropic redistributor, but as an agent of resource distribution... and this is the source of the most extraordinary reforms on the horizon as we enter the seventies."[18]

In the face of "inevitable social change," the "medical guilds" are trying to avoid the "attack on traditional privileges." This is to be expected because "the rise of the right to health and its acceptance by society means the end of the reign of practitioners and guilds over the medical world." The state must "eliminate the decrepit old form of remuneration by act and replace it by salaries for all doctors. [Salaries] should be fixed annually in relation to the areas where the need is greatest so manpower resources can be used optimally. They should be determined on the one hand through negotiations between the state and the unions, and on the other, on the basis of a certain number of indicators of efficiency in the maintenance of the level of health." [19]

"It might be objected that the medical profession and the health professions in general would not be efficient if they were controlled in this way.... The medical profession is a system composed of excellent soloists but it needs to be brought to see itself as a whole, with its various parts working in close harmony.... Efficiency means coordination of these virtuosos so that they play a tightly knit arrangement under the direction of a competent conductor." [20]

The objective of social medicine is "the restructuring of the health care delivery system and thus the powers that preside over it." [21]

That these kinds of articles were regularly published in the journal indicates a clear awareness on the part of the FMOQ of the transformations underway in the health sector. It is also possible that the Federation was preparing its position for the confrontation with the new state authorities and even to defeat them if necessary when they passed from talk to action concerning the integration of the general practitioners within the new health system. I will come back to this point in Chapter Five.

In the area of social services, a new wave of university trained social workers arrived in the field during the 1950's and was soon to attempt to overthrow the tutelage of the Church over the institutions of public assistance. Two events are particularly significant in this "emancipation" of social workers. Firstly, the decision to form a professional corporation in 1960 gives some indication of the effort to "professionalize" social work and to free it from the terms of religious ideology and the grasp of the clerical élites within the social service institutions. Secondly, the Boucher Report officially sanctioned the professional social work model and recommended its widespread adoption in the various agencies and within the provincial government department on the basis that it would increase the overall efficiency of services. By supporting the actions of the professional social workers and by separating the recognition of their professional acts from the management of the funds of public assistance which were to henceforth be in the hands of the state, the Boucher Committee succeeded in undercutting the powers of the clerical faction of the traditional petite-bourgeoisie. The material basis which permitted it to reign over the distribution of charity was removed and at the same time it was clearly stated that the solution of individual and collective social problems demanded a specialized form of training which must be scientific and no longer simply based on a morality of "human relationships." The support which the state provided for the social workers (who were organized along corporatist lines, not as a trade union) allowed it to win over a sizeable part of the new petite-bourgeoisie and thereby gain new allies in its struggle against the traditional petite-bourgeoisie which was still dominant in the social service sector. [22]

It must be noted, however, that the corporative form of association of social workers was only of temporary importance. The association was never able to win real autonomy for the profession, nor was it able to obtain for its members the material and symbolic advantages of full professional status.

Four types of problems were to come up during the sixties which made this impossible. A rough analogy can be drawn with the situation in the health sector although this must be considered with caution because the medical and social work professions are at very different levels in the hierarchy of professions, and consequently the ways in which their activities were integrated into a new organizational model of services were also quite different.

(1) In the general atmosphere of the "war on poverty," a group of social workers, most of whom were connected with the Conseil des œuvres de Montréal (an institution which did research on social problems and policy as well as coordinate community services), decided to set up a new form of social action in low-income urban areas. The objective was to encourage the urban poor to form "citizen committees" which would be instruments to help them to identify their needs and to find ways—either within their own community or through pressure on competent authorities—to solve their problems.

59

These social workers called themselves "animateurs sociaux" (community organizers), and sought to "encourage the population to take charge of its own problems." This manner of envisaging the role of the social worker implied a serious critique of professionalism with its specialized and clinical techniques and was thus in contradiction with the principles upon which, only a few years earlier, the social workers had founded their new professional association. A radical wing soon formed within the ranks of the social work profession whose platform was similar in many respects to that of the GP's when they used their journal to promote the cause of a health programme based on front-line care, prevention, group work, and so forth. What is even more significant is the similarity of the underlying ideology: modernization, efficiency and rationality. The relationship between the community organizers and the association of social workers was similar to that which existed between the GP's and the College of Physicians. The community organizers were the most receptive to the new forms of technocratic management of social services and were thus the ideal vehicle for the technocratic critique of professionalism within the ranks of the association. The technocratic project sought to encourage progressive integration of social workers into a new model of services, organized and administered by the state. This model could only reinforce the split developing within the profession between those who would plan and administer the new programmes (the technocrats) and those who would put them into practice (the technicians). Some indication that the community organizers did in fact constitute the vanguard of the technocratic initiative can be found in the fact that a large number of them rose to fill the ranks of management when the health and welfare reform was implemented at the beginning of the seventies.

(2) The economists also appeared on the social services scene and played much the same role as their counterparts in the health sector. They proclaimed a new perspective for social services based on a scientific and rational approach to the question of poverty. The most striking example of this approach can be found in the work done by a group of researchers at the Conseil des œuvres de Montréal (COM). In

addition to its general responsibility for the coordination of community services and community organization projects, this institution sponsored a group of young technocrats, economists, sociologists, urban planners and social workers, who had specialized in the planning and administration of social services. The group published a series of research projects, one of which soon became widely known: *Operation Social Renovation: A strategy to reduce socio-economic inequalities in the low-income areas of Montréal* (December 1966). Through a detailed analysis of census tracts, this project sought to identify the priority areas for social intervention in the Montréal area according to various social indicators such as income, education, characteristics of the labour force, housing conditions, and in particular, rates of infant mortality and juvenile delinquency. The authors emphasized that this study was undertaken in response to the demands of various citizen committees which were beginning to doubt that the "war on poverty" had any clear strategy.

> "The citizens of all the city-core neighbourhoods are beginning to get impatient and think it is time that something gets done.... Their impatience is more than justified and it is in this context that the Conseil des œuvres de Montréal decided, during the summer of 1966, to get a group of specialists working on this project and to start suggesting some answers."[23]

The COM, then, attempted to legitimize its efforts on the basis of popular demand from the poor themselves. The fact that it was also the COM which sent in the community organizers whose job it was to set up the very groups who made these requests means that, in reality, we are looking at a closed system of legitimation. The ultimate function of this process seems to be to integrate the whole range of social services into a new perspective, a new management model. This example also serves to illustrate the hypothesis that I mentioned in the introduction concerning the ultimate functions of the dramatization of the poverty question. It seems quite clear that this manner of raising the issue is part of a technocratic strategy to integrate the social services into a new perspective. It is important to note, in this respect, that of the sixteen members of the research group who worked on *Operation Social Renovation*, over half were soon to be hired as researchers for the CIHSW, and in 1970 one of them became deputy minister for planning in the department of social affairs. He was chosen, the minister explained, on the basis of the excellent brief submitted to the Commission by COM. This brief, entitled *A Social Policy for Québec* (October 1967), was prepared under his direction.

The ideology that underlies this document is typical of the technocratic approach to social problems.

It is obvious just how the issue of poverty is used as a justification for technocratic action, in the sense that the only possible solution is the technocratic one with its integrated, systematic, overall approach, with its call for a radical redefinition of the mission to be accomplished and the professional groups involved.

In the same sense that medical programmes should no longer be viewed within the narrow confines of a struggle against sickness but rather within a general framework designed to maintain and improve the state of health of the population, so the objectives of the social programmes should no longer be limited to piecemeal charitable measures in the struggle against poverty. Instead, a positive approach to "social development" should be adopted. This approach, suggests the report, is the starting point for the most important change in the field of welfare and social services during the sixties.

This new ideology was the expression of a project for functional integration of various piecemeal aspects of the social service system. Social policy and the programmes for the sectors of the population not involved in the active labour force were to be coordinated by the new actor in this field: the state. Through this integration process, the state would administer the welfare programmes in accordance with its new functions of social management.

The brief clearly states this goal of modernization and the global approach to welfare and social services:

"... In the past... 'welfare' has been... identified with measures designed to compensate extreme poverty and to help the victims of individual, family or social misfortune.

It was taken for granted that an ordinary citizen would be able to look after his own problems. Economic development was supposed to entail social development...

It is only recently that the theories of liberal economics have begun to be demystified and that the twin scandal of the twentieth century has been clearly revealed: that is, the growing gap between rich countries and poor countries on the one hand and the existence of poverty even within the most affluent societies. Quite clearly, economic progress does not ensure social progress.

Over the last few years, the term 'welfare' has come to mean much more than... a minor back-up policy... it [now] is seen in terms of a dynamic state of equilibrium between individuals and society....

In this sense, social welfare is a long term objective of all social policy and every society.

Economic reality and social reality should be seen as interdependent. Ultimately, each conditions the other.... The fundamental objective of economic development is to ensure the welfare of each citizen in his social environment. In this sense, we believe it is urgent to coordinate government policies, [to] conceive of welfare... within the context of an integrated, global approach to social reality....

The state in today's world has the urgent and unquestionable duty to define a true social policy.... Priority must be given to investments in human resources.... The progress of a nation in both economic and social terms is measured, above all, in terms of the quality of its human resources.

The directing principle for modern social policy must be *equal opportunity* for all citizens....

It is essential that all citizens participate actively in the process of definition of a social policy for Québec.... Vast sectors of the population have been neglected. Participation, for all practical purposes, has been reserved for the owning classes, for an 'élite' which controls economic and political power. It is essential, if equal opportunity is to have any real meaning, that all citizens can make their voice heard... in other words that there be no second-class citizens.

In recent years... the poverty which afflicts vast sectors of Québec society, close to 25%, has been severely criticized. This situation... is not acceptable within a prosperous society and every so often a 'war on poverty' is declared.

But this war cannot be won if we do not pay the price. There is only one way to remedy this situation and that is to recognize that we are all responsible for this scandal, that the poor are poor because they are victims of multiple inequalities and collective inertia. We must make the social investments necessary to overcome these handicaps through coordination of our efforts, by emphasizing redistributive policies and through health, work and housing programmes.

In this perspective, we believe that priority must be given to the needy in the practical application of a social policy for Québec." [24]

63

This language is typical of the new technocratic authorities whose new social morality calls for the state to act as a rational manager of economic and social behaviour in both the public and private sectors with a view towards correcting the most flagrant inequalities. The reference to the scandal of poverty can best be understood as a form of rhetoric by the new technocratic élite which is rising to state power and which, in Québec, as in all advanced capitalist societies, is trying to establish its political legitimacy.

By attacking poverty and by explaining it in terms of "collective inertia" and social exclusion, the technocratic argumentation justifies the necessity for a "neutral" authority which arbitrates particular group interests in favour of the common good. The relative absence of the poor must be remedied by encouraging them to form pressure groups. This "neutral" but active authority of the state means that its powers and functions must be broadened if it wishes to deal effectively with the situation of growing economic concentration. This approach to the question of poverty opens up a breach in the dominant liberal ideology and enables the technocratic class to offer its services for the management of the new functions of the neo-liberal state. This is the significance behind the twin terms of "economic development" and "social development." They constitute a direct reference to the two main forms of power in modern society: economic monopolies and the state in its corresponding "monopolist" form. "Social development" now includes all measures of redistribution and regulation by the new state. It is, in fact, the main function of the state in the new economic and political regime. Social development, in its widest sense, covers much more than just the areas traditionally reserved for welfare and social agencies. It is practically the vision of society of the technocratic state. The extension and coordination of social policies enable the state to intervene effectively in a process of economic and political regulation of society.

This process was already well underway by the end of the sixties, and the rhetoric concerning the war on poverty, which clothes the programmes of community organization and participation, also tended to provide the symbolic motivation necessary for the reform of state administrative machinery

64

while opening the doors to state power for the new élites.

The dramatization of the poverty issue as a means of legitimation for the new technocratic reorganization of services was equally present in the health sector, and it is in this light that the social and political functions of the community health model can be more clearly seen. Take, for example, this warning from an American expert which is quoted in *Le Médecin du Québec*:

"Health care for all can be realized if physicians surrender solo practice and form groups to treat people—rich and poor alike.... Unless the private sector of medicine comes up with a plan for providing comprehensive health care to all people, the federal government will have to take over, and if private medicine defaults or fails to solve the health problem of the *poor*, then private medicine may not survive."[25]

At this point, we may examine more closely the analogy indicated earlier between the researchers at COM and the health economists. This, of course, is the reason why we have chosen to put their commentaries side by side in the preceding paragraphs. Each group sought to win the support of the least qualified sectors of the profession. The health economists looked to the general practitioners and the researchers looked to the community organizers. The only thing these two groups have in common is that they are not specialists, that is to say, that their work is defined more by its social function than by a clearly distinguishable body of knowledge. This is the significant advantage from a technocratic point of view. It is not a particular body of knowledge that counts as much as the organizational process itself. It is above all one's position in the organization that is the important factor. We must be careful, however, not to take this analogy between general practitioners and community organizers too far because physicians do possess socially recognized knowledge, which is not the case for the social work professions. It is precisely this knowledge which permits them to develop an effective strategy of resistance to the threat of total technocratic subordination. By the same token, the absence of such a body of knowledge for the community organizers meant that a good part of them were to become the mainstays of the new technocratic management model of social relationships. It was the lack of professional legitimacy, or expressed another way, the lack of a body of

65

knowledge which can be reduced to a definition of tasks and responsibilities, which constituted the main difference in the case of the community organizers.

(3) If we turn now to look at another analogy between the health and welfare sectors we can observe the situation of the doctors who are the object of constant pressure by the state, through its cost-reduction strategies, to delegate a major part of their tasks to the nursing personnel. The social workers were submitted to the same type of pressure when the state decided to revise the training programmes for social workers and to create a three-year programme for technicians of social assistance at the junior college level. In practice, the technicians often obtain tasks equivalent to those of professional social workers. The social agencies, which are themselves administered by professional social workers, were faced with a difficult problem: either they encourage the hiring of technicians whose salary is about one half that of the professional social workers, in which case they contribute to the general deterioration of the status of the profession, or else they choose to support the profession at the cost of efficient management. The existence of two categories of personnel, which in spite of differences in social status are most often called upon to fulfill similar tasks, allowed the department of social affairs in the late sixties to play one against the other and thus to succeed in its attempt to relegate social workers to the places allotted for them in the new state-run organization of social services.

The social workers' association tried to defend the status of its members by emphasizing the specialized nature of their work. They refused to present a brief to the Castonguay-Nepveu Commission, or CIHSW, in conjunction with the technicians, preferring to present their brief with the psychologists. Nevertheless, the sign of the times was clearly given when, at the same time, an important unionization campaign was underway which included both professional social workers and technicians.

(4) As the state gradually took over the administration of social services and began its process of rationalization, it became more and more clear to the social workers that their traditional organizations for defending their interests were no longer adequate, and this led them to massive unionization. In

66

this sense, their behaviour was similar to the ranks of the paramedical personnel in the health sector, and especially the nurses. The sharp division of labour and the abrupt change in labour relations (from the paternalism of the Church-run hospital to the functional administration of government hospitals) had led to the unionization of these groups in the mid-sixties.

The social workers who had succeeded by 1960 in creating a professional association were irretrievably divided over the problem of the new social and technical division of labour imposed by the technocratic organization of social services. Some of them were to rise to fill management positions and vigorously defended the professional ideology in the vain hope of counteracting the social effects of the division of labour, while others, who were in subordinate positions, joined forces with the technicians and adopted a union strategy to defend, just as vigorously, their interests as a new form of service workers, as the technicians of the new petite-bourgeoisie. The profession split apart.

Organizational change and the effects on the institutions: the issue of regionalization

By the sixties, most of the hospitals in Québec were already being run by a new generation of administrators who had succeeded in breaking down the strongholds of clerical power. Each hospital, however, remained completely independent and little had been done to resolve the problem of the haphazard localization of hospitals throughout the province, and even less had been attempted in the way of public health.

The experimental training programme underway at the medical school of the University of Sherbrooke, under the direction of Thomas Boudreau, had chosen the university hospital as a pole of attraction, as the centre of a comprehensive regional organization of medical resources. The university hospital was thus something more than just a teaching hospital; it was also an attempt to develop a new health care delivery system on a *regional* basis. The choice of this hospital was motivated by the presence of community health experts who were given the task of completely reorganizing the antiquated hospital structures.

This emphasis on the regional organization of health care systems was neither new nor unique. In the United States, a law concerning the regionalization of health services had been adopted in 1966, and in Canada, federal government task forces had been emphasizing the need to reorganize health care systems on a regional basis since the beginning of the sixties. The new approach to health could be successfully pursued only in conjunction with an overall reorganization of health services, and the *region* was of strategic importance in the *planning* process. Regional centres were also responsible for a new health unit on the local level, the Neighbourhood Health Centre, whose principal function was to facilitate the adaptation of existing resources to the new situation. This new type of local health centre—which was being implemented in the United States as part of the war on poverty programmes— was based on the principle of polyvalent health teams which would be active on the neighbourhood level and which could increase the effectiveness of health care by adapting it to the particular needs and "culture" of the local area. [26]

The pilot project in the Sherbrooke area was created by the Planning Committee on Health Services for the Eastern Townships. The work of this committee, under the direction of Thomas Boudreau, had a determining influence on regional health policy not only in Québec but for all of Canada. Boudreau's influence was considerable. The main government inquiries on health care by both federal and provincial governments, in which he actively participated, clearly show the stamp of his experience of this combined project of innovative medical training and regional organization of health care. The Sherbrooke project was certainly one of the most influential in Canada.

The Eastern Townships Planning Committee was supported by both the federal and provincial government. The only other pilot project of a somewhat similar nature was being undertaken in California under the auspices of the Kaiser Foundation. In this sense, the Sherbrooke project was a prototype for the young technocrats, both in Québec and in Canada, and its success or failure would have a major impact on the attitudes of all the professional groups involved. The stakes were high and the experts wanted to proceed cautiously.

The Committee was made up of thirty-three members, chosen by the various hospitals of the area. A physician and an administrator represented each of the major institutions; one or the other for the smaller ones. Neither the population as a whole nor patients were represented on the Committee. The Committee had also hired a group of experts, mostly from the social sciences or management schools—there were three administrators, four economists, four sociologists, and one geographer, in addition to four doctors, two nurses and one social worker.

The objective of the Committee was to improve the level of health of the population while at the same time reducing costs. This was to be attained through the integration of all existing medical establishments within a single rationalized system. The director of the Committee expressed his idea in the following way:

"The citizen or the patient can no longer remain the patient or the client of a single physician or a single institution. He must become the patient or client of a regional system in which all the component parts are functionally related." [27]

The first task of the Committee was to gather statistical information necessary for the study of social epidemiology and the particular needs and resources available in the area.

The process of elaboration of the master plan for the area during the period 1969 to 1971 is a good example of how the experts of the Committee sought to implement their technocratic strategy. From the beginning, there was no attempt to unilaterally impose the reform. On the contrary, on the basis of the model they had worked out, the experts sought to negotiate with each institution the best way of implementing the specific changes necessary. A conference was organized in the fall of 1969 to set the tone. The main speaker explained that there were basically two ways of proceeding with regional reorganization. The first consisted of simply putting the question in the hands of the professionals and telling them to work it out between themselves through an informal process of coordination and harmonization. The second was based on the work of experts who study the needs of the population, the existing resources, and attempt to come up with a coherent and effective health care delivery system which would then be imposed without consultation on the professionals involved.[28] The Eastern Townships Committee sought to combine these two approaches by working out an effective system in conjunction with all groups concerned. The objective was to establish an effective means of coordination and cooperation between technocrats and professionals of the health system.

At the same time that this pilot project was being carried out in the Sherbrooke area, the other hospitals, sensing what was in store for them, began to work out their own regionalization project. In 1968, they suggested that a permanent committee be set up in the department of health to oversee the application of a rather timid attempt at regionalization. This committee was to be composed of hospital administrators but was not to include experts from outside the hospitals. This initiative was an attempt to propose a strictly professional model of regionalization as opposed to the techno-professional model favoured by the Eastern Townships Committee. The hospital administrators sought to develop their model along the lines of the giant multinational corporations in which local branch plants had a large degree of independence. This model permitted management personnel to acquire considerable practical experience on the local level and thus to create a pool of competent personnel who could eventually take on greater responsibilities.[29] The administrators, not surprisingly perhaps, thought of the reform in terms of a "chief executive," a kind of chairman of the board, who would be solely responsible for his decisions. He would be sensitive to the needs and opinions of his subordinates and collaborators, of course, but it was his leadership and management qualities that constituted the best guarantee for efficient operations. This project can thus best be understood as part of a defensive strategy on the part of the local administrators in the face of the growing threat of centralized government control by the technocrats. The latter were attempting to develop a strategy of cooperation with professionals on the basis of their knowledge rather than bureaucratic authority.

Whereas the administrators felt threatened by the new role being played by the technocrats on the regional level, this was not the case for the general practitioners. The FMOQ quickly perceived the advantages of a policy of regionalization and collaboration with "outside" experts. The Federation immediately moved to support the project. During the Congress of the FMOQ held in 1966, on the issue of regionalization, one of the most influential members of the Federation spoke in these terms:

"It is our task to be fully prepared for these new structures which will significantly alter traditional methods of practice. We must realize that this evolution will not only affect the hospitals.... it will radically transform medical practice itself. Rather than fearing or opposing these changes in the name of outdated ideas, we should seek to play an active role in their implementation." [30]

The Federation's journal also regularly published articles concerning the Sherbrooke project, which is an additional indication of the objective alliance which existed between the general practitioners and the technocrats. Article after article appeared describing, discussing and defending the new medical model in operation in Sherbrooke. The authors emphasized the necessity of getting rid of the antiquated and irrational traditional medical structures which had proved so incapable of ensuring "public health." The Federation invoked the main technocratic themes to defend the project: cost reductions and greater effectiveness. The issue of regionalization was also an important theme in the brief presented to the CIHSW in 1968. The regionalization model proposed was not limited to professionals. It was, in fact, identical to the Sherbrooke model and involved coordination and cooperation between technocrats and professionals. [31]

The Eastern Townships project enjoyed strong financial support from the provincial government, which also firmly backed the general trend to regionalization. As early as 1962, the provincial government had worked out a plan for the regionalization of hospital services which sought to relieve the pressure on hospital occupancy rates. In 1965, a committee of physicians and administrators had been set up to study ways of integrating hospitals in the Montréal area on a regional basis, but it was only in 1966 that the department of health officially adopted the objective of integrated regional structures as a model for the health care delivery system. In 1967, at the annual congress of hospital administrators, the minister of health announced that regional planning and administration was to be implemented and called for a policy of consultation and participation of all concerned. [32] The constant support and increasing financial aid for the Sherbrooke project by the provincial government made it quite clear that a new policy of regionalization was in the making. At a conference in Sherbrooke on regionalization in 1969, the deputy minister congratulated the committee on its work and hailed it as a "prototype that will soon be applied to the whole province." He continued:

"The ideal health care delivery system should not be thought of on the level of a village, a local community or even a city; it is a system or a functionally integrated network.... This concept subordinates the local interest to the general interest ... by means of intelligent coordination, and thereby avoids petty local considerations." [33]

The Sherbrooke experiment can thus be seen quite correctly as a model for the future which opened the door to general reform on the basis of participation by professionals in conjunction with the technocrats who served as catalysts or modernizing influences. The model worked because it was able to organize consensus, without severely disturbing the established interests in the health area. As such, it was an example of liberal reform on the regional level.

This experiment was no doubt in the back of the minds of the authors of the CIHSW Report on Health (Volume IV, tome II). Nevertheless, the goal of joint techno-professional health management, symbolized by the Sherbrooke project, was largely rejected by the principal architects of health and welfare reform in favour of a more authoritarian and purely technocratic model.

During the sixties, the social service agencies had joined together to found the Federation of Social Services for the Family (FSSF) which was meant to serve as an organization for the defense and consolidation of the professional status of social workers. The effective monopoly which it enjoyed provided the young profession with exclusive rights in a specific area, and the independent source of revenues which it possessed enabled the Federation to seek hegemony over the social services in spite of growing state activity. The growing importance of the FSSF, however, forced it to become more and more an administrative body linked to the state. Whereas during the first years of its existence the Federation sought to promote the interests of all sectors of the social work profession, it was later to become more closely identified with the interests of the management personnel at a time when union organization was making strong headway amongst the subordinate categories of personnel.[34] The progressive implementation of technocratic reform with its profound effects on the division of labour prevented the Federation from simply defending professional interests and led to its becoming an organization for the defense and consolidation of management interests. These interests were under attack on two fronts: on the one hand, the status of the profession was threatened by the process of unionization, and on the other, professional autonomy was threatened by a situation in which the job of social workers was increasingly being defined as a series of administrative tasks. The administrators of the social agencies were thus torn between their job and their profession. Their decisions and strategies were determined by the temporary instability of their position within a structure in transition.

It was in the name of defending the standards of the profession that the administrators attempted to resist the bureaucratization of their profession. "The Federation strongly opposes bureaucratic state interference and considers that professional prerogatives justify a reduction of controls."[35] FSSF positions constantly tended to reinforce the image of specialized professional action as the only possibility for effective action,[36] at a time when the state was promoting exactly the opposite policy in the health sector. The strategy of the Federation, then, had little chance for success. Above and beyond the defense of professional interests, however, loomed the sharpening conflict with the state and the breakdown of the alliance between social workers and the state which had been created by the Boucher Report.

In 1967, when the conflict broke out into the open between the professional administrators and the technocrats in the department of family and welfare, the former fought through their boards of directors. The Federation had joined

73

forces with agency administrators in an attempt to unite the existing local and regional authorities against the growing power of the state. This explains why the boards of directors of the agencies played such an important part in the Federation's strategy. The FSSF demanded that the state respect the juridical status of the agencies which guaranteed their legal independence from the state even if they were financed almost entirely through public funds. In contrast to the project of centralized state control under the direction of a new technocratic class, the Federation fought for the independence of local agencies controlled by a cast of techno-professional administrators.[37]

In 1968, the department of family and welfare modified its strategy and accepted the Federation's proposal for a joint committee on private social services. Satisfied with this new "partnership" status, the Federation ordered its agencies to undertake a "programme of rationalization of their services and administrative machinery." The top-level personnel of the Federation started working more closely with the government department, and as one author noted: "The state discovered that it could now find supporters of technocratic reform in the strong-holds of the professional ranks."[38]

We must mention here also the evolution of the Regional Welfare Councils (RWC), that is, the various charity federations and councils, welfare councils or social development councils as the case may be, which were in charge of raising funds for social and charitable projects, of planning community services and occasionally of encouraging research on social questions.

Most of these councils, especially in the rural areas, had become the refuge of the traditional petite-bourgeoisie. In the urban areas, however, and particularly in the case of Montréal, as mentioned earlier, these councils were an important source of contestation of the traditional powers and energetically supported the new technocratic ideology of social services.

These welfare councils played an important role in spreading the ideology of the "war on poverty." In 1965, they organized a symposium on poverty which constituted a turning point: the task at hand was no longer to efficiently consolidate the charitable efforts of the community but rather to mount an attack on poverty.[39] Poverty was defined as the absence of participation in the centres of decision concerning wealth, power and knowledge. The response, therefore, was to ensure that all had access to knowledge and power and to guarantee a minimum income for everyone. Once again, we discover the strategy against poverty as formulated by the technocratic faction of the petite-bourgeoisie. Social development and, not surprisingly, regional planning and participation, figure as the two main lines of attack on poverty. Coherent and coordinated action by the state should seek to aid the population to rationally adapt to the new necessities of economic production. This action should be undertaken on the local level, in the neighbourhoods and regions. The RWC suggested that an inventory be made of local conditions and that a system of "socio-economic accounting be developed in each region as an essential instrument for the planning of social development."[40] The activities of the Conseil des œuvres de Montréal described above were recognized as primordial.

After the symposium of 1965, two main positions appear. Some of the councils call for systematic state intervention. This was the position expressed in the brief *A Social Policy for Québec* presented to the CIHSW by the COM in 1967, which, as mentioned above, emphasized the importance of planning and coordination of resources, together with a system of citizen participation. The effective power, however, would remain in the hands of the state while the regional bodies were to be centres for consultation, participation and implementation but were not to be called upon in the planning process.[41] The second position, which was defended by the more traditional sectors of the petite-bourgeoisie outside Montréal, sought to modernize the mechanisms of local coordination and financing of regional social development. This group also emphasized citizen participation but demanded a degree of autonomy in relation to the state.

The issue of regionalization, then, was supported for different reasons: on the one hand by the local élites of the traditional petite-bourgeoisie and on the other by those favourable to the integration of local services into a coherent programme of overall state planning.

The fields of health and welfare were increasingly submitted to a process of technocratic reorganization. The traditional élites attempted to protect their interests and to work out satisfactory compromises in a situation in which the movement towards concentration of power in the hands of the state seemed inevitable. It is in this context of reorganization of the principal health and welfare institutions that the CIHSW began its work in 1966. Before turning to examine the work of this commission, however, we must analyze more carefully the initiatives of the federal government because they constitute the driving force behind the changes on the provincial level.

Footnotes

1. Rivard, Jean-Yves, *L'Évolution des services de santé et des modes de distribution des soins au Québec*, CIHSW, Annex 2, Government of Québec, 1970, pp. 30 and ss.
2. See, for example: Monière, Denis, *Le Développement des idéologies au Québec*, Montréal, 1977, pp. 115 and ss. Touraine, Alain, *Les Sociétés dépendantes*, Bruxelles, 1976, pp. 98-99. Renaud, Marc, "Québec: New Middle Class in Search of Local Hegemony," in *International Review of Community Development*, Rome, Summer 1978. "Changement social et rapports de classe" in *Sociologie et sociétés*, Vol. 10, No. 2, October 1978.
3. *Report of the Study Committee on Public Assistance* (Boucher Committee), Government of Québec, June 1963, p. 60.
4. CIHSW, *Health Insurance*, Government of Québec, 1967, pp. 275 and ss.
5. CIHSW, *Social Services*, Vol. VI, Part I, Government of Québec, 1972, p. 41.
6. Rivard, Jean-Yves, *op. cit.*, pp. 60-70.
7. Lemieux, Vincent, Renaud, François, and Van Schoenberg, Brigitte, "La régulation des affaires sociales: une analyse politique" in *Administration publique du Canada*, 17, 1, Spring 1974, p. 43.
8. *Report of the Study Committee on Public Assistance*, *op. cit.*, p. 21. Note that one of the three members of this committee was Claude Morin, a senior civil servant for the Québec government who was responsible for the most important negotiations with the federal government concerning social security. He was the main architect of the Parti-Québécois strategy for independence and minister of intergovernmental affairs in the Lévesque cabinet from 1976 until 1981.

9. *Ibid.*, p. 60-61.
10. *Ibid.*, Recommendations 1, 2, 3, 4 ,5, 16, 61, 62, 64, 65.
11. *Ibid.*, Recommendation 18, p. 126.
12. *Ibid.*, p. 127.
13. *Ibid.*, p. 118.
14. *Ibid.*, p. 110.
15. See Desrosiers, Gilles, "La naissance du syndicalisme médical," *Le Médecin du Québec*, 1,1, Montréal, 1962, p. 14.
16. *Le Médecin du Québec*, June-July, p. 378.
17. Paquet, Gilles, " Vers une médecine rationnelle, *Le Médecin du Québec*, 5,3, March 1970, p. 113.
18. *Ibid.*, p. 116.
19. *Ibid.*, p. 119.
20. *Ibid.*
21. Paquet, Gilles, "Comment régler le problème de l'aide aux médecins," *Le Médecin du Québec*, 6, 8-9, August-September 1971, p. 441.
22. See Renaud, Gilbert, *L'Éclatement de la profession*, masters thesis, École de service social, Université de Montréal, 1978, pp. 78-107. Later published by Éditions coopératives Albert Saint-Martin, Montréal, 1978.
23. Conseil des œuvres de Montréal, *Opération rénovation sociale*, Montréal, December 1966, p. 13.
24. Conseil des œuvres de Montréal, *Une politique sociale pour le Québec*, brief presented to the CIHSW, Montréal, October 1967, pp. 5-11.
25. Swan, Lionel F., "Group Approach to Medical Care," cited in Paquet, *op. cit.*, 1974.
26. Rutstein, D.D., *The Coming Revolution in Medicine*, Cambridge, Mass., 1967. Geiger, J.H., "The Neighborhood Health Center," *American Journal of Public Health*, June 1967. Gibson, C.D., "The Neighborhood Health Center: The Primary Unit of Health Care," *American Journal of Public Health*, July 1968.
27. Boudreau, T., "Les Cantons de l'Est à l'avant-garde," *L'Hôpital d'aujourd'hui*, XVII, Feb. 1971, Montréal, pp. 15 and ss.
28. Rochon, Jean, in *L'Hôpital d'aujourd'hui*, XV, 12 Dec. 1969, Montréal, pp. 15 and ss.
29. Deschênes, Jean-Claude, editorial, *L'Hôpital d'aujourd'hui*, XIV, 5 May 1968, Montréal, p. 3.
30. Desrosiers, J., in *Le Médecin du Québec*, Montréal, June 1966, p. 225.
31. FMOQ, "Mémoire présenté à la CESBES," *Le Médecin du Québec*, Montréal, Aug.-Sept. 1968, pp. 11 and ss.

32. *L'Hôpital d'aujourd'hui*, XII, June 1967, p. 39.
33. *L'Hôpital d'aujourd'hui*, XVI, Jan. 1970, p. 34.
34. Renaud, Gilbert, *op. cit.*, p. 116.
35. *Ibid.*, p. 170.
36. *Ibid.*, p. 174.
37. *Ibid.*, p. 201-210.
38. *Ibid.*, p. 232.
39. Gourvil, Jean-Marie, *Fractions de classes et stratégies régionales au sein des C.B.E.R.*, École de service social, Université de Montréal, Aug. 1978, p. 4, unedited.
40. Gourvil, Jean-Marie, *op. cit.*, p. 12.
41. See Gourvil, Jean-Marie, *op. cit.*, p. 16.

CHAPTER 2
Federal Initiatives in the Field of Health and Welfare

As mentioned above, the initiatives of the federal government in the late fifties and early sixties were the determining factor that forced the provincial government to undertake the process of modernization of its health and welfare system. By virtue of the Canadian constitution, the federal government does not have the power to legislate directly on health and welfare policy. It can, however, propose cost-sharing arrangements to the provinces on the condition that the provinces administer programmes which meet federal requirements. This approach was used extensively during this period. It was the federal legislation concerning hospital insurance and unemployment insurance which set the reform process in motion. The Health Insurance Act of 1968, the Public Assistance Act of the same year, and the new law on social services passed in 1977 culminated this process. No new federal initiative in the health sector has been undertaken since 1968.

In addition to these financing laws, however, the federal government was able to manifest its presence through the creation of several commissions of inquiry, task forces and research projects. Because of the specific role of the federal government in this area, the reports produced were invariably concerned with ways to reduce costs and improve productivity. As such, they constitute an invaluable source of clear and explicit information on the economic strategies to increase productivity which inspired the various organizational models for the health and welfare systems of the provinces. It is from this perspective that I shall now examine the main reports of the federal government written during this period.

In most cases, these reports were published a few years before major governmental decisions in Québec, and there can be little doubt but that they had considerable influence on the reform process in Québec. They are thus of considerable importance for this study. It is interesting to note, in this respect, that the report of the Commission of Inquiry on Health and Social Welfare (CIHSW) in Québec (Castonguay-Nepveu Commission), in spite of its public image of complete independence and originality, was also largely influenced by the federal government reports.

The formulation of health policy: The Royal Commission on Health Services (Hall Commission), 1961-1965

In 1957, the Canadian parliament decided to establish a universal programme of public hospital insurance to be financed jointly by the federal government and the provinces, which agreed to implement the programme. Cost-sharing programmes were frequently proposed by the federal government after the war in an attempt to sidestep the thorny constitutional problems concerning the respective jurisdictions of the provincial and federal governments. The British North America Act stipulates that the fields of health, social assistance, education and culture are matters of purely provincial jurisdiction. In the successive phases of modernization of the Canadian state, characterized on the one hand by the transition from competitive capitalism to monopoly capitalism, and on the other hand by a growing dependency in relation to the United States, the central government used its powers of financing to propose cost-sharing arrangements to

80

the provinces on the condition that they modernize the key sectors of the economic and social infrastructure which are under their exclusive jurisdiction. In particular, the federal government encouraged action in all areas related to improvement in quality of the work force.

As early as the 1920's, in response to public pressure and union demands, different federal cabinets had studied the possibility of providing health insurance, but the enormous constitutional problems that this implied, due to the fact that health is an area of purely provincial jurisdiction, prevented these projects from seeing the light of day. It was only after the Second World War that the social democratic party in power in the province of Saskatchewan decided to set up a provincial programme of hospital insurance. Most provinces, however, and in particular Québec, remained resolutely hostile to anything which resembled socialized health care. The result was a situation in which access to health care varied greatly from one province to another. The potential threat that these disparities posed for the political integration of the provinces within Confederation, the perceived threat to national unity — which has always been an obsession for the central government — forced action in the health field in spite of opposition from Québec. In 1957, the Canadian Parliament unanimously adopted a law on public hospital insurance to be jointly financed by federal and provincial governments.

In spite of the fact that this measure constituted an infringement of provincial rights, the provinces, on the whole, were favourable because the federal contribution provided needed financial resources. The major pressure groups also supported this law, including the powerful Canadian Medical Association. In fact, this first piece of federal legislation in the health field met unanimous support except from the Québec government. From this point on, the area of social policy, particularly in the fields of health, social assistance and income security, was a constant source of conflict between Ottawa and Québec. The pattern, once set, was often to be repeated. The central government time and again took the initiative of proposing financial incentives in order to encourage the provinces to modernize their social policies, and the provinces, sooner or later, ended up accepting these pro-

81

grammes, often after some years' delay.

The implementation of public hospital insurance led to a spectacular increase in the number of hospital beds, to spiralling costs, and to an increased emphasis, on the part of both the medical profession and the public in general, on a type of health care directly related to hospitalization, clinical and biological research, specialized medicine and a sophisticated technological infrastructure.

At the same time, there was a general decrease in the prestige of general practice and simple health measures such as home care and community clinics, as well as a growing indifference to such issues as public health, prevention, rehabilitation, and so forth.

These changes were incredibly abrupt. Of course, the hospital insurance law was not the sole cause, but it certainly played an important role in the process. In this context, the following hypothesis can be put forward: the hospital insurance law and the large measure of support it received, particularly from the most powerful pressure groups—physicians, hospitals, pharmaceutical and medical industrial groups—corresponded to the necessary process of socialization of the costs of production of health by the state which was in a period of transition towards its new monopolist functions. The role of the state at this juncture was to consolidate the health field in the form of a medical and hospital industry and to take the measures necessary for the development and expansion of this industry along the lines of a greater concentration of power and more rational management.

This law opened the floodgates of consumer demand for hospital care and at the same time opened the way for technocratic action—or what is more euphemistically termed "modernization of the health care delivery system." The state soon discovered, however, that it was urgent to take another step. Uncontrolled consumption of hospital services very rapidly became financially unbearable and regulation of consumption became essential. Barely three years after the implementation of the hospital insurance law (1958), the federal government set up a Royal Commission on Health Services (Hall Commission) in 1961. The recommendations of the report which were handed down four years later were to

82

include a public health insurance scheme which, in the opinion of the experts on the commission, would have the effect of decreasing consumption of hospital care and thereby curtailing health expenditures dramatically.

It should be mentioned that, once again, the federal government had been preceded in this area by the social democratic government of Saskatchewan in 1962 and by the small "l" liberal regime in Alberta in 1963. These provinces had implemented obligatory public or semi-public insurance programmes for non-hospital care. The federal government had to move quickly, but this time not just to compensate for new disparities in health care between the provinces but also in an attempt to control the health costs which its earlier policy had sent skyrocketing. In this case, the political function of protecting national unity and the economic function of balanced expenditures were closely connected. Together these two functions indicated the growing role of the state—used here in the sense of both federal and provincial governments— in areas in which it had been absent or restricted to a simple support role. State intervention now became synonomous with an active role in the double process of political and economic management. The Hall Commission was to articulate the first coherent technocratic policy for the health care system in Canada.

The Hall Commission, like all commissions of inquiry, was composed of two types of commissioners. There were what we can call "political" members — that is, commissioners chosen by the government because of their representativity of the main interest groups affected by the work of the Commission; and the "experts" — that is, the research staff, which is chosen for its technical and scientific qualifications. The work of the research staff is generally published in the form of appendices to the main report of the Commission and, at least in principle, constitutes the scientific basis upon which the commissioners justify their recommendations. Scientific considerations are thus dosed with political considerations. This distinction between the two types of personnel and their respective roles in the work of the Commission is essential. The task of the "political" members, whether or not they are consciously aware of it, is to effect the transition from one state

83

of social relationships and ideology in a given field to a new form of these social relationships together with the new legitimating ideology. The task of the "scientific" personnel, on the other hand, who in this case were composed of representatives of the medical élites, and in particular, a new figure in the field, the health *economists*, the specialists of social and community medicine as well as representatives of other disciplines from the social and administrative sciences, is to develop new organizational models, to propose fundamental redefinitions of roles, functions and relationships for the main actors in the field. As such, the scientific personnel is called upon to act as a kind of vanguard for the new technocratic rationality in the health sector. The two groups, however, have one function in common which unites them and which stems directly from the authority that gave them their specific roles. The ultimate function of the Commission as a whole is to legitimize, both politically and scientifically, the role of the state as a new and important partner in the health field. Through its action, the state structures the field and thereby confers upon it a new functional coherence.

The first concern of the political subgroup in the Hall Commission was to establish the necessity of state intervention in the health field. They refer explicitly to the initiatives taken by some of the provinces and conclude that there exists a desire on the part of the Canadian people for a universal health care insurance programme. The attempt to legitimize the federal government's action in this area, then, is undertaken in reference to already existing provincial programmes. It is not their social-democratic character which is set forth as an example. On the contrary, the commissioners take pains to steer clear of any rhetoric which questions the nature of liberal society. It is rather the *organizational* solution which is referred to by the commissioners and the way this can better meet the needs of the population:

"Saskatchewan established an all inclusive plan [of medical services] on a compulsory basis.... [This initiative] is based, we believe, on the recognition that government action in the personal health care field is overwhelmingly desired by Canadians.... [However] the lack of harmony [of the plan] points to the danger which Canada faces if health planning and health care coverage is

84

left solely to the initiative and financial ability of individual provinces, without regard to adequate standards of health services for Canadians from one end of the country to the other... and without making the most effective use of Canada's health resources, both existing and those that will be forthcoming through integrated and cooperative health planning on a non-political Canada-wide basis."[1]

Arguing in favour of quality health services and their necessary coordination on a non-political basis, the Commission outlined its technocratic project for national management of health and called for the collaboration of all concerned.

"We need the fullest participation, both in planning and implementation of the health professions, health agencies, voluntary organizations, governments and of the public."[2]

This reference to the national demand for health care conceals the recognition — albeit reluctant, as we shall see — of the necessity for state intervention in the health sector to the extent that it constitutes a way of socializing the indirect costs of production and thus helps to maintain economic growth.

"The national interest requires that the risk must be spread over the whole productive population to cover everybody and not only those who choose to insure volutarily."[3]

The reference to voluntary adhesion is an attempt to gloss over the economic factors which influence this "free choice." Quite obviously, access to private health insurance schemes is simply not possible for the working classes and this entails important medical and social consequences. Pure liberalism, the ideology of "each man for himself," which is typical of competitive capitalism, is recognized here as a failure and as totally inadequate for the new needs of the work force in today's economy.

"[There is a] growing awareness of the cost to society as a whole of failure to be concerned and to act on behalf of its members.... The Sickness Survey of 1951... showed the appalling social and economic cost to Canada of ill-health, proving that the family and the nation pay heavily in terms of lost production for failure to make available to all Canadian citizens the standard of health service we know how to provide. Nor is it only in loss of production that we pay. (In 1961, 52,700,000 man-days were lost through sickness.) Many of our so-called 'welfare' expenditures are the end result of illness, disability and premature death.

To the extent, then, that health expenditures prevent or shorten

85

periods of sickness, reduce the extent of disability, postpone death, and contribute to the productivity of citizens, then to that degree health expenditures are investments in our human resources, with the prospect for rich dividends....

No enlightened government can ignore that the economic capacity of its citizens to be productive depends upon their health and vigour as much as upon their educational attainment."[4]

The new technocrats are trying here to convince the ruling economic class that it is in its interests, that is, that it can best perpetuate its class power, if it welcomes the state as a new partner in certain areas of social management.

The role of this new partner, however, poses some problems for the dominant ideological system which legitimizes the existing order. State intervention is generally viewed with suspicion by the liberal ideology of individualism. The state is simply supposed to guarantee individual freedoms. The Commission had the task, therefore, of producing a new ideology that would attempt to resolve what the dominant ideology had previously presented as being contradictory. This argument of the Commission sought to obtain recognition of the necessity of state intervention while at the same time reaffirming the necessity to maintain all the ideological and organizational prerogatives and characteristics of a society based on free enterprise.

The Commission recognized "the necessity to extend the advantages of prepayment to all Canadians" and continues: "the public interest... is clearly supportive of the individual's interest in his own health."[5] The report emphasizes "the individual's responsibility for his personal health and that of the members of his family." This means "temperate living" and "wise and prudent use of health services." It means, furthermore, that "he must assume responsibility as a member of organized society for meeting a fair share of the costs of providing health resources for the nation." The Report takes pains to add: "These obligations and responsibilities are perfectly in line with the democratic belief in the individual in a free and independent society."[6] The fundamental principles of liberal society, then, do not seem to be endangered. Individual freedom is vigorously defended. It is only the inconveniences which need to be corrected. Nevertheless, state intervention, even if it is seen as essentially compensatory, constitutes the first step towards a new model of society which is gradually being implemented in the health sector and elsewhere.

Although state action involves reorganization and planning of human and material resources, the Commission still loudly proclaimed that:

"We are opposed to state medicine, a system in which all providers of health services are functionaries under the control of the state. We recommend a course of action based upon... the cooperation and participation of society as a whole... upon freedom of choice on the part of the citizen, and on services provided by free and self-governing professions. By safeguarding these elements, so vital to a free society, we believe we have avoided difficulties inherent in a programme which attempts to nationalize the services which one group provides for others."[7]

This last comment was no doubt designed to avoid confusion between the propositions of the Hall Commission, based on a neo-liberal ideology, and the nationalized health scheme that the social democratic government of Saskatchewan had adopted and which provoked a doctors' strike in 1962. The Report comments on the Saskatchewan plan in the following terms: "a plan... attended by much needless friction..."[8] and then mentions the alternative proposals of Alberta and Ontario which "basically provide for voluntary coverage of certain medical services with subsidies for specified categories of citizens to help with the payment of premiums with such plans administered by private carriers, both profit and non-profit."[9] The state, in the view of the report, should intervene in a limited fashion and, in no case, enter into competition with private enterprise.

The Commission sought to portray state intervention as simply that of a new partner alongside and not above the other partners. The role of the medical establishment is clearly recognized and the Report calls for cooperation and collaboration:

"We have tried our best to see that the Report does not give primacy to any one area while at the same time recognizing that health services consist of many interdependent elements with the physician as the central figure. Cooperation of all elements must be of the essence of any properly conceived health service. The programme we visualize is rooted in this concept of close cooperation of all health services personnel with the physician and the administering agency or agencies."[10]

The freedom of the health professionals and the supremacy of the medical profession is explicitly reaffirmed when the Report recognizes "the right of members of health professions... to free choice of location and type of practice and to professional self-government."[11] "No profession is nationalized; no professional is turned into a state employee. Private practitioners or voluntary organizations will continue to provide the bulk of health services."[12] It is apparent, then, that in this initial phase of state intervention, it is what I would term the *techno-professional* model which is dominant. The emphasis is on good faith, understanding and collaboration with a view towards integrating services provided by various institutions. "For hospitals... [freedom and self-government] means freedom from political control or domination and encouragement of administration at the local level."[13] The new health experts exist only to facilitate this coordination. If the state was simply concerned with implementing free medical care this view of things might be plausible, but it is clear, especially when we turn to look at the work of the scientific group, that state action is envisaged sooner or later on a much greater scale. The time when the state limited itself to a role of support is over. The state must now begin to assume its role of leadership.

Similarly, the Commission professed its respect for the existing private organizations and community resources and simply stated its desire to improve the collaboration and integration of public and private sectors. There was no question of nationalizing any institutions. The Report only expressed the hope that it would be possible to efficiently coordinate resources on the regional level through voluntary cooperation. The creation of regional planning councils was suggested but there was no call for new institutions, only new mechanisms for facilitating discussion and coordination.

In fact, it seems that it was almost with reluctance that the commissioners recognized the necessity for state intervention: "We are convinced that, however much we prefer voluntary to public action, nothing but public action and support at every level of government can correct the imbalance

88

[between regions]."[14] Nevertheless, public action should scrupulously respect the prerogatives of voluntary action. "Outstanding among our impressions was the constructive work of many voluntary agencies."[15] The public sector relies on private initiative for innovation. Needs are first detected by voluntary agencies and then picked up by the public sector. "We believe that this process of interaction of voluntary and public action and, hence, this progress, will continue."[16] The Report emphasized "the necessity of retaining and developing further the indispensable work of voluntary agencies in the health care field"[17] and therefore recommended "that voluntary organizations have an integral place in any comprehensive health care programme and that they participate actively in the work of the various planning councils."[18]

The view of the community and community organizations and services expressed in the Report is very much tributary to the liberal ideology of independence, individual freedoms, and the relationship between the state and the individual as described above. The community is the ideal level for the private sector and voluntary initiatives while at the same time constituting the most logical level for organizing a coherent delivery system. Instead of trying to compete with or contest these local initiatives, the state should seek to encourage them and to make them more efficient through a process of coordination and planning. There is no trace in the Report of the potential conflicts which were to come to the surface in later years, between the interests of the community and the state. In other words, for the Hall Commission, the state simply seeks to coordinate and plan. It does not centralize power; it does not impose a systematic organizational model in the field of health.

The recommendation to create "on the local, regional, provincial and federal levels, representative health planning councils in order to ensure public participation concerning the goals and objectives of health care and to respond more closely to the needs of the population"[19] seems to indicate a reference to the type of community organization that had been developed since the beginning of the century in the welfare sector in North America along the lines of "grass-roots democracy" and community councils.[20] These councils were seen as res-

89

ponsible for coordination and planning health and welfare resources. Their operations on the community level (town or neighbourhood) are meant to be representative of both public and private bodies as well as professionals and non-professionals within the population. As such, they constitute an institution typical of North American industrial society of the period before and after the Second World War when health and welfare establishments were largely financed through public charity for the poor.

It is striking to note how the Commission's report emphasized the respect and development of these structures and the extent to which it considered that the state would be able to play an active role in them. The novelty of these councils seems to lie in the planning role which the Commission attributed to them and the fact that they should exist at "all levels of government: federal, provincial and municipal."[21] This seems to indicate a desire for vertical integration—and not just horizontal integration on the community level—of health planning. In this sense, one is left with the impression that they are eventually meant to be major instruments of state action. In addition, the Commission mentioned the importance of planning and research for the future which should also be the concern of these councils. It is possible, then, to guess the lines along which state action will develop, but for the moment there is no question of centralization, and therefore no mention of decentralization: two of the major concerns of the technocrats in the following years who were to look on the community in quite different terms. As we shall see, there was an important mutation in the ideology of the community. The image of the community as a relatively homogeneous and closely integrated social unit in which the members have common interests, is gradually replaced by the definition of a community as a jurdico-geographic unit, an administrative level within an integrated system of health care delivery. It may correspond to the geographic area of the sociological community, but not necessarily. It is only *a posteriori* that there is an attempt to recreate community life within the framework of the new bureaucratically defined subdivisions.

The rationalization of health organization

(a) The Hall Commission and health organization

We now have some understanding of the political relations which the Hall Commission intended to establish with the dominant figures of the health sector. Quite clearly, the desire was to keep as much of the liberal order intact as possible. It is interesting, in this context, to look briefly at the orientations of the technical and scientific personnel of the Commission who were particularly concerned with the administrative and professional organization of health care. This means, first of all, that we must consult the *appendices* which were written by experts in various areas, and then attempt to retrace the impact of these studies on the commissioners' report. With this in mind, then, we shall refer either to the annexes or to the parts of the report itself which are influenced by them, as the work of the "scientific" group. This distinction between the two groups within the Hall Commission clearly reveals the very different and apparently contradictory functions of each group. Whereas the "political" group appears to be quite conservative, the "scientific" group was technically innovative and proposed a major revamping of the whole organization of the health sector. While the concerns of the first group were to reassure the existing élites and to protect their privileges, the second group called into question the traditional powers and privileges in the field and proposed sweeping reforms in the name of science and the needs of the population. There is no doubt that this was a very subtle strategy for change and we come across this "division of labour" again and again in the various commissions of inquiry connected with health and welfare reform throughout the sixties. This situation reflects the functions of change and modernization of power relationship that the state fulfills during the transition from a competitive capitalist society to a monopoly capitalist society. The models proposed by the "scientific" group are in perfect harmony with the new roles of the state in the process of the socialization of the costs of production. In this sense, their work is directly related to the establishment of a universal state programme of health insurance which was the primary objective of the Hall

91

Commission.

The propositions put forth by the scientific personnel of the Hall Commission were in essence to be repeated, in one form or another, by all the commissions, task forces and research groups that tackled the question of the organization of the health care system over the following years. This is an indication that the transformation of social relationships brought about by the process of concentration of the productive forces had penetrated the entire social organization, its ideologies and its praxis.

The establishment of a health insurance scheme corresponds to the administrative and political necessity to compensate for the disastrous effects of the first law concerning hospital insurance which, by covering all medical consultations and by encouraging the growth of hospital out-patient clinics, had sent hospital expenditures spiralling. The first measure had the effect of reinforcing the powers of physicians and hospital administrators. The health insurance scheme, however, was meant to be a measure through which the entire organization of the health sector could be implemented. At the very moment that the "political" group of the Hall Commission was proclaiming that it recognized and accepted the existing model of health care, the experts were in the process of defining the main characteristics of a radically different model. It was this concern for a new health organization model which provides the explanation as to why their work on a public health insurance scheme led them to a complete re-examination of existing medical training programmes, the development of paramedical professions, group practice, out-patient clinics, community services and home care. Social objectives and organizational reform were inextricably related. The insurance plan could not be financially viable unless the health care system was completely reorganized in order to increase productivity. The task of the experts, then, was to find solutions to this situation and it was in this context that they sought to reorganize the health sector along the lines of technocratic reform. The main thrust of their efforts was concentrated on the consolidation and development of non-specialized health care on the community level in an attempt to reduce consumption of specialized medical care in the hospitals. The role of the "community" in this model was different, and in many ways contradictory to prevailing conceptions. It was no longer seen as a pre-existing sociological entity which could serve as a coherent unit for the distribution of health care. In the eyes of the reformers, the community was an administrative level which played a strategic role in the reorganization of the health sector along the lines of industrial efficiency. The community was seen first and foremost as a means to increase operational efficiency.

Two general trends in contemporary medicine were singled out by the report:[22] on the one hand, a *wholistic* approach to medical care with the emphasis on the patient as a social being rather than merely as a disease entity; on the other, a tendency towards specialization. This latter tendency, however, creates new problems. Fragmentation of medical practice has resulted in the fragmentation of the patient. "The task of putting the patient together again... is an essential next step in the progress of medical practice."[22a] Already, in 1964, the Commission was expounding this criticism of specialized hospital care, its over-concentration on pathology and the lack of attention to the importance of the social environment. This criticism was to come back again and again in the various government reports over the next decade. Consequently, the Hall Commission deplored the medical training programmes which put too much emphasis on specialization[23] and suggested that the general practitioner should be the key figure in the new model of health care. "You might call this man a patient-oriented community based physician."[24] In the eyes of the commissioners, the importance of the GP should be more fully recognized and his training should be oriented towards a comprehensive care approach. He should be involved in other sectors of health care such as treatment of patients within a family or community context, care for the chronically ill and the aged as well as family planning and mental health. He should be concerned with both the social and medical dimensions of rehabilitation, home care, prevention, and so forth. On the whole, then, the general practitioner was supposed to provide a continuous and comprehensive approach to health care and for this reason should be closely integrated into the community with which he worked. He should be the "neighbourhood doctor," the key figure on this primary level of the health care delivery system. As such, the role of the general practitioner was to be profoundly transformed, and the report suggested that departments of general practice be set up in medical schools. "[T]eaching in medicine should include preparation in sociology, psychology, statistics, and economics, which are the basic sciences necessary to an understanding of organized community health work and to... social medicine." [25]

The main thrust of the strategy for the reorganization of the health care system was concentrated on this new conception of the role of the general practitioner. In this sense, we are looking at a *techno-professional* model, based on an alliance between technocrats and professionals.

To ensure the effectiveness of this model, the organization of health services had to be "rationalized":

"Gains in productivity which have reduced costs tremendously in most lines of production in the industrial countries have not been so noticeable in the service industries.... The organizational revolution, which has been responsible for many of the gains in productivity in the economy generally, has largely by-passed health services." [26]

Several methods of increasing the productivity of non-hospital health services were seen as crucial if expenditures were to be brought under control.

Group practice, for example, was strongly encouraged:

"Medical services of comparable quality can be provided at a lower real cost in a group setting than they can under conditions of solo practice. These gains can be attributed to the fact that practice is organized to take advantage of specialization and division of labour [and] to use capital equipment efficiently...." [27]

"[It would be highly desirable to] provide the incentive to bring about staff organization using the known techniques of record review, case conference, medical audit, staff education as well as those informal contacts which go to make group practice a 'way of life'." [28]

Furthermore, the report suggested a greater division of labour within the medical profession and the development of the paramedical professions which are capable of performing much of the work usually reserved for physicians, at a significantly lower cost. In the same sense, the nursing staff should be seconded by "auxiliary nursing personnel and clerical staff so that skilled nursing time may be used to full

94

advantage."[29]

Concerning the *organization* of health services, the report recommended that "out-patient services benefit as a condition of any further payment in respect of in-patient benefits"[30] and that out-patient services should have priority.

The report also recommended that a major programme of hospital or community-based *home care* should be launched and a "full-scale hospital-based home care programme should be required before any request for hospital bed expansion is considered."[31] One of the annexes to the report devoted a major part of its attention to the question of organizing home care services.[32] The aged and chronically ill were singled out as prime candidates for home care. "Obviously this does not eliminate all costs. It shifts some of them from the community to the patient or his family."[33] A coordinating agency for home care should be established to which physicians could refer their patents just as, at present, he refers them for admission to the hospital.[34] "Where there is close contact between the hospital and a home care programme, we have, in fact, a model for coordinated health services in the community."[35]

Coordination is to be the new priority. "Health services are becoming increasingly interrelated with and often depend on other community services."[36] One of the experts recommends that health and welfare services be amalgamated.[37]

The report therefore suggests "promoting an institutional environment which will facilitate a coordinated approach"[38] on the local level while at the same time creating Regional Health Services Commissions (and eventually Health and Welfare Commissions) which could organize community health services and eliminate costly duplication of services.[39] Effective coordination can only be implemented by competent administrative personnel which should be recognized as a new health profession in its own right.[40] This new profession should be organized around the "health services coordinator" whose functions should be:

"First of all, those of a medical *administrator* who is equipped to plan, to administer and coordinate, and to evaluate services. In the second place, he should be the local consultant and expert in *epidemiology* and *community health research*, not only for communicable diseases but also for newer problems of the public's health,

95

such as cancer, heart disease and the chronic diseases in general. He should be involved in the provision of adequate community services for home care, the care of the aged, accident control, rehabilitation, mental health and family planning...."[41]

The three key figures, then, in the social and community health model are the general practitioner, the medical health officer and the health administrator. It is hardly surprising, in this context, that some ten years later, the Québec government would try to implement an organizational reform of health services very much along the lines suggested in the Hall Report. The Local Community Service Centres and the Departments of Community Health which will be analyzed in Chapter Five are eloquent examples in this regard. These institutions grew out of the recommendations of the CIHSW (Castonguay-Nepveu) Report, which six years after the Hall Commission, made similar recommendations which it heralded as major innovations in the field of health organizational practice. In point of fact, however, there was precious little innovation. Both the CIHSW Report and the Hall Commission Report were largely based on the theoretical and experimental work that had been underway in the United States since the end of the 1950's in certain universities like Harvard and Johns Hopkins or the Kaiser Foundation in California. It is probably more correct, in this case, to speak not of innovation but rather of the process of penetration of new modes of health organization which are coherent with characteristics of monopoly capitalist societies, that is, from a society in which the process of industrial and financial concentration is the most advanced.

(b)   The Task Force Report on the Cost of Health Services in Canada (Willard Report), 1969

The report of this task force comes to largely similar conclusions concerning community and social health care as those of the Hall Commission and the CIHSW Report. What is more surprising, and at the same time more significant, is that these recommendations are suggested from a strictly economic point of view. Here we are dealing with the language of accountants rather than that of visionary social reformers concerned with promoting a "revolutionary" new model of health care in the interests of social justice. A more convincing demonstration of the technocratic nature of this health organization reform can hardly be made.

The objectives and composition of this task force leave no doubt as to the motivations involved. Several sub-sommittees were set up by the federal government in order to come up with suggestions for severely curtailing the rate of growth of expenditures on health care:

"The cost of health services has risen so rapidly in Canada in recent years that three alternatives are now imminent:
— the standards of health care now available can be reduced, or;
— taxes, premium or deterrent fees can be raised even higher, or;
— ways must be found to restrain growth of cost increases through better operation of the health service structure now in existence, and serious consideration must be given to a future major revamping of the entire system."[42]

Quite obviously, it is the third solution that was the focus of attention for the experts called together by the federal government. Nearly a hundred civil servants, hospital administrators, physicians, economists, university professors and researchers were grouped together in seven work committees on the following themes:

- consumption patterns of medical care
- administrative efficiency
- salaries and wages
- hospital beds and equipment
- medical care distribution methods
- costs of medical care
- costs of health services.

"The object of the exercise was... to put into economic focus a vast patchwork of separate services.... Four main points emerge: (1)...Health is a labour-intensive *industry* and may in years to come be the second largest employer of labour in Canada. Even now, seventy per cent (70%) of health costs are fees, salaries and wages.... Costs of health services related closely to wage and salary levels in all industries and additional cost increases in this area may occur. However, increased productivity and better operation of the health care system can reduce the impact of these increases upon total costs. It is necessary that the efforts of this vast force of... people be deployed with the utmost skill to ensure *maximum productivity*.

(2)...The remorseless escalation of [health care] costs should not continue. Selective use of federal and provincial contributions should, in future, be aimed at encouraging economy in the health services and avoiding financial rigidity which can lead to arbitrary procedures and entrenched inefficiency.

(3) Every task force which touched the question, clearly felt that *regional* organization of all health services involving *central coordination* of many facilities and agencies was essential to cost efficiency.... Coordination among federal and provincial governments is essential....

(4) The health care system exists solely to serve all the people, and without their understanding and cooperation, attempts to reorganize and strengthen it through cost efficiency will be infinitely more difficult.... The most obviously desirable alternative... would be for the present structure [to] be reformed in all its aspects.... It is a vital challenge to all involved, which means every Canadian, layman or professional, and particularly those in positions of leadership and responsibility."[43]

This statement, which reflects the essential concerns of the sub-committees, was formulated by the government itself. In other words, here again, it is the political personnel which intervened to summarize the technical work of the experts and to "put order" into the various recommendations. The political function of management of social relations is acutely obvious. The postulate that health can be considered primarily as an industry is clearly accepted. It is on this condition that productivity can be increased. All efforts must therefore converge towards transforming the various independent parts of this system into a coordinated, integrated industry. Regional organization is one of the main strategies for attaining optimal performance. The question of wages and salaries was identified as the principal source of cost growth. Honoraria, wages and salaries were analyzed in the most sophisticated manner but no consideration was given to the enormous disparities between these forms of remuneration nor to their respective rates of growth. The veiled reference to private industry seems to suggest that the primary objective concerning wages and salaries was to be greater control over wage increases, that is, over the revenues of the support staff, and there is little doubt that this was meant as a warning for the trade unions. Federal-provincial relations were discussed with the hope that the provinces would come to support the objectives of the federal government. The diagnostic of the situation, then, was, not surprisingly, couched in terms of collaboration between all classes and sectors of the society to work in harmony for the common interests of all health care consumers under the guidance of the new organizational experts who will resolutely defend our national health. The collusion between technical expertise and the political interests of a social class can scarcely be more obvious than in the quotation cited above.

This task force was active in 1969, at the same time that the CIHSW in Québec proposed its own health reform project. The first sub-committee of the federal task force (on health care consumption patterns) outlined the general framework and the guiding principles for organizational reform. This group particularly stressed the importance of regionalization. Thomas Boudreau, whom we mentioned earlier, acted as a special consultant for this committee. The president was one of the foremost physicians of the Sherbrooke medical school and in general a good number of the experts involved in this task force had also participated in the work of the Hall Commission and were to be involved in later commissions of inquiry as well. In fact, it is possible to trace the itineraries of a solid group of technocrats which, from the beginning of the sixties through to the present day, has been active in adapting the Canadian health system to the necessities of economic and social development.

The fact that the federal government is not responsible for the daily operations of the health care system while at the same time is responsible for financing them, means that it can be brutally clear concerning its objectives for the transformation of the health and welfare sector to adapt it to the requirements of monopoly capitalist society. It is the federal government which acts as the vanguard for the implementation of technocratic reform in this sector. Federal government policy papers, which were more concerned with developing an overall strategy, are much more explicit and direct than the policy papers of the various provinces. These documents produced by the federal government constitute a clear expression of the aims of the state in monopoly capitalist society:

"Only government commands the financial and organizational resources and the authority to undertake the required changes."[44]

The main propositions formulated by the sub-committees were the following:

The key concept in the new definition of health organization was that of the *integrated system* which can be

99

achieved only through the reinforcement of governmental authority—both federal and provincial. This authority is considered essential in the areas of planning and programming which necessarily implies a process of centralization of power in the hands of the state. In this context, the state considers that it has acquired the overall responsibility for the health system. The various actors and institutions each pursue particular and sometimes contradictory objectives, and it is considered to be the role of the state to bring them "into line" (that is, to recognize the ultimate coherence of the system). This can be done only in the name of the common good, and in particular, in the name of the disadvantaged.

This new conception of the health system explicitly recognized for the first time the role of active leadership for the federal government in the health sector. This becomes clear when we examine the four levels of organization proposed for the health sector: local, regional, provincial and national.

"Administrative arrangements should be made to provide full coordination of the total health care delivery system at the provincial level, with health services, welfare services, mental health care, hospital care and medical and ancillary care as elements of a single function and overall plan. Greater emphasis should be placed on defining the needs of elderly, low-income and other disadvantaged groups.... The federal government should ensure that national standards and guidelines are available and coordinate its legislation to the highest degree possible to further the objectives of provincial governments, so the Canadian citizen has available the resources necessary to meet his or her needs."[45]

The *regionalization* of health care is one of the major propositions of the sub-committees. This policy should be closely integrated within an overall planning programme based on systems analysis:

"The concept of area-wide or regional planning for health facilities and services... is required if integrated and balanced health care *systems* are to be achieved. The need is so evident, and the economies and improvements so significant, that regional planning should proceed immediately.... A true partnership of comprehensive health planning between the government and voluntary sectors is essential in each province. Only at the regional level can sufficient perspective be gained to effectively organize and integrate the varied health resources of the area concerned. Depending on population and geographic area, an entire province, or more than

100

one province, could constitute a region for certain services or planning purposes." [46]

It is clear from the passage quoted above that planning is to include both public and private resources. Furthermore, effective planning implies the creation of a new political unit: the region. The state, in its attempt to implement the new economic and political rationality of monopoly capitalism, must break down the outdated political and geographical structures of competitive capitalism. If the provinces are too small, they should be grouped together. If they are too large, they should be sub-divided. The CIHSW Report in Québec follows the same logic when it suggests dividing the province into three health and welfare regions. Similarly, outdated definitions of jurisdiction within the medical profession must be abolished. The traditional separation between hospital care and medical care must be overcome. The sectorial division between health and welfare services is questioned. The Report emphasizes that effective population management of the most disadvantaged sectors of the population necessitates an integrated approach to health and welfare policies. We can see, then, that the regional planning process with its objective of creating an integrated system of state action in the health and welfare field implies a complete transformation of prevailing ideological, political and administrative categories.

The efficiency of a system from this point of view is, of course, directly related to the efficiency of management techniques. The task force pronounced a severe verdict in this respect: "Industrial management techniques and standards have not been employed to maximize the contribution of financial resources allocated to the health services industry." [47]

The report suggests, amongst other measures:

"... an adequate incentive plan for hospitals and their employees.... Industry experience shows that effective productivity rates of 80 to 85% of performance standards are routine without incentives; with incentives, rates of 120 to 130% can be reached and maintained. It follows that incentives should not be paid for performance which is below established norms." [48]

"The Research and Statistics Directorate of the Department of National Health and Welfare [should] undertake an ongoing programme to compare productivity in hospitals with that in other industries." [49]

101

The report also strongly emphasizes the advantages of a greater division of labour for a more efficient use of personnel. A detailed analysis of the professional qualifications necessary to accomplish each task would allow greater use of non-medical personnel.

"It is becoming increasingly evident that allied health professionals such as public health nurses, social workers, physiotherapists and dietitians can and should be employed to form a health care team which would relieve physicians of the execution of many routine duties which can just as ably be performed by other, less highly paid, professionals. The medical care plan should cover the services of allied health professionals working under the direction of practising physicians."[50]

The report recommends a similar policy for hospital services:

"The needs of the individual patient... should be met in the most economical manner possible.... The capital cost of an acute care hospital bed is often more than $40,000. The patient in that bed should actually require the range of services the investment provides. Otherwise less expensive levels of care should be used."[51]

It is for the same reason that the development of ambulatory and home care services are strongly encouraged. Hospitalization should only be considered when absolutely necessary and for the shortest possible duration.

It is also from this perspective that the Report suggests the establishment of Local Health Centres, staffed by general practitioners, which would provide the full range of medical services connected with prevention, diagnosis and curative treatment but would not include hospital beds. These centres were also meant to organize full-scale home care programmes as one of the major priorities in a strategy designed to reduce costs and alleviate pressure on hospitals.

This, then, is the picture of the new integrated system of regional health care as seen from the viewpoint of economic performance. The over-riding concern with the norms of industrial productivity was the most revealing and most significant contribution of the Task Force Report on the Cost of Health Services in Canada. The integration of voluntary community organizations, the encouragement of Local Health Centres, and the emphasis on regional organization are all meant to be measures designed to improve the economic

102

performance of the new health care system.

(c) The Report of the Study Group on Community Health Care (Hastings Report), 1972

Three factors motivated the creation of this task force by the Department of National Health and Welfare. Once again there is the over-riding concern with the rate of growth of health care expenditures, and particularly those related to acute care hospitalization. Secondly, there is the determination to provide alternatives to acute care and to traditional medical views on treating diseases rather than promoting health. Thirdly, there exists the necessity to encourage more effective mechanisms of coordination of resources on a local basis.

"In summary, community health services are increasingly seen as an important means for slowing the rate of increase in the cost of health services and for more fully reflecting the objectives, priorities and relationships which society wishes to establish for health care in the future."[52]

"The real question is, therefore, not how much we will be spending but what will we be getting for our money. How may community health centres help in achieving the potential economies of a health service system?"[53]

It is clear, then, that this report, the last in a long series of studies concerned with organizational reform in the health sector, continues in the footsteps of the Task Force on the Cost of Health Services in Canada. With the creation of this task force, the government explicitly recognizes that community health care constitutes a major element in technocratic health management, especially in the light of its effectiveness as a cost reduction strategy.

Of course, this in itself was not particularly new, since both Great Britain and especially the United States, with its Office for Economic Opportunity and its Health Maintenance Organizations, had been forerunners in the field of community-based social policy. Furthermore, the legislative measures concerning health reform in Québec had been adopted in late 1971. One of the principal features of this reform had been the creation of Local Community Service Centres (CLSC) which were modelled along lines similar to those mentioned above.

In addition to their strategic importance as a means of reducing health costs and of providing a viable alternative to

103

acute care hospitalization, the community centres played a key role in the technocratic effort to modify traditional modes of medical practice. The community centre postulated multi-disciplinary group practice and thus favoured salaried remuneration for all practitioners, including physicians. It was seen as a small-scale, flexible organization with a minimum of bureaucracy and a maximum of adaptability to the needs and resources of the community. Most importantly, its main concerns were to be prevention and a comprehensive approach to health care. It is clear, then, that the community centre was meant to be the institutional form for the type of social health programme so often described in the various governmental reports.

"In every case, the community health centre should be an integral part of a wider health services system.... Only in this system setting will its full economic and service potential be achievable."[54]

The community centre was not only meant to take into consideration the needs and resources of the community; it was also meant to encourage an authentic form of client participation concerning health problems. The objective to "involve individuals more fully in decisions about services provision as well as in personal and family health care"[55] was, in itself, a strategy for cost reduction. In much the same way, home care was encouraged as a means of involving the community and the patients themselves in responsibility for their own health problems. In this sense, to encourage participation, whether it be of patients, members of the community at large, or hospital staff, is also an attempt to re-allocate power within the decision-making process by reducing the relative importance of the established powers (in particular those of the hospital and the physicians). The objective here is not so much ideological or political as it is economic. The over-riding concern is to discourage unnecessary use of the most expensive components of the health care system, and team-work, a community approach and participation are all means by which this objective can be reached.

"The central concept of the community health centre is teamwork. The kind of teamwork which is meant is not the kind of teamwork which has been developed in hospital operating theatres, a paramilitary system to deal with inert patients, but the milieu therapy approach, developed first in mental hospitals, and later in community psychiatry. This approach recognizes that all those who have contact with the client may influence his behaviour and his self-concepts, but that professionals have a special responsibility in making their interventions not only to help the patient but to help others to help him, and to help him to help himself. The focus is not upon the physician as team leader but upon problem-solving processes for the client/patient.... This approach focuses upon helping the patient to take greater responsibility for his own health and the community to take greater responsibility for its members."[56]

The community centre was seen as an important means by which health consumers could progressively take responsibility for their own health care services. By providing basic, comprehensive and preventive health care services, the community centres help to demystify the traditional clinical model of medical practice with its almost exclusive reliance on chemical therapy. The main efforts of the community centres were to be concentrated on health education programmes designed to modify both health maintenance behaviour and health service consumption patterns. It is in this sense, then, that individual responsibility for one's own health is stressed.

"Community health centres can and should provide a setting for formal and informal education necessary to change attitudes. The public should understand that modern scientific medicine is limited in what it can accomplish — many ills cannot be remedied. Individuals must take real responsibility for personal and family health (diet, smoking). They should be made to feel confident that nurses and other non-physician personnel can give high-quality care and that community health centres can provide many services as effectively and safely as hospitals."[57]

This vast ideological campaign in favour of a "new" health model is directly related to the state's objective of reducing by all means possible the cost of public services and particularly the most expensive ones such as health care. In the face of the so-called uncontrollable rise in health care expenditures, the state attempts to place as much of the burden as possible on individuals and their families. The strategy employed consists of an attempt to control demand for hospital care at the source by erecting a series of ideological barriers designed to prevent the demand for health care from reaching the more expensive levels of treatment. In 1972, when this report was written, the economic crisis was well

105

underway and there is little doubt that these economic pressures played an important role in the minds of the authors. The miraculous progress of medical science so loudly proclaimed during the fifties and sixties was no longer the favourite theme of the day. The time had come to realize the enormous benefits that simple, basic solutions could provide to health problems. In this perspective, the community health centres were seen as the most effective means of implementing the recommendations of the Task Force Report on the Cost of Health Services (1969).

(d) The white paper *A New Perspective on the Health of Canadians* **(1974)**

This reorientation of health policy towards progressive withdrawal by the state from the health sector culminated in the white paper of the Department of National Health and Welfare entitled *A New Perspective on the Health of Canadians.*[58] Its impact was considerable not only within Canada but also internationally.[59]

"To my knowledge, it is the first time in the capitalist world that an official government document stated that it is no longer sufficient for governments to reorganize and reform the service delivery system but rather that they must make significant changes in the present situation of resource allocation. The report states that serious efforts should be made to switch from a curative approach to a policy of prevention, from reliance on medical care to action which can eliminate individual risk factors (cigarette and alcohol consumption, poor nutrition habits, lack of physical exercise, and so forth) as well as risk factors in the environment. Even if this policy statement proves to be empty rhetoric, the fact that it is so widely publicized is a clear indication of the way in which the fiscal crisis can influence changes in the orientations of health policy. Even the most ardent defenders of modern medicine scarcely a decade ago have been forced by this fiscal crisis to revise their perspective and their priorities."[60]

The main thrust of this widely publicized government paper was organized around two themes in vogue in the field of health management throughout the world at that time. The minister linked these themes together in an attempt to justify the new orientation of national health policy:

— Specialized medicine with its costly institutional and technological requirements imposes impossible demands upon society. Cost growth in this sector is unlimited unless a clear policy decision is made to put a halt to this situation.

— In spite of massive investment in the health sector, the overall level of health has not improved. Worse, it has declined. Why? Because the cause of sickness today is related to our modern way of life: pollution, lack of exercise, eating habits, and so forth.

"It is evident now that further improvements in the environment, reductions in self-imposed risks, and a greater dnowledge of human biology are necessary if more Canadians are to live a full, happy, long and illness-free life.... The Government of Canada [therefore] now intends to give human biology, the environment and lifestyle as much attention as it has to the financing of health care organization..."[61]

In this white paper, the federal government announces a new health ideology which will guide its policy decisions in the field. The main emphasis in this document is on the process of demedicalization of health. Although the report admits that the causes of poor living conditions cannot be solely attributed to individual factors, its practical recommendations are nevertheless directed towards the individual with the idea that each individual is ultimately responsible for this own health.

"Personal decisions and habits that are bad, from a health point of view, create self-imposed risks.... Individual blame must be accepted by many for the deleterious effect on health of their respective lifestyles.... If we simply give up on individuals whose lifestyles create excessive risks to their health, we will be abandoning a number who could have changed.... The deterministic view must be put aside in favour of faith in the power of free will.... The ultimate philosophical issue... is whether, and to what extent, government can get into the business of modifying human behaviour, even if it does so to improve health.... One must inevitably conclude that society, through government, owes it to itself to develop protective marketing techniques to counteract... abuses. The marketing of social change is a new field which applies the marketing techniques of the business world to getting people to change their behaviour, i.e. eating habits, exercise habits, smoking habits, driving habits, etc...."[62]

As we can see, this paper is perfectly consistent with neo-liberal ideology which seeks to plan and "rationalize" society to conform to the dominant economic interests while at the same time extolling the virtues of freedom of choice and individual responsibility. In fact, the emphasis is on individuals as levers for social change. Since the state is unable to control the growth in the supply of health care services, it tries to influence the demand by persuading consumers, not simply that they should limit their consumption but rather that they should realize that there is no direct relationship between health care consumption and their general state of health. As individuals, they are able through personal discipline not only to stay in good health but also to reduce the rate of growth of expenditures on health care.

It is in this context that particular attention is paid to "high-risk sectors of the population" rather than individual cases of disease or sickness. These sectors can be effectively aided only by a health strategy designed to reduce risks.

"*Risk* is a statistical term which is expressed in percentages or odds.... One does not profess to make predictions about individuals but about the likelihood of an event occurring in a population of given characteristics."[63]

To illustrate this notion, the report gives examples of health control for problems such as Downs' Syndrome (mongoloidism) and coronary-artery disease, but it soon becomes apparent that the real issue at stake is one of *social* control.

"Sickness and death rates for [the 5 to 14 age group] are low.... [However,] pre-adolescents are a 'threshold' population which will shortly be taking decisions that will determine whether they will become high-risk or low-risk individuals in later life.... One could identify, within a general population aged 5 to 14, certain individuals whose behaviour is not only negative as it affects themselves but who also exercise a strong influence on their susceptible acquaintances. The phenomenon of adolescents adopting the values and habits of rebellious peers, rather than the values of society in general or those of their parents, is not new, but the scale on which it is now happening is truly alarming.... [A recent study] points out the prevalence... of such attitudes as wanting to be older than they are, of rebelliousness against authority and social norms, of impulsiveness and risk-taking and of poor academic performance.... There is no doubt, therefore, that there is a readily identifiable sub-group within the age-class 5 to 14 who are not only themselves at high risk but who pull many others along with them. This sub-group may well be a target population of the first order...."[64]

Health control is thus inseparable from social control. A

108

"scientific" approach using social indicators legitimizes a medical interpretation of social behaviour while at the same time, the struggle against deviancy becomes one of the main ways in which the effectiveness and productivity of the health system can be improved.

In addition to stressing the importance of identifying target populations whose "lifestyles" and environment constitute major cases of morbidity and mortality, the report called for a new priority to be given to various sectors of the population who do not receive adequate health care because their conditions "do not satisfy the healing instincts on which the health care system thrives": [65] the disabled, the chronically ill, the retarded, the mentally ill, and the aged. The growing importance of these sectors of the population forces the state to insist upon a reorganization of health care in these areas based on less costly methods such as home care and the use of paramedical personnel. Along the same lines, the report suggested that the proportions of acute care hospital beds be reduced in favour of beds for the chronically ill, thereby reducing overall hospital operation costs. Lastly, the report emphasized that it is the neglected segments of the Canadian population... "the economically deprived, the troubled parents and others who are either at a high risk or are receiving insufficient health care" [66] who will benefit by the greater coverage offered by this new perspective on health policy.

A New Perspective on the Health of Canadians can thus be seen as the most advanced conceptualization of the contradictions confronting the state in the health sector. It attempted to formulate a strategy which would enable the state to assume its double role of supporting economic development while at the same time legitimizing the social costs involved.

The formulation of welfare policy

The Canadian Public Assistance Act of 1966 provided, for the first time, a plan for sharing costs of public welfare programmes between federal and provincial governments on a 50-50 basis. The result, of course, was a tendency towards uniformity of the various provincial programmes and, through financial incentives, creation of new programmes. Not surprisingly, social welfare programmes entered a period of considerable expansion. The 1966 law, however, soon proved inadequate in that it covered only programmes of direct public assistance whereas it became increasingly evident that social services had to be expanded to include other sectors of the population. During the period 1973 to 1977, the governments sought to amend the law in line with a new national policy of social security which had been defined in 1973. This new perspective on social policy was stated in the following manner:

"Social and job-related services [are] essential if full employment and income maintenance strategies are to be effective: vocational training and counselling, rehabilitation programmes, family auxiliaries and child care facilities."[67]

In addition, this social security policy included a community job creation programme to be administered by the Depatment of Manpower in an attempt to "stimulate community initiatives and resources and to provide jobs for the unemployed."[68]

This new presence of the federal government in the welfare sector had the effect of integrating social assistance programmes into an overall strategy of economic development. The function of the state was thus no longer merely one of passive support. On the contrary, the state intervened more and more directly in the regulation of levels of employment and collective consumption. The objective was no longer to provide support for individuals but rather for the economy. The more the process of economic concentration is advanced, the greater the role of the state. In the same sense, one can say that the greater the scope of application of health and welfare policies, the more they become essential instruments for the ideological and economic management of monopoly capitalist society. "The new law allows the federal government to help the provinces adapt to the changing priorities in the field of social services."[69]

The new law of 1977 defines social services as "services which seek: to help people become useful... [and] self-

110

supporting members of the community; to contribute to the prevention of individual and social inequality and handicaps; to encourage participation of individuals, families and groups in social and economic life.... to encourage the development of individual and community resources as a means of increasing economic and social well-being."[70]

The law pursued the same objective as the various documents examined above in relation to the health sector. The criteria of admissibility broadened—"the law recognizes that not all persons in need of social services are necessarily welfare recipients. Need for social services can be unrelated to one's economic situation"[71]—as part of an overall strategy to reduce costs. The attempt to improve the cost/benefit performance of the welfare system led the state to encourage the continued presence of private charitable organizations as well as requiring individual financial contributions for the use of certain services such as day care centres, family auxiliaries and family counselling.

At the same time, it was felt that the most effective manner in which to reduce costs was to intervene energetically in three main areas: (1) alternatives to institutional care for the disabled and the aged; (2) rehabilitation and support measures for the handicapped; and (3) day care for children. The first area was in fact closely related to similar priorities in the health field—discouraging reliance on institutional care. The terms of an official government statement in this respect were quite clear: the law sought to "encourage people to help themselves...[and] to become or to remain self-supporting."[72] This theme of "self-support" is, of course, in perfect harmony with the state's objective to reduce institutional care, and at the same time it legitimizes the progressive financial cutbacks in an area which the federal government considered it could no longer afford. The second major area of government action was also concerned with home care but equally with the attempt to force as many of the handicapped into the job market as possible. This was also the underlying motive in the development of day care services which were specifically designed to encourage women—particularly those classed as head of household—to find a job in the labour market. "When certain services allow people to find a job this means that the

111

government is no longer obliged to provide financial support. On the contrary, income tax revenues increase."[73] Furthermore, child day care is a means to discourage placing children in various types of centres or institutions: "Specialists have long since realized that traditional solutions such as reliance on foster parents... is too expensive and does not always meet the needs of those concerned...."[74] The attempt to reduce institutional care expenditures is guided by the following principle:

"Almost any programme which provides an alternative to institutional services (including prisons) will provide substantial financial savings."[75]

Similarly, the importance of prevention and strategic support for families in difficulty leads the government to stress the importance of familly counselling: "To remove children from their natural family setting in times of stress does not produce results comparable to those obtained by providing the means to overcome the stress, or better yet, of preventing it."[76]

These services were oriented towards the family, the handicapped and the aged in order to reduce demand on institutional services and to help those who have jobs to keep them.

All these measures—embodied in various laws and administrative regulations—constitute an integral part of the reform of the welfare sector in Québec, which in turn grew out of the vast reform of income-security policy in 1973. The underlying economic logic is clearly related to the role of the state in monopoly capitalism and it is only in this sense that one can understand how the areas of health, welfare and income security were moulded together during the seventies into a single socio-political strategy: "social development." The action of the federal government over the past two decades is the key to a thorough understanding of the major reforms in the health and welfare sectors in Québec.

Footnotes

1. *Report of the Royal Commission on Health Services* (Hall Commission), Ottawa, 1964-65, Vol. I, pp. xx-xxi.
2. *Ibid.*, Vol. II, p. 1.
3. *Ibid.*, Vol. I, p. 10.
4. *Ibid.*, pp. 5-6.
5. *Ibid.*, pp. 3-4.
6. *Ibid.*.
7. *Ibid.*, p. 13, and Vol. II, p. 211.
8. *Ibid.*, Vol. I., p. xx.
9. *Ibid.*.
10. *Ibid.*, p. xxi.
11. *Ibid.*, p. 12.
12. *Ibid.*, Vol. II, p. 211.
13. *Ibid.*, Vol. I, p. 12.
14. *Ibid.*, p. 9.
15. *Ibid.*, p. 3.
16. *Ibid.*, p. 7.
17. *Ibid.*, p. 12.
18. *Ibid.*, Vol. II, recommendation 224, p. 292.
19. *Ibid.*, Vol. I, recommendation 10, p. 21.
20. See, for example, Dunham, Arthur, *Community Welfare Organization, Principles and Practice*, New York, 1962, pp. 224 and ff.
21. Hall Commission Report, *op. cit.*, Vol. I, p. 12.
22. *Ibid.*, Vol. II, pp. 240 and ff.
22a. Somers, H.M., and Somers, A.R., *Doctors, Patients and Health Insurance*, The Brookings Institute, Washington, D.C., 1961, p. 33, cited in Hall Report, *op. cit.*, Vol. II, p. 241.
23. Hall Report, *op. cit.*, Vol. II, p. 243.
24. *Ibid.*, p. 242.
25. Hastings, J.E.F., *Organized Community Health Services*, appendix to the Hall Commission Report, Ottawa, 1964, p. 76.
26. Boan, J.A., *Group Practice*, Appendix to the Hall Commission Report, Ottawa, 1966, p. 2.
27. *Ibid.*, p. 5.
28. *Ibid.*, p. 6.
29. Hastings, *op. cit.*, p. 76.
30. Hall Commission Report, *op. cit.*, Vol. I, recommendation 105, p.55.

31. *Ibid.*, p. 61.
32. Kohn, R., *Emerging Patterns in Health Care,* appendix to the Hall Commission Report, Ottawa, 1965.
33. Boan, *op. cit.*, p. 2.
34. Hall Commission Report, *op. cit.*, Vol. II, p. 247.
35. *Ibid.*.
36. *Ibid.*, p. 251.
37. Hastings, *op. cit.*, p. 87.
38. Hall Report, *op. cit.*, p. 243.
39. Hastings, *op. cit.*, pp. 87 and 36.
40. Hall Report, *op. cit.*, p. 256.
41. Hastings, *op. cit.*, p. 76.
42. *Task Force Report on the Cost of Health Services in Canada* (Willard Report), Government of Canada, Ottawa, 1969, p. 1.
43. *Ibid.*, pp. 6-8 (my emphasis).
44. *Ibid.*, p. 13.
45. *Ibid.*, pp. 13-14.
46. *Ibid.*, p. 19 (my emphasis).
47. *Ibid.*, p. 43.
48. *Ibid.*, p. 51.
49. *Ibid.*, p. 90.
50. *Ibid.*, pp. 78-79.
51. *Ibid.*, p. 61.
52. Report of the Community Health Centre Project, *Community Health Centre in Canada*, Vol. I, Government of Canada, Ottawa, 1972. (Hastings Report) see foreword.
53. *Ibid.*, p. 12.
54. *Ibid.*, p. 9.
55. *Ibid.*, p. 19.
56. *Ibid.*, pp. 10-11.
57. *Ibid.*, p. 19.
58. Lalonde, Marc, *A New Perspective on the Health of Canadians*, Ottawa, April, 1974.
59. Ivan Illich mentions this document in the French edition of *Medical Nemesis*, Paris, Seuil, 1975.
60. Renaud, Marc, "Crise de la médecine et politiques de santé, les leçons de l'histoire" in *Possibles*, 1, 2, Montréal, 1977, p. 37.
61. Lalonde, *op. cit.*, p. 6.
62. *Ibid.*, pp. 32, 26, 36.
63. *Ibid.*, p. 39.
64. *Ibid.*, pp. 40-41.
65. *Ibid.*.

66. *Ibid.*, p. 64.
67. Conseil national du bien-être social, *Le Gouvernement et les services sociaux*, Ottawa, March 1978, p. 8. Cf. Lalonde, Marc, ministre, *Document de travail sur la sécurité sociale au Canada*, Gouvernement du Canada, Ottawa, 1973, 10ᵉ proposition.
68. Ministère de la Santé et du Bien-être social, Gouvernement du Canada, *Communiqué*, 20 June, 1977, p. 2.
69. *Ibid.*, p. 3.
70. Conseil national du bien-être social, *op. cit.*, p. 9.
71. Ministère de la Santé et du Bien-être social, Gouvernement du Canada, *Communiqué, op. cit.*, p. 3.
72. *Ibid.*, p. 1.
73. Ministère de la Santé et du Bien-être social, *Questions et réponses, législation fédérale sur les services sociaux—1977*, p. 7.
74. *Ibid.*, p. 4.
75. *Ibid.*, p. 6.
76. *Ibid.*, p. 2.

CHAPTER 3
The Québec Commission of Inquiry on Health and Social Welfare (CIHSW)

Characteristics of the Commission

The origins of this commission of inquiry, the characteristics of the personnel involved, and the way in which they sought to fulfill their mandate are all particularly significant of the stakes involved in the health and welfare reform of the late sixties. It is with these elements in mind that I shall begin the discussion here.

The CIHSW was established in 1966 with an incredibly vast mandate from the Québec government. All aspects of reform in the health and welfare sectors were to be studied: economic, administrative, organizational and professional. More specifically, the Commission was asked to study the following questions: (1) the establishment of a public health insurance scheme; (2) reorganization of the whole system of hospital care as well as all other forms of health and welfare services; (3) redefinition of the health and welfare professions with special emphasis on the way that training programmes and research priorities could be developed; (4) definition of roles and status of paramedical personnel; (5) modes of remuneration for professionals, particularly physicians; (6) definition of relations between professional associations and the state; (7) reorganization and integration of existing piecemeal legislation concerning public assistance into a single coherent policy; (8) a general policy concerning citizen participation in the management process of institutions; and finally, (9) the question of regional organization of the delivery system.

The mandate was enormous, and it should be mentioned at the outset that the Commission did not try to narrow it down. Quite the contrary. Its work went on for five years and resulted in a report divided into seven major sections, many of which included several volumes and hundreds of recommendations. In addition to the report itself, twenty-eight often very bulky appendices were published, and hundreds of briefs from various interest groups were submitted. The Commission travelled extensively throughout the country and indeed the world, holding dozens of hearings and collecting expertise from over three hundred and fifty specialists. Its budget totalled several million dollars. These facts are mentioned simply to give some indication of the political and strategic importance of this commission of inquiry in Québec at the end of the sixties.

The objective, as stated by the report itself, was nothing less than a definition of a new model for Québec society. One might think this claim to be empty rhetoric if not simple foolishness. I do not think so. It can be understood only if we consider the particular situation of Québec in the early sixties. The development of monopoly capitalist social relations in Québec society had forced the process of modernization of the state apparatus, which in turn had given rise to a new type of ruling class. This ruling class sought to consolidate its economic and political power through the only means at its disposal: the state.

In this context, the CIHSW can be seen as the product of two powerful and contradictory social forces. It is the interplay of these forces which shaped the work of the Commission from the outset and throughout its investigations.

(1)   The key figures in the CIHSW were representative of the new local élites seeking power. The dependent nature of

118

Québec society, however, made it impossible for these élites to become an independent ruling class. It is clear that they could exercise political power in Québec only if they submitted to and accepted the domination of the international economic system within which Québec lies. At most, they could hope to establish local hegemony.

(2)   At the same time, in order to establish this local hegemony while maintaining a relative autonomy in relation to foreign ruling classes, these élites were forced to invent forms of political leadership which tend to minimize the negative effects of foreign domination and to win the allegiance of the local population.

Of course, every ruling class presents its vision of the world as harmonious and free of conflict, and the model presented by the CIHSW is certainly no exception in this regard. Nevertheless, it is also true that every ruling class must deal with two fundamental exigencies: (1) how to work within the international economic order as it presently exists, and (2) how to establish and maintain its political power on the domestic level. It is in this light that the work of the CIHSW will be analyzed.

The vast scope of the mandate given to the CIHSW should not, therefore, be simply dismissed as fantasy. The mandate was nothing less than the task of defining the forms of political leadership necessary for establishing the hegemony of these local élites in Québec society. The members of the Commission, the way they were brought together and worked together, are all extremely significant factors for the interpretation of their final report.

The government's choice of the members of the Castonguay-Nepveu Commission was clearly motivated by the desire to acheive a balanced representation of the various élites. Of the eight commissioners, two were from the economic sector (a senior business executive and an actuary), two were from the legal profession, two were from the medical profession, and two were from the social work profession. Furthermore, taken as a whole, they also tended to be representative of the various interest groups in the health and welfare field: the government, the financial sector, the insurance sector, the College of

119

Physicians and Surgeons, the professional corporations, the Church, the social services and charitable organizations. All of them were, of course, university trained, and four of them taught at various universities. When we consider their socio-professional background, it appears that three of them can be clearly identified as part of a "traditional" élite, while three are more closely linked to a "new" élite.

The chaiman of the Commission, Claude Castonguay, was an actuary and can be considered as a representative from the economic sector. Since 1951, he had pursued his career in various life insurance companies in Québec which are all closely tied to American multinational corporations. In addition to this career in the private sector, he had been given responsibility, in the late fifties, for the elaboration of the various public insurance schemes of the Québec government. In 1970, he was to be named minister of health, family and social welfare (which became the department of social affairs in 1971). This department, in itself, administers one-third of the total budget of the Québec government. He left politics in 1973 to return to the private sector, and in 1977 he became president of one of the largest life insurance companies in Québec. At the same time (1977), he became director of the Committee for Canadian Unity which was set up immediately after the Parti Québecois came to power in Québec.

As we shall see, the departure of part of the personnel and the new posts they took up play a key role in our understanding of this Commission. In addition, it is particularly significant to note the *real* order (not numerical order) in which the various volumes and appendices were published together with the themes and frames of reference particular to each of them.

What becomes clear is that the Commission was in fact composed of two main groups, one of which was clearly dominant. The dominant group, which represented the interests of a modern, economically oriented, technocratic élite, was by far the most dynamic. The other group, much more traditionally oriented, characterized by its humanistic, moral and clerical outlook, was simply out-classed. The first group, under the firm direction of the chairman of the

Commission, undertook its work with the help of experts and various research groups and think tanks. Quite rapidly, this group was able to establish its superiority over the other members of the Commission. Apart from the volume on health insurance, which grew directly out of the work already done by the task force on health insurance which Castonguay had headed since 1965, the other volumes were written by the experts, while the commissioners were mainly occupied with holding hearings and collecting briefs. Some of the commissioners, however, did participate directly in the writing up of certain volumes of the report. In all cases, these commissioners were among those associated with the "traditional" group. It is interesting to compare the methods of operation of the two groups. The first group legitimated its work on the basis of academic, scientific expertise—in particular on the basis of its regular consultation with experts at Harvard University. Apparently, regular weekly reports were sent to the commissioners by consultants for detailed criticism and feed-back. The traditionalist group, on the other hand, relied mainly on its consultations with practitioners in the field:

"This report is... the result of a combined process of... compiling information, field investigations and scientific research. Four types of investigation were used: (1) direct evidence was sought... [from] social service personnel and clients.... (2) scientific and practical research work was undertaken, (3) four seminars were organized with a group of experts.... and finally, (4) numerous individual consultations were held with administrative personnel (in the field of social services)."[1]

For the moment, the technocratic group can be considered as relatively homogeneous which, in any case, seems to have been the situation at the outset. There were seeds of dissension, however, which came to light only when the chairman of the Commission became a government minister in 1970. The conflict centred around three questions: (1) the centralization of power; (2) the administrative organizations on the regional level; (3) the role and functions of the various professional associations. In this sense, we see the same type of division between the technocratic and techno-professional options which were examined in Chapter Two. It is clear, however, that this latter option is in no way synonymous with the

121

traditionalist point of view.

The main volumes of the report were published in the following order: Volume I: *Health Insurance* (1967), which contains a brief explanation of the philosophy of the CIHSW; Volume IV: *Health*; Volume VII: *Professions and Society* (1970); Volume V: *Income Security* (1971). (This last volume was already written in 1970.)

These volumes are unmistakably the work of the technocratic group. Their orientations and concerns clearly predominate. It should be noted also that this work was completed (or in the final stages of completion) by the spring of 1970. Sixteen of the twenty-eight appendices were also published by this time: concerning the health sector (inventory of resources, costs, modes of remuneration, research, etc.), the organization and licensing of professional practice, and the cost of a guaranteed minimum income. The work of the Commission can be divided into five main parts: (1) health insurance (the problem of access to health care); (2) health care administration (the problem of productivity); (3) the professions and their relation to the state (which, as we shall see, included all the "liberal" professions and not just those related to the health and welfare sector); (4) income security (the various forms of social insurance); and, finally, (5) the social services. Of these five sectors, it is clear that the technocratic group controlled the first four.

That leaves the fifth sector: the social services. This area was the bastion of the traditionalists. Two volumes were published: Volume III: *Development* (1971), and Volume VI: *Social Services* (1972). Although the volume on development was presented as a general introduction to the whole report, there can be little doubt that the technocratic faction must have had some difficulty in accepting the frame of reference and vocabulary in this part of the report. On the other hand, perhaps the problem never really arose since this volume appeared only in 1971, a full year after the theoretical work of the technocratic group had been completed. As will be shown, however, even the volume on development is not written from an entirely traditionalist perspective. It was also influenced by the technocratic approach to this question which had been elaborated in Appendix 25[2] and published in 1970. Most

122

probably the technocratic group considered this appendix as its point of reference for the question of development.

As far as the volume on social services is concerned, it is the result of a shaky compromise between the two groups, which probably explains why this volume took so long to be published. On the whole, it seems to be the work of the traditionalist group. The terms of reference, the moral judgements, the frequent reference to religious literature, and even to the social doctrine of the Church, all point to their influence. At the same time, however, parts of this report deal with questions related to the administrative and organizational reform of social services and we find the same kind of concerns as those mentioned earlier for the health sector (hierarchical organization of institutions and functions, regionalization, an interdisciplinary approach, citizen participation, etc.). The compromise, then, was a delicate one. In fact, this volume contains two radically different approaches to the question of social services, but each group had an interest in preventing open conflict. The technocratic group sought the implicit support of the élites who traditionally controlled this sector as long as they could proceed with the overall organizational reform of the health and welfare field. The traditional group, on the other hand, sought to conserve its symbolic and ideological frame of reference concerning the services themselves while at the same time appearing to be modern in its acceptance of the new organizational reforms.

It would be a mistake to simply dismiss these two volumes as archaic and outdated and to neglect the function they fulfill in the report as a whole. On this level, the overall orientations of the CIHSW are perfectly clear. We shall come back to this point.

A few of the twelve appendices concerning social services were written from a traditionalist point of view but most of them are clearly the result of a technocratic analysis. The key appendix, in this regard, seems to be Appendix 25, written by the sociologist Gérald Fortin, entitled *La Société de demain: ses impératifs et son organisation* ("Tomorrow's society: its imperatives and its organization"), which was published in 1970. This volume which sings the virtues of the

123

"abundant society," seems designed to work out a process of transition between the traditional group, which controlled the work of the Commission in the social service sector, and the technocratic group, which needed a modernized framework of reference for organizational reform.

The careers of the commissioners and certain of the research staff is an extremely significant factor. In the spring of 1970, the work of the Commission was completed, as we have said, except for the part concerning the social services. At this point, the chairman, Claude Castonguay, resigned and in May he was appointed minister of health, family and social welfare in the new Liberal government which had just come to power in Québec. His closest collaborators soon joined him. The health adviser for the CIHSW became deputy minister in June 1970. The legal adviser of the Commission became the minister's adviser on social policy, and the economic adviser followed the same route. Many of the research experts also obtained important posts in the department. Only the social welfare adviser stayed on with the CIHSW. In his place, a young technocrat, who had been active in the social service sector but whose university training had been in economics, was chosen as senior adviser on welfare policy for the government. He had come to the attention of the commissioners when he had presented a brief entitled "Une politique sociale pour le Québec."[3]

Other more minor transfers also occurred. Two of the lawyers of the Commission were appointed to government posts. For all practical purposes, the Commission was dismantled. The chairman and his closest advisers—in other words, the core of the technocratic group, which had solidly dominated the work of the Commission for the first three years—now appeared to have decided to put their ideas into action in the most important department of the government. They may even have felt that they could work more freely in the government than on the Commission, where incessant wrangling whith the traditionalists forced them to accept certain limitations. In any case, it soon became evident that the group in government meant to go even further along the road to technocratic reform than had been recommended by the Commission. Three examples are particularly significant in

124

this regard: (1) Contrary to the Commission's recommendation, the department of health and the department of family and social welfare were merged into a single gigantic department of social affairs. (2) Health and welfare institutions were to be administered through extremely centralized bureaucratic structures rather than through regional offices. (3) The Local Health Centres which had been proposed by the Commission became Local Community Service Centres (CLSC) (and thus included administration of social as well as health care services). This latter measure was put into effect even before the Commission had submitted its report on social services, and when the report finally did come out, no mention was made of such an idea. The general impression that one receives when reading the volumes on the social services is that the authors were on the defensive and completely incapable of providing a clear and articulate proposition for reform of their own. Government legislation concerning the reorganization of health and welfare services was presented and adopted in 1971, a year before the Commission submitted its report on social services. Not surprisingly, this situation provoked a rather bitter reaction from the commissioners: "The consultants feel that this bill may have started off badly. Premature at least for the social services—the place given them is sought in vain. The bill... is characterized by a spirit of centralization contrary to the recommendations of the Commission. It is difficult to see how this will not produce increased bureaucratization."[4]

The members who stayed on with the Commission chose the former secretary as president and attempted to complete the work that had been originally planned. They published the volumes on development and social services but it is clear that their work was to have little influence on the government. It was now in the government itself that the main process of reform was underway.

The picture that emerges, then, is the following: it is not so much Claude Castonguay as an individual who is important here as the social significance of his qualifications and of those of the group of individuals with whom he worked. It is the analysis of these qualifications which enables us to see the class interests behind the strategy for reform in this area.

There was, in fact, an alliance of class interests brought together under the leadership of a representative of the economic sector. This group, composed of individuals of various professional backgrounds, had in common the fact that they were all relatively young, recent university graduates of prestigious foreign universities (London School of Economics, Harvard, etc.) with a technical, scientific approach to the analysis of problems in the health and welfare sector. It was a small group, barely more than a dozen individuals, who were clearly representative of the new petite-bourgeoisie that emerged from francophone universities [5] and which controlled the provincial state apparatus since the beginning of the sixties. More than half of them were economists; the rest were either lawyers or doctors. They were united by their technical competence which constituted the new basis of legitimation for exercising power in the health sector as well as by their common belief in the objectivity of their research methods.

This mode of legitimation constitutes in fact a form of expression of their class power and enables them to refuse to consider all problems which are not of a technical nature, that is, which are not amenable to a technical mode of analysis. The technocratic outlook considers the economic environment simply as one variable amongst others which has to be considered in an analysis of the health and welfare sector. In this way, it was possible, at least temporarily, to construct an alliance between the technocrats (economists and jurists) and the professionals (especially the physicians) within an all-encompassing technocratic framwork.

The CIHSW Report: ideology as rhetoric

The main objective of the rest of this chapter is to analyze the ideology of the CIHSW. It should be realized, however, that ideology is both *rhetoric*—in the sense of an ideal representation of society, independent of class relations, founded on a more or less coherent set of abstract principles — and *action*—by the dominant class which, in the case at hand, means the specific choices it made concerning the organization of services. These choices grew out of the ideological perspectives of the dominant class to take the forms of concrete institutional reality.

In the following section, we shall look at ideology as rhetoric, as the representation of reality by a specific class, profoundly influenced by its situation as an intermediate ruling class within a context of world capitalism. This aspect of its ideology is most evident in the volumes of the report dealing directly with the economy, that is, the volumes on health insurance and on income security, as well as the volume which attempts to define the basic ideological orientations of the CIHSW, the volume on development.

In another section of this chapter, I shall look at the organizational transformations proposed by the CIHSW as expressions of the active or operationalized aspects of its ideology in the areas of health and welfare as well as its legislation concerning the professions. I shall then attempt to show how these organizational reforms are related to the ideological orientations which we will now examine.

(a) Health insurance

The preparation for introducing a universal public health scheme had already begun in Québec before the CIHSW had been created. A year before, in 1965, the government had set up a Task Force on Health Insurance under the direction of the two most important figures in health and welfare reform in Québec: Claude Castonguay was named chairman of the task force and Thomas Boudreau, an economist, was responsible for the research activities of the group. As mentioned earlier, these two men represented the two main approaches to state reform of the health and welfare sectors. Castonguay was the champion of the technocratic approach while Boudreau represented what can be called the techno-professional approach.

This task force had been set up as a result of the recommendations of a federal government commission of inquiry (the Hall Commission), which had emphasized the necessity of implementing universal public health insurance schemes in all Canadian provinces financed jointly by the federal and provincial governments.

This task force, which was on the point of producing its

127

recommendations, was suddenly disbanded when the Union Nationale unexpectedly came to power in the 1966 provincial elections. The preparation of a public health insurance programme was dropped. In its place, the new government, under considerable pressure from the trade unions and the federal government, decided to use delaying tactics by setting up the CIHSW with its enormous mandate in the hope that the whole problem would get lost somewhere along the way. It was Claude Castonguay, however, already a very influential public figure, who was appointed chairman, and he was able to use almost all of the work which had already been completed by the former task force. For this reason, the Commission was able to publish the first volume of its report on health insurance almost immediately after it was created.

The work of the Task Force on Health Insurance was mainly directed towards legitimizing the necessity of state intervention in the health field. It is clear that the task force itself recognized that this necessity had been brought about by major social and economic changes which were no longer compatible with the normal regulating effects of a "free market," characteristic of a traditional liberal economy.

"At present, our economy produces enough to maintain a sufficiently high level of consumption while at the same time allowing a satisfactory rate of capital accumulation. In fact, the problem now is more one of consumption levels than production levels. What portion of our resources should be directed towards consumption? What goods should be purchased, to what extent and by whom? These problems... cannot be resolved... solely through the unfettered operation of individual self-interest. The complexity and dynamism of modern society make it impossible for the individual to maximize his personal welfare all by himself; collective public action is necessary to maximize the general social welfare."[6]

For the task force, health care was one of the areas in which "the free interplay of market forces does not result in an optimal allocation of resources and in which, therefore, state intervention is justified."[7]

The necessity for state intervention can hardly be recognized more explicitly. The role of the state is to use its authority to ensure the "optimal allocation of resources" in certain areas such as health. This intervention is justified mainly on economic grounds. It is only the state which can assume responsibility for management of the labour force as a whole and in this way facilitate the transition from a competitive capitalist economy to an era of monopoly capitalism.

The economic justification of state intervention can be summarized in three major points:

(1)   Poverty is a cause of ill health and ill health is a cause of poverty. Sickness often reduces or even eradicates family income. It necessitates major expenditures. "In the struggle to improve living standards, people who are in good health, who have abundant reserves of physical and intellectual energy, have a better chance than those who suffer from physical or mental deficiencies."[8] This statement, of course, is simply an expression of the liberal ideology of "equality of opportunity" as it is applied to the health sector. Health insurance is seen as necessary because it is no longer sufficient to simply provide assistance to the poor: "It is necessary to determine the causes of poverty and to attempt to eliminate them.... Sickness is one cause of poverty."[9]

(2)   Health care can no longer be considered as simple consumer goods and services. "In recent years... it has become apparent that health care expenditures should be considered as *investments in human capital* and, as such, can provide high social dividends."[10] The College of Physicians and Surgeons of Québec clearly supported this viewpoint in its brief submitted to the Québec government in 1964:

"The fundamental question which must be answered is the following: to what extent do improvements in the human capital of a given society produce economic progress?... As an investment, the attractiveness or desirability of health care expenditures should be measured in terms of the return that can be obtained from these investments."[11]

The task force quoted this passage in its report and went on to explain how billions of dollars and millions of work-days are lost each year due to sickness. The commissioners concluded by stating that "the state of health of the population can have major economic implications for the society and that the state has a direct and immediate interest to invest in this sector."[12]

(3)   *Market mechanisms* are insufficient to regulate health care consumption. "The present level of health care consumption does not permit Québec society to maximize

benefits."[13] In other words, the upper classes which, at present, are already capable of maximizing benefits of health care consumption, must be convinced that it is to their advantage to open this market to the society as a whole by providing external incentives for consumption independent of the economic status of consumers.

There is thus a clear, explicit recognition, by the task force, of the relationship between state intervention in the health care market and major transformations of the economic structure. The liberal ideology of individual freedom, of unfettered competition, of the self-regulating capacities of the market, was severely criticized. The state must intervene to reduce the social costs of ill health and to increase the quality of the labour force. In this way, it is able to contribute to the growth of national income. Health care, which had traditionally been seen as a strictly individual and private concern, now became an investment. In addition to its task of regulating the most extreme forms of social inequality, the state must now directly participate in the process of modernization—and "industrialization"—of the health sector through its support of the new economic and professional élites in the field. As Thomas Boudreau put it: "Health insurance does not just pay bills. It is a means for planning the health sector."[14]

The work of the task force had thus already done the groundwork for the CIHSW on the question of health insurance and the Commission quickly published its first report in 1967. The arguments used in this report to justify the new role of the state were similar or perhaps slightly more sophisticated than those used in the task force report. What was new was the theme concerning the magnificent discoveries of Science, and how, when put to work for "Humanity," these discoveries can make the goal of universal public health possible. This theme has the overall effect of masking the importance of the economic factors behind the reform process. Perhaps this shift in emphasis can be explained by the fact that the work of the CIHSW was meant to influence public opinion whereas the task force was more of an internal research group for the government.

As already mentioned, the rhetoric and action of a ruling class is characterized by the refusal to explicitly

130

recognize class relations. Quite likely, it is also an important way through which dominant classes, seeking to maintain and develop their position, are able to convince themselves and the subordinate classes that, in the face of the obvious consequences of domination, it is those who suffer who are mostly or solely responsible for the situation.

This tactic is nowhere more evident than in the Castonguay-Nepveu Report. In order to legitimize its project, that is, to make it seem like the best solution for all concerned, the Report refers to a value system, or a "cultural model" which at first view seems self-evident but which, at the same time, allows the specific class interests which underlie it to appear as common sense or as the "public interest." In traditional societies, it was in the same of God that dominant classes sought to establish a particular form of social organization. For the CIHSW—that is, the Commission on *health* and *social welfare*—it is in the name of *Science* on the one hand and *Mankind* on the other that the attempt was made to justify the respect of a dominant economic order and the restructuring of social relations.

It is at this point that we begin to see how these two themes—health and social welfare—were perceived as fundamentally complementary within an overall management strategy of Québec society, and it is only with this in mind that one can grasp the underlying logic which runs throughout the work of the CIHSW.

In its effort to justify the dominant economic order, it is the reference to *science* as a cultural model which serves as the ideological underpinnings for health and welfare reform.

"Public opinion" can scarcely protest against a proposal to reorganize society under the direction of a new ruling class which will provide unlimited access to the marvelous discoveries of medical research. Who can be against waging an effective war against sickness and disease and in favour of a longer, more healthy life?

"The degree to which treatment is used by a community does not constitute a goal in itself; the goal is the prevention of illness, to reduce the number of sick and to increase life expectancy. The improvement of health, an essential element in raising the collective standard of well-being, is the ultimate goal of social action in the

131

health field.... Medical research ensures continuous progress in the field of medicine... and health insurance, which has the immediate goal of providing treatment, puts the discoveries and results of medical research at the disposal of the community.... The extension of life implies continuous recourse to medical consultation or medication.... [T]he establishment of health insurance results in a major increase in the use of treatment because, as the emphasis is placed on the importance of health, it fosters a collective awareness of the need for treatment." [15]

The proclaimed objective, then, was "to raise the level of security and well-being of the community," [16] which, in fact, means "medicalizing social relations." This was only the first step, however. What is more significant is the relationship of this ideology to the economic system and to the realities of class domination:

"An essential instrument in the planning and coordination of the fight against illness, health insurance is also one of the mechanisms available to society in its efforts to achieve a complete, integrated and optimal programme of *investment in human resources*.... Society has come to understand the necessity of taking full advantage of its *collective human capital*. Among the general measures taken with this goal in mind, those that tend to raise the standard of health and education of the community are in the forefront since they are part of the vital concerns of developed societies. Expenditures on health maintenance are, in reality, investments... [which] promote economic and social progress. The direct cost... affects society by depriving it of potential manpower.... The cost of health therefore can be considered as an *investment in human capital*. As such, the social benefits one can expect are great.

For example, it is known that illness is the main cause of absenteeism in the work force. In Canada, statistics show that... in 1962... 27 million man-days [were] lost to production, that is, a loss more serious than that caused by all the strikes which have taken place in Canada since 1947.

The progress [in health care]... is expressed therefore by a quantitative increase in manpower. Already impressive, the advantages stemming from health expenditures are nevertheless underestimated. Little account is taken, in fact, of the inter-relation between the fields of health and education. The loss of manpower wipes out the *investment* in human resources during the entire training period....

...The relationship existing between health and the quality of productive resources... is explicitly recognized in the economic theory which attributes the rate of growth of technical progress to

132

the cumulative effects of improvement in the level of human knowledge, of training, health and the technological quality of the labour element. That is the reason why there is insistence on the investment character of expenditures for the purposes of health and education, and why *gains greater than those realized from physical capital* now are attributed to this emphasis on human capital. From the point of view of long-term growth objectives, health policy... becomes a valuable *ally* of economic policy."[17]

A coherent health policy, however, is concerned with investing in "human capital" not only as a means to improve its productive capacity but also to improve its consumption capacity which, of course, is the other essential element necessary for a healthy economy:

"Illness has an unfavourable effect on the overall demand for goods and services because a person who is ill has a reduced income. It also has a negative effect on the use of production factors which become immobilized, thereby causing serious economic losses. To the extent that the health insurance plan will contribute to a decrease in absenteeism, in total or partial disability or even premature death, it will have a favourable effect of the same scope on the overall demand for goods and services and on the use of resources.... Through its favourable repercussions on the productive capacity of the economy, health insurance... constitutes an investment and contributes to economic growth."[18]

A health policy, based on a health insurance scheme, can thus "profoundly influence the relationship between economic progress and social progress."[19]

The Report does not just emphasize how the economic and social sectors play complementary roles. At times, it explicitly recognizes the predominance of the former over the latter and the necessity to subordinate the labour factor to the interests of capital. In this same volume on health insurance, the authors attempt to explain how social security is an essential element in an overall health and welfare policy:

"It is impossible to dissociate social and economic life because of the profound interdependence between these two fields of human activity.... Social security, which sought to correct the consequences of economic inequality, was nevertheless part of the very framework, structure and process of an economic system which caused disparities in income. As one observer recently stated: 'Social security policies have the advantage of producing maximum benefits with a minimum of change in the economic order. They are in no way steps towards equality'."[20]

133

Social security plans seek to eliminate the gap between the needs of individuals and the financial resources at their disposal.... The economic structure does not contain any special process to correct these gaps between resources and needs. On the contrary, the evolution of productive systems tends to widen them. If there is no compensation... the evolution of manpower requirements contributes to an increase in wage disparities.

The development of social and manpower policies is a necessary and irreversible phenomenon.... This concern over the balance or adaptation of social benefits to the movement of production clearly illustrates the principle by which *economic development determines and conditions social legislation.* Thus, in the interplay of the two partners—the economic and the social—*the former sets the pace.*

This economic philosophy... is based on the priority given to production... but if one takes into account the productive aspect of the human factor and the possible value of social expenditures for the improvement of this factor... [then they] should be considered as productive in the same way as real capital investment. The facts go further. In highly developed countries, long-term possibilities of increasing production are directly related to investments in human resources.... Social security can be considered equally indispensable for economic as well as social progress." [21]

The conclusion, then, is exactly the same as for health and health insurance "investments" and we discover the same determination to deny the preponderant influence of the economic sector over the social. Even after explicitly recognizing that the two sectors do not have the same relative importance, the report continues to consider them on an equal basis and tries to get around the problem by inventing the concept of "overall socio-economic development" which becomes *the key concept* in their commentary on human resource management. "Social progress and economic development are complementary and must be coordinated in order to achieve the total balanced development of a society.... Only coordination will permit the full realization of the overall aim of global socio-economic development." [22] There, in a nutshell, is the essential ambiguity which the CIHSW used consistently in order to obfuscate the question of class domination.

To grasp the full significance of this attempt at ideological integration within the framework of a dependent society, we must realize that it is not simply a means by which a local ruling class attempts to justify its intermediary role between foreign dominant classes and the local subordinate classes. It is also most certainly the ideal image that this class has of itself, an ideal image of its own autonomy. In other words, it is not surprising that such a class, which can exist only through its collaboration with the established order, tries at the same time to elaborate a vision of society and its role within it, in which it is master both of its own future and that of the society it leads. What better way to convince oneself of this than by proclaiming a symmetrical relationship between the economic sector (over which this class has little control) and the social sector (over which it exerts significant control)? If we pursue this idea a bit further, we note that in many cases, the Castonguay-Nepveu Report goes to the other extreme and tries to convince itself that, in fact, it is the social sector (high quality human capital) which can provide the means to control the economic sector:

"In highly developed countries, long-term possibilities of increasing production are directly related to investments in human resources.... Technical progress... is essentially a result of general progress in human knowledge.... It is connected to the level of education, health and professional competence found in the manpower pool. Modern theories of economic growth attach great importance to investments in human capital since these must make up for major lags in development." [23]

"The relationship between the level of expenditures for health and education and the economic growth rate is now clearly established. In some cases, it is illustrated by obstacles to economic progress in developing countries; in other cases, it explains the situation of depressed and marginal regions within countries where the economy is strong; sometimes, finally, it is confirmed by comparative calculations of the product of investment in human and material capital in countries of high technical development.... At the present time... investment in human resources is more productive than investment in technical capital." [24]

"In all economically developed countries, it is conceded that research is the most important factor in economic growth and social progress. Québec cannot be an exception to this rule; taking into account its late start, particularly in economic development, it must invest more than any other society in research." [25]

With G. Fortin, this argument is brought to its apotheosis:

"Although the secondary sector continues to play an important part in the creation of wealth, it is no longer the driving force behind economic growth. Modern economists hold the view that the sector of research, education and intellectual creativity in general

135

plays just as important a part, if not more so, in the development of the North American economy. If Québec chooses to move boldly into this fourth sector of the economy, *the relative underdevelopment of the secondary sector could turn out to be an advantage.*"[26]

From these examples, it is quite clear that we are floating in the realms of triumphant technocratic ideology as expressed by American management élites in the mid-sixties. This theme of constant adaptation to change, as expounded by such figures as Robert MacNamara, emphasized progress in the field of education and knowledge as the essential conditions for further economic development. The same theme was taken up in France by J.-J. Servan-Schreiber in his bestseller *Le Défi Américain* (Paris, 1967).

There can be little doubt that we are at the heart of the Utopia of this dominated ruling class when we read: "Social policy must not serve to palliate the nefarious consequences that the economic system engenders among individuals and societies. Economic development must always be considered as a dimension of social progress."[27] The reversal is complete— except for one detail: the language used is no longer one of analysis but of moral or voluntaristic incantations. What else is there to do, in the face of the facts?

And the facts are the results of the historical state of dependency of Québec society. The CIHSW repeatedly points to the precarious state of general health in Québec as compared to the Canadian average: (1) infant mortality rates are higher;[28] (2) in 1961, there was no health insurance plan for 40 to 45% of the population (i.e. the vast majority of the working class);[29] (3) 60% of those insured had only minimal coverage,[30] and so forth. The commissioners also noted that Québec had the highest rates of unemployment and of those living on welfare and was plagued by persistent and serious problems of regional disparity. The average income in some outlying areas of Québec was little over a third of what it was in Montréal. Infant mortality rates in low-income neighbourhoods and regions were three to four times what they were in the richer areas, and so on.[31] In brief, the picture painted was one of the social consequences of economic dependency.

The volume on health insurance constitutes an excellent synoptic view of the overall work of the Commission. Although it is mainly concerned with the implementation of a universal public health insurance plan, this does not prevent it from dealing with many of the most important issues concerning the reorganization of health care services which later volumes treat more extensively. Questions concerning medical staffing, training and research, administrative structures, decentralization and modes of association for professionals are all touched upon. The health insurance volume also gives us a clear picture of the type of social relations that the CIHSW seeks to establish in the health and welfare sector and in this sense contributes to our understanding of the way in which its project is part of the process of production and reproduction of social relations of domination within Québec society.

The preponderant role that the state assumes in the financing of the health sector legitimates its global reassessment of both production and distribution of health care services. It is in the name of increased productivity—as the only response to increased consumer demand brought about by free access to health care—that the state seeks to impose a vertical and horizontal reorganization of both resources and personnel. This reform process, although it is presented as a purely technical and functional question, necessarily implies *social* consequences since it involves destructuring and restructuring the established interests and their bases of legitimation in this field.

"Rationalizing requires that high-priced technical capital be used to its full capacity. Unnecessary barriers between distribution systems—hospital care, medical care and preventive care—barriers between professions, and independent practice of these professions are all factors preventing maximal use of technical capital."[32]

The guiding principles for reorganization were clearly stated: the existing state of affairs was seen as "irrational" in that it did not permit maximal use of the most expensive equipment (i.e., specialized care hospital resources). Health care services were not integrated into a coherent system to provide an appropriate response for each situation.

Three main sources of expenditures were identified:

(1) The technical factor (including hospital accommodation and equipment);

137

(2) The professional factor (physicians);

(3) The time factor (i.e., the fact that prevention is neglected in favour of a curative approach).

These factors were to be dealt with by providing various levels (1) of modes of treatment (from home visits to hospitalization); (2) of professional practice (from the nurse to the specialist); and (3) of temporal intervention (by placing the priority on prevention rather than curative measures).

The "barriers" to rational use of health care services which the Commission often referred to should be understood as both a technical and moral criticism. The technical critique refers to the intrinsically fragmented nature of the present situation as opposed to a more open, unified administrative system. On the other hand, the moral reproach implicit here is that this situation is due to the selfish and particular interests of institutions and professionals who are simply trying to protect their own power and privileges. This negative moral judgement, especially concerning physicians and social workers, is clearly present throughout the CIHSW Report. Rationalization of the system demands a coherent definition of legitimate power. We shall now look at the way in which the Commission sought to deal with this question.

One can only say that the commissioners proceeded with extreme caution concerning the question of physicians and hospitals as a cause of exorbitant expenditures. Quite clearly, the political weight of the new technocratic élite was not up to the level of its rhetoric. When it came to proposing specific, concrete measures of reform, the Commission was well aware that the power of physicians was no technical detail. As in the case of the federal commissions of inquiry examined above, an indirect approach was suggested. The objective was to transform the modes of production of medical care furnished by physicians so as to increase the overall level of productivity of the health system. This meant that the exclusive jurisdiction of physicians over this system had to be weakened. It was with this in mind that the Commission emphasized the importance of group practice, delegation of responsibility for a large number of medical acts to paramedical personnel, preventive instead of curative care, and an increase in the proportion of general practitioners in relation

138

to specialists. On the other hand, the Commission retained the principle that physicians should receive fees for services rather than become salaried employees. This seems to have been self-evident for the commissioners: "In the present situation, the need for physicians and other professionals in the health field justifies... retaining the fee for services system."[33] The fact that the Commission seems to justify this suggestion on the basis of the present shortage of professional resources could indicate that this was a temporary concession and that the government might eventually choose to establish a salary system for physicians at a later date. This interpretation is all the more probable in light of the Commission's suggestions concerning medical practice in disadvantaged areas and regions which, as is often the case, were considered as trial grounds for technocratic experimentation:

"The Commission believes that even in cases where fees for service remuneration may be negotiated, a salary scale should be negotiated at the same time.... [This] formula encourages group practice... and may interest a good number of doctors or other professionals, particularly those practising in depressed areas."[34]

The suggestion, then, was to call for two systems of remuneration: as a rule, the fee for service arrangement should apply, but in particular cases (that is, for the lower echelons of the profession, working directly with the disadvantaged) a salary scale should be implemented. In other words, it appears that there was an attempt to introduce the salary system for physicians by beginning with the weakest link in the profession. This strategy, in its early stages at least, would not be particularly effective in increasing the productivity of the health care system. That the commissioners stopped short in this regard can only be understood within the context of the relative strength of the medical profession in relation to the technocrats at that time. For the time being, the only solution, from the point of view of the technocrats, seemed to be to work towards a gradual transformation of medical practice which could be integrated into a modern system of health care services. This could be achieved only by making an important — and costly — concession on fees for service remuneration.

Another aspect of the CIHSW strategy concerning

139

remuneration of physicians was to recommend a single fee schedule for both general practitioners and specialists. This measure was meant to discourage the increase in the proportion of specialists (62% of physicians in 1967) as compared to general practitioners. This attempt to reduce the proportion of specialists allowed the technocrats to take advantage of the divisions within the medical profession. The government was able to use this measure as a means of winning the support of the general practitioners who had insisted on the single fee remuneration schedule as a preliminary condition for their participation in the health insurance plan which was then being implemented for welfare recipients. There is little doubt that this plan was perceived, by all concerned, as a pilot project for a universal public health insurance scheme.

Concerning the level of remuneration, the Commission stated that:

"It thus appears essential that the fee schedules or salaries negotiated must be reasonable and take market conditions into account.... [G]enerally speaking, professionals in the health field should not be given the right to charge fees in excess of the negotiated fee schedule.... The Commission recognizes, however, that certain exceptionally competent and renowned practitioners may be authorized to charge fees in excess of the negotiated schedules...."[35]

It should be noted that in 1967 the income of physicians was seven times greater than the average salary in Québec and fourteen times the level defined as the poverty line. In 1977, general practitioners were earning six times the average salary; the specialists, eight. In relation to the poverty line, these ratios were ten to one for the general practitioners and about 12.5 to one for the specialists. While it is clear that the Commission was bent on breaking down the traditional professional—and social—hierarchy which had developed over the years, it should also be mentioned that it sought to establish a new division of labour characterized by three types of physicians: those working in disadvantaged areas would receive a salary; the large majority of general practitioners and specialists would receive indentical fees for identical services independently of their professional qualifications; and finally, "exceptional competency" would be allowed to charge more than the fee level agreed upon. The principle of

140

stratification within the medical profession was thus maintained but was redefined in a way which had little to do with the traditional categories of the profession.

Another indication of the cautious and circumspect approach of the CIHSW in its dealings with the medical profession is evidenced by its insistence on the necessity of maintaining a legal distinction between physicians and "ordinary" employees: "the mode of remuneration has nothing to do with the definition of a *salaried* person as described in the Labour Code: 'any person who works for an employer in return for remuneration'."[36] Since labour legislation did not provide a legal framework for negotiations with non-salaried individuals, the Commission recommended that *ad hoc* legislation be put into effect. A distinction should be made, the Report stated, between laws concerning the relationship between the state and salaried employees covered by the Labour Code and this new situation which necessitates negotiations with non-salaried persons. The Commission went even further when it stated that salaried status should not in itself be the primary criteria as to whether the Labour Code should apply or not. "This means that the mode of remuneration has nothing to do with the definition of 'non-salaried' and the fact that a person might be remunerated at a fixed salary would not prevent him or her from being 'non-salaried' for the purposes of the legislation proposed."[37] In other words, the Commission wants to avoid at all costs an amalgamation of "professionals" and "employees." In any case, "only conditions governing professional practice over the short term, such as setting a fee scale or any other form of remuneration, and related working conditions should be the subject of formal negotiations with the state...."[38] Certain rights were recognized such as the right to opt out of the health plan and the right to strike. The key question of essential services which had always been the stumbling block in labour relations between the public sector employees and the state was resolved in favour of the physicians:

> "There would be no question of declaring... the services provided by non-salaried professionals, doctors or others as essential and to oblige them to provide services under threat of injunction.... The law should expressly charge the syndicates with full responsibility

141

to the public for the maintenance of emergency and essential services."[39]

These "rights" should be situated in their context. The amendments to the Québec Labour Code in 1964 which put public sector employees on an equal footing with private sector employees concerning the rights of association and the right to strike, were seen as a major union victory. No doubt, it was an important concession by the government but it should also be interpreted in the context of the vast reform of governmental institutions which was underway at that time. Quite clearly, the success of this reform hinged on a complete overhaul of working conditions in the public sector. Furthermore, this new labour legislation contained an important limitation on the right to strike, that is, the "essential service" clause. Public employees could not legally strike unless essential services were guaranteed by a formal agreement between the two parties or by a decision from the Labour Court. Furthermore, the law stipulated that a Superior Court judge could, after inquiry, grant an injunction prohibiting a strike if he considered that it endangered the health or safety of the population or if it threatened to compromise the education of a group of students. The clause on "essential services" is thus a legal means by which the state-employer can abolish the right to strike in the public service wherever and whenever it chooses to do so. [40] The history of strikes in this sector shows that the various governments have not hesitated to use this clause. At the very moment that the volume on health insurance was being written, for example, the government withdrew the right to strike for teachers. This action constituted a turning point in the history of public sector negotiations. Relations between the government and the union movement continued to deteriorate to the point that the main union leaders were imprisoned in 1972 which in turn led to even more massive union agitation in 1976. It should be kept in mind, then, that the period during which the CIHSW was preparing its report was characterized by a growing antagonism between public-sector unions and the state.

These comments serve to indicate just how determined the Commission was to protect the privileged status of physicians and to prevent them from being considered as employees

142

subject to the Labour Code in spite of the fact that their income came from and was negotiated with the state. The CIHSW was attempting to maintain privileges of their former status as part of the traditional petite-bourgeoisie while at the same time integrating them into a new system of health organization controlled by a technocratic state. Two factors tend to explain why physicians received special consideration and treatment while a process of "devaluation of labour" was underway for the other employees and professionals of the health and welfare sector: firstly, there can be little doubt that the circumstances at that time favoured an alliance between physicians who could henceforth be considered as part of the new petite-bourgeoisie and the new technocratic class who needed this reform in order to consolidate the basis of its class power. This alliance was obvious even in the choice of the members of the Commission. Secondly, it should be noted that the medical profession in general, and especially the physicians, symbolized more than any other profession the viability of the "cultural model" of Science. In this sense there was a strong ideological affinity between the technocrats and the physicians.

Nevertheless, in spite of this attempt to work out a compromise with the physicians, the new technocratic class did not hesitate to spell out its own interests in this reform, in particular as they related to the necessity of centralized control in the hands of the state.

"The goal sought in the operation of this [health] system is the utilization of the various types of care and services in a combination... which will bring about, as quickly as possible and at the lowest cost, the desired standard of health. How can this be achieved without some centralization of decisions?... In this context, the Commission is of the opinion that complete integration of overall health services under the ultimate authority of the Minister of Health is essential."[41]

The centralization process and the way in which the department of health exercised its authority was not meant to affect all sectors and all personnel in the same manner. The Commission sought to enlist the active collaboration of the medical profession in the implementation of the government health plan and was therefore willing to recognize certain prerogatives for physicians.

"Taking into account the inherent complexity of the therapeutic relationship and in order to facilitate quick and smooth adjustments to rapid technological evolution... the administrative system recommended for the health insurance plan must allow for the participation in its operations of the health care professions.... There must be close cooperation between persons well-versed in professional practice and experts in administrative matters.... A plan administered by the government alone might compromise certain major principles of professional practice in the health field, while a plan administered solely by the health professions might not fully serve the public interest.... In order to promote the participation of groups involved in health, the Commission believes that *the administration of the health insurance plan must be submitted in a less direct way to the authority of the Minister of Health than services for prevention, public health and health education.*"[42]

There is thus a hierarchy of health care and services and consequently of professional practice which is in direct relation to the economic efficiency of the various services. At the same time that the reform brings a new participant into the health and welfare sector—the state—it also creates a new *social* hierarchy. This can be schematically represented as a continuum which stretches from the basic, preventive community services performed by non-medical and medical personnel alike at the one end, to the most specialized services and clinics equipped with the most sophisticated technology available and staffed by highly specialized medical personnel at the other. This continuum can also be seen in terms of costs, or more precisely in terms of the volume of circulation of capital. It should also be noted that state intervention varies as one moves from one end of the continuum to the other. It intervenes in a direct, authoritarian manner at one end, while at the other, it respects the prerogatives of private economic and professional interests and takes measures to ensure the profitability of private capital investment by pharmaceutical and medical equipment companies. The objective of the state, however, in taking over the sectors of prevention, community health and primary health care, is to reduce the relative importance of specialized and ultraspecialized care within the health system as a whole. In this sense, it also breaks down the

144

exclusive control which the institutions and professionals of these sectors had previously exercised. In other words, the state sought to implement a reform which would restructure the power relations of the professional and economic interests in this area by forcing them to work within the constraints of an integrated, coherent, hierarchical organization of health services.

That this reform had to take place within the constraints imposed by the situation of economic dependency of Québec society is clearly evident when we look at the attempts made by the technocratic class to obtain a share of economic power. The Commission was particularly interested in the pharmaceutical industry since the possibility of a health insurance plan which would cover the costs of medication was being seriously considered. The possibilities of taking over a part or all of this industry were studied. The conclusions of these studies were particularly revealing, given the highly monopolistic structure of this industry. We can clearly see the strategies employed by a new bourgeoisie seeking to benefit from the development of monopoly capitalism in the health and welfare sector. Through its new position of dominance within the state apparatus, this class sought to reinforce its power as a ruling class.

Health insurance, from the point of view of this class, should be as extensive as possible and should cover all health costs, including medication. In this way, it becomes a means for the state to exercise economic leverage through control of the insurance sector and the local production of the pharmaceutical industry. The argument used by the Commission was, of course, in terms of reducing drug costs and thereby providing another advantage of a public health insurance scheme.

The Commission notes: "[T]he abusive prices of drugs... are largely due to the non-competitive nature of the market... the concentration of the pharmaceutical products industry (in 1960, 40 companies supplied 90% of all prescription drugs in Canada)... the foreign control over the Canadian pharmaceutical industry... and a form of collusion in price setting."[43]

145

In light of this situation, the Commission proposed various measures designed to stimulate *competition* in the pharmaceutical sector. The changes suggested were mainly concerned with amending existing legislation. In particular, the Commission severely criticized the federal government laws on patents and trademarks which favour the foreign-controlled (American) pharmaceutical corporations. "These laws help curb competition.... Effectively, they grant the owner a monopoly on manufacture, importation and distribution...." [44]

In the spirit of the Quiet Revolution, the Commission proposed limited participation by the state in the pharmaceutical sector, especially in the area of research: "The Commission feels... there would be major advantages if the public sector was to contribute in various ways to this type of research" (that is, to basic research, which studies undertaken for the Commission showed as representing only a small part of the cost of production in spite of the claims by manufacturers that the high costs of their products were justified by the vast sums spent on research). "Initially, the state might intensify research by granting subsidies to universities. Eventually, it could coordinate authentic research as a whole by creating a pharmacology research centre." [45] Given that research and development operations are almost always located in the same country as the head office, it would seem that the only measures a local bourgeoisie could take in order to gain some degree of economic power would be to encourage state financing of basic research and to change legislation in such a way as to encourage competition. The only institutional means of action available to this class is the state, and even there, the instruments at its disposal are relatively limited. Since this class does not control the economy, it can only act in the areas of research and education on the one hand and legislative action on the other.

"The Commission believes that public authorities should act on drug prices by implementing a series of legislative or other measures capable of stimulating competition in the market and by intervening at the production-cost level. Public authorities can modify advantageously certain characteristics of production... [by] financing... basic research.... (This will have no short-term effect on the price of drugs because pharmaceutical firms do not

146

conduct basic research in Canada. However, it will have long-term effects to the extent that it encourages the development of a competitive Canadian industry, independent of the foreign cost structure.)" [46]

The strategy is not elaborated in more detail, and the Report is forced to admit that:

"There is no doubt that Canadian or Québec authorities can create mechanisms and adopt regulations to incite industry to behave in a given way, but they cannot force compliance without incurring the risk of seeing the companies move into other sectors of activity or establishing operations elsewhere. This is the nature of private enterprise and the result could be a loss of jobs and revenues for the community unless the state itself intervenes at the manufacturing level." [47]

When it comes to concrete proposals and recommendations, the suggestions are much more modest and the ruling class agrees to limit its action to the sphere of consumption by using pressure group tactics. By becoming a collective buyer, by establishing a list of the most common and essential drugs and by requiring that they be sold under their generic name rather than their trademark, the state sought not only to obtain better purchasing conditions but also, by encouraging individual consumers to buy the least expensive products, to force other manufacturers to lower prices. All the recommendations of the CIHSW concerning the pharmaceutical industry boil down to this one strategy. Since this class controls neither the sphere of production nor the sphere of distribution, it can only count on its power to organize consumption. The state thus contributes, once again, to the growth and concentration of dominant economic interests while it tries to defend, from a position of weakness, the interests of the population as consumers.

(b) Income security

The relationship between the Castonguay-Nepveu Commission and dominant economic interests is also clearly evident in the volume concerning *Income Security* (two tomes, 1971). Basically, the Commission sought to examine policies which could reduce the negative consequences of dependent development. State intervention was not to be oriented towards the sphere of production as such, but rather towards the structure of income distribution—that is, consumption. The sphere of consumption in this context constitutes the only field of intervention for the social management of dependency.

The scenario in the income security volume is much the same as that described in the health insurance volume: state intervention should seek to make its action more effective by pursuing a policy of rationalization and integration of piecemeal legislation on the federal and provincial levels into a single coherent system.

The unquestioning recognition and acceptance of the dominant economic order is obvious even in the structure of the volume on income security. The whole emphasis is on policy proposals for supplementing incomes, when for some unspecified reason, they drop below acceptable levels. For the CIHSW, economic problems are essentially problems of insufficient income, not problems related to the economic structure or to the social relations of production. The state explicitly recognizes that it must submit to the demands of "economic progress" and considers its role to be that of dealing with the social consequences. What is more, it sees its role of "rationalization" as a means by which it can be more effective in making economic investment profitable:

> "The search for full employment must support the objective of an economy at maximum efficiency since a modern economy requires emphasis on the productivity of labour. This search for a high level of productivity... is necessary to keep the Québec economy competitive.... New activities must therefore be developed within the framework of an accelerated integration of technical progress with the economy.... In channelling investment towards peak sectors, high-paying jobs will be created." [48]

The state should thus contribute directly to the development of the monopolistic sectors where productivity is highest. These types of investments should be a priority and can be pursued in three ways: (1) direct aid to multinational corporations in an attempt to influence their decisions concerning investment and development; (2) efforts to improve the level of qualifications of the labour force; (3) support for either low-productivity sectors of the economy in order to prevent them from being eliminated too rapidly by multinational corporations, or, when this happens, support for the sectors of the labour force which have been excluded from productive activity by rapid structural transformations of the economy.

148

On the whole, however, the strategy pursued is oriented towards supporting the monopolist sectors and although the Commission admits that there is a high level of structural unemployment in Québec, it nevertheless concentrates all its efforts towards forcing inactive workers back on to the labour market. In this sense, the Report clearly implies that the main causes of economic problems, defined in terms of insufficient income, are due to the characteristics of the labour force (low levels of qualification and mobility, poor health, etc.) and not to the structure of the social relations of production.

More precisely, it should be noted that the Commission does explicitly recognize the structural inadequacies of the economy but by limiting its interpretation of economic problems to the question of insufficient income, it is unable to deal with the relationship between the structure of production and income distribution. It simply reduces the problem to considering ways of acting on the labour force. In other words, the only influence this dependent ruling class can exercise on the economic system controlled by multinational corporations is through its capacity to transform the characteristics of the labour force. It is not surprising, therefore, that this class identifies the characteristics of the labour force as the main source of economic problems since this optical illusion has the effect of providing a political goal and legitimizing its action as a dependent ruling class.

The themes of poverty and income insufficiency serve as "intermediate levels" in the construction of the socio-economic ideology of the Commission. These are the concepts which permit the ruling class to see itself as an intermediary between the dominant economic structure and the social consequences on the local level with which it must deal.

"It is astonishing to observe the scope of poverty in the richest modern societies." [49]

"... Our own studies show that the situation is more serious in Québec than in Canada as a whole or in the United States.... It should be noted that the permanent nature of inadequate income strongly contrasts with the growth rate of savings." [50]

"We are struck by the extent of inadequate income. Even when government benefits are taken into consideration... 43.8 per cent of persons living outside the family... and 35.3 per cent of persons

149

living within families, that is 1.7 million persons, had incomes below the poverty line in 1961. Income inadequacy is so great that government subsidies (in the form of family and school allowances) would have to be tripled (from $160 million to $463 million) in order to eliminate the problem."[51]

"Privation of financial resources affects about a third of the Québec population even after the payment of social benefits."[52]

"In Québec, more than in Canada as a whole, income inadequacy affects the immediate potential of the labour force as opposed to groups which for particular reasons are not part of the active labour force.... Lack of jobs is a major factor behind income inadequacy in Québec. The level of unemployment and economic conditions in Québec are such that the portion of the labour force which is slightly below average educational qualifications encounters much more difficulty in being absorbed into the labour market.... The differences between Québec and Canada are even more pronounced if the Québec situation is excluded from the calculation of the Canadian average."[53]

"Poverty in Québec does not result mainly from inability to work but rather from unemployment, insufficient employment and low salaries."[54]

"The proportion of welfare recipients is much higher in Québec than in Canada as a whole. This is particularly the case when we compare welfare cases which are directly related to a lack of jobs. During the fiscal year 1968-69, 44% of all Canadians who received assistance allowances lived in Québec."[55]

The ideology of the Commission tended to put the responsibility for income inadequacy on the shoulders of the individuals concerned even if it made an effort to avoid moral judgements. There was no attempt to establish a hierarchy in the causes of poverty, no mention of privileges and charity; the emphasis was on such terms as "basic needs," "public risks," "poverty lines," "income security," and so forth.

"Income security policy attempts to ensure that all unattached individuals and families will always have the financial resources necessary to meet essential needs... whatever their status and whatever the circumstances depriving them of an adequate standard of living."[56]

This process of "homogenization" of the notion of "need" (in the sense that it is no longer considered necessary to justify the *causes* of this need) is paralleled by the "homogenization" of the notion of "risk" (in the sense that their *effect* on income is the same). At the same time, the term "income,"

150

and especially "income security," denotes a shift in emphasis from the world of production to the world of consumption, from working conditions and the social relations of production to the way in which one uses one's salary for the consumption of goods and services. The worker is no longer defined by what he produces but by what he is able to buy. Consumption, in this sense, is perceived as a stimulus for production, over which the worker has no control or from which he is excluded:

"[The] exclusive purpose of income security measures [is] to replace or supplement the purchasing power of individuals...."[57]

The notion of "risk" is thus a highly ideological conceptualization in that it avoids the question of the causes of income inadequacy, which for the most part are related to the conditions of production, and only attempts to deal with the effects which are seen in terms of the individual's relationship to the sphere of consumption.

"Income security plans cover a social or economic risk which generally threatens the individual with the temporary, prolonged or even permanent loss of a job and consequently, with income deficiency.... The types of situation which generally involve income deficiency or inadequacy... are: loss of a job, illness, disability, mental or physical infirmity, death or absence of the breadwinner, age and... inadequate job or earning possibilities."[58]

It is clear that this notion of "risk" is a key element in the process of ideological conceptualization of the causes of exclusion from the sphere of production. Nevertheless, we find the same gap in the Commission's analysis of income inadequacy as was noted above concerning unemployment. In the same sense that the Commission recognized the structural nature of unemployment and yet persisted in dealing only with the characteristics of the labour force and the effects of unemployment, so, in the case of income inadequacy, it recognizes that, in fact, there are two significantly different situations of "risk-need": there are those in which the individual is incapable of working due to age, disability or illness, and there is the situation caused by the unavailability of work on the job market.[59] In other words, the distinction is made between individual causes and structural causes, or more precisely between causes which for the most part are indirectly related to the structure of production (retirement, sickness,

151

work accidents, etc.) and causes which are directly related to the structure of production (i.e., unemployment). What is interesting here is that the ideology of income security claims to abolish this distinction and considers it no longer relevant in the context of a project which seeks to universalize the concepts of risk and need. Inherent in this universalization process is the notion of the *right* to income security. This apparent generosity, however, cannot conceal the fact that income security measures remain repressive and tend to reproduce existing social relationships in that they must always contain incentives for beneficiaries to return to the labour market (by providing a level of assistance which is lower than the level of income which could be obtained on the job market) and must always be linked to policies encouraging adaptation and reorientation to the demands of the job market. [60]

The Commission described the situation in the following terms:

"Attitudes towards social assistance measures imply the following challenge: to cease considering them as simple consumer subsidies and indirect forms of encouragement of dependency but rather as essential elements in a programme for the development of human resources." [61]

The liberal state characteristic of competitive capitalism is thus forced to abandon its passive auxiliary role concerning social policy in favour of an active strategy of support for the growth and development of monopoly capitalism. In this context, social assistance programmes are designed to adapt the labour force to the new requirements of economic activity through an energetic policy of job retraining programmes. "The income security system [must be] converted into a system of prevention and reintegration... it can be considered as a contribution towards a programme of human resource development." [62]

The objectives of a manpower policy are directly related to the question of income security: "A manpower policy must: (a) provide each worker with the possibility of finding work, (b) allow each worker to use his capacities to the fullest in accordance with his own aptitudes and openings in the job market." [63]

152

The income security measures suggested by the CIHSW should thus be seen as part of the more general process of development of the state in monopoly capitalist society. The process of concentration of capital and the consequences for small and medium-sized firms accentuates the need for social and economic assistance. The state is thus called upon to enlarge its scope of action, and for this reason attempts to "rationalize" its various social programmes by integrating them into a single, coherent "income security" system. In addition to financial assistance programmes as such, which as we have said are designed to encourage participation in the job market, this system includes two other aspects which clearly reveal the social and political functions of this policy: on the one hand, the state is called upon to support the declining sectors of the local economy by supplementing the salaries of workers in these sectors; on the other, job retraining programmes and manpower mobility incentives should be provided in order to make the labour force more attractive for new private investment. This latter aspect also has the effect of putting the burden of proof on the shoulders of the workers to show that their situation of unemployment is not a result of any lack of willingness to work on their part.

"The operating rules of the economy provide a part of the population with a share in economic power which largely satisfies their needs and aspirations. These same rules, however, place other parts of the population at a disadvantage and give rise to situations of insecurity.... [The] objective is to cushion the negative effects of this situation and to improve the chances of success for individuals in search of work and adequate remuneration."[64]

The Commission explicitly encourages the trend towards economic concentration and its effects on the labour force when it states: "Full employment must cease to be an immediate and instant objective.... A modern economy requires emphasis on the productivity of labour."[65] At the same time, the disastrous effects on employment of this policy can be compensated by providing support for small and medium-sized local firms: "Since, by definition, the present levels of productivity in these sectors do not allow adequate remuneration, an income supplement may be paid directly to the workers."[66] The Commission's policies concerning the workers can be summarized as follows:

153

— to attempt, through job training programmes and mobility incentives, to adapt the labour force to the requirements of monopoly capitalism:

"First of all, manpower policies bring about a better use of production potential.... Secondly, the quality of the labour force influences technical progress. Technological advances in physical capital require increasingly qualified manpower, failing which technical progress is slowed. Finally, highly qualified and mobile manpower is a factor of economic stability."[67]

— to use economic and psychological incentives to assist the least qualified sectors of the labour force in the weakest sectors of the economy.

— to administer programmes of assistance for those who are excluded from productive activity.

These comments help explain the nature and scope of the General Social Allowances Plan (GSAP) which the CIHSW envisaged as a general policy of social management of the labour force in the context of a dependent economy. The Report summarizes this policy as follows:

"Essentially, the GSAP assures universal access to a minimum standard of living; this is an essential condition for the development of the person. It must encourage the person to acquire, preserve or re-establish a certain economic independence. Certainly, establishment of such a plan is based on behavioural characteristics of the individual and on the functioning of the economy. The assumptions advanced should be briefly summarized:
1. economic policies, within reasonable periods, assure a sufficient number of jobs to allow all groups of workers to participate in the labour force;
2. manpower policies provide adequate instruments to readapt manpower, allowing the reclassification of workers and improvement in their productivity;
3. these readaptation policies bring about the creation of outlets for the benefit of the least favoured workers;
4. income security policy can be integrated within overall measures to heighten human resources;
5. a minimum income level is a fundamental condition for access to these measures as a whole;
6. as long as participation in economic activity improves his income possibilities, the breadwinner will prefer work to unemployment;
7. far from hindering the rational choice of an individual in regard to his employment, recreation and income possibilities, social assistance, like every other measure which heightens human resources, can contribute to his motivation."[68]

154

The plan was the product of a coherent ideological system of domination founded on the premise that society can provide full employment and income through participation in the labour market; consequently, social policy must contribute to the reinstatement of workers in the labour market. Yet not only was this basic premise in contradiction with the hard facts (the transformations in the mode of production aggravated by the structures of dependence); the economic options proposed elsewhere by the Commission itself (in particular concerning the maintenance of full employment)[69] gave the lie to this assumption. The proposed plan thus threw the brunt of the structural contradictions on working people, thereby actively strengthening the domination of the ruling class that devised and would administer the system of social policies and income security.

The ideology was based on a hierarchical and individualized vision of society and the social relations that shaped it: "normally" the dominant economic system allows individuals to survive, and above all to *develop personally*. It was therefore their individual responsibility to take advantage of the system as fully as possible and to rise in the social hierarchy. It was true, of course, that part of the population was "disadvantaged" by the system and lived in economic insecurity, in poverty. Thus the state, as the administrative channel for redistributing social wealth, had the collective responsibility for providing individuals with the material means of attaining the threshold of security and personal development; once this was achieved, they became active competitors like everyone else. This was the logic behind the establishment of a "guaranteed minimum income," the definition of a "poverty line" and the idea of "equal opportunities."

The goal was to allow for a certain degree of redistribution of resources, while at the same time explicitly subordinating this concern to ruling economic interests and thereby reproducing fundamental social inequalities:

"In principle, equalization of opportunities to enter the labour market is an objective of manpower policy. But it is so roughly in the same way as a just sharing of income would be an objective of economic policies. In short, it is rather a secondary objective playing the role of constraint in the maximization of output or efficiency."[70]

155

This essentially ideological view of social relations and the way it shaped policy can be seen even more clearly when we examine the volume on development.

(c) Development:the management of local social relations

As pointed out earlier, the volume entitled *Development* clearly reflected the influence of the traditional faction within the CIHSW. This can be seen in the descriptive nature of the presentation; the arguments grounded in a recognition of "universal" values such as Man, the Common Good, Justice, Solidarity, etc.; the philosophical language used; the explicit references to the social doctrine of the Catholic Church; the dramatization of current social trends; and so on. These and many other characteristics betray the cultural and institutional roots of the volume's authors: representatives of a crumbling clericalism, schooled in the neo-Thomist theology that came to predominate in Québec by the end of the 19th century as the clerico-petit-bourgeois alliance consolidated the domination it was to preserve through to the 1950s. [71] But the anachronistic language and categories used should not blind us to the more important fact that the volume is actually a vigorous reaffirmation of economic liberalism or, to be more precise, neo-liberalism, inasmuch as it clearly acknowledges the need for state intervention in the management of social relations. Paradoxically, this acknowledgement sounded the end of the domination of the clerical faction that had fiercely fought state intervention right up until the Quiet Revolution. What this ideological shift in fact reflected was the subordination of the clerical faction of the traditional petite-bourgeoisie to the new technocratic class. To understand this, it is useful to note that the new technocrats had set up their own parallel working group on the ideology of social development. Their vision was expounded in Appendix 25 of the CIHSW Report, *La Société de demain: ses impératifs, son organisation* ("Tomorrow's society: its imperatives and its organization"), written by the sociologist Gérald Fortin and published in 1970, a year before the volume on development came out. The significance of these two parts of the Report can only be understood in the context of the power struggle between the representatives of the two factions in the field of social development, social services and poverty. Since these problems had traditionally been left to the Church, the technocrats were in a relatively weaker position here than they were in the fields of health and income security.

The report *La Société de demain* was written by a sociologist actively involved in the process of the Quiet Revolution. It summed up the discussions of a working group "charged by the Commission with defining the general framework for welfare policy in Québec."[72] The group was composed of three sociology professors, a professor of law, four social work professors all clearly indentified with the modernizing school of social work, a professor of industrial relations, the Commission's expert on public administration (who was in fact the real source of inspiration for the Commission's models for reorganizing social services), and economic and medical advisers who were prime examples of the technocrats soon to head up the ministry of social affairs. Appendix 25 was without a doubt the result of a strategy aimed at outflanking the traditional group on its home ground. Indeed, it took this group only eight working sessions to agree on an ideology of social development[73]; in contrast, the volumes assigned to the "clerical" group were published a year or two later than all those produced by the technocrats' group. The technocrats' efforts in the field of welfare were not limited to writing Appendix 25, however; much of what is said there is repeated in the volume on development, which as a result tends to read as a compromise, as does the volume on social services. In other words, the technocrats used the appendix to lay the vital cornerstones of the coming reform, concentrating especially on the role of the state, the economy and social policies, leaving external details and internal organizational questions in the hands of the traditional group. I will thus treat Appendix 25 and the texts in the volume on development as a whole.

As mentioned previously in relation to the report on health insurance, the CIHSW used a "cultural model" of science in its management of social relations. This was repeated in *Development* with its discourse on Man, its idealist vision of Man as both individual and community, free of social relations and material constraints, Man as the supreme value of a teleological and voluntarist vision of society united in a common endeavour of progress, accomplishment and com-

157

munion in the "Common Good"—accompanied by some stale whiffs of neo-Thomism and seasoned with doses of social catholicism, Teilhard de Chardin and even Saint-Exupéry on the one hand [74] and of the "development" ideology of international agencies on the other. The Commission asserted that Man was progressing, thanks to Modern Science, and quoted B.A. Houssay's words at a United Nations conference in 1963:

"Science and technical knowledge have now become essential to our life, for our health, agricultural and industrial production, wealth and well-being all depend on them. The relatively underdeveloped countries have two choices: science or poverty. Either they will recognize the merits and importance of science and scientific applications, or else they will condemn themselves irretrievably to ill health, economic and cultural underdevelopment and continued lives of poverty and stagnation. Other countries that are more but still insufficiently developed will in turn have to choose between science and mediocrity.... The developments and improvements in the world so far are the result of the great scientific discoveries made and put into practice and not, as many seem to wrongly believe, of talks and political events." [75]

Confronted with a choice between science and wealth, or ignorance and poverty, the Commission had no trouble making up its mind!

To establish local political and social control, to reorganize the structure of local domination, means that a ruling class has to organize class relations on a hierarchical basis, thus confirming the inequality of classes. It has to stay at the top of the hierarchy while at the same time trying to give the impression that the "new" forms of its domination seek to encourage greater social equality. It must also make sure that the social costs and consequences of its domination are borne by the dominated classes.

One of the advantages of the volume on development is that it gives a very straightforward, unambiguous statement and justification of this social hierarchy, and thereby enables us to better understand one of the fundamental orientations underlying the work of the CIHSW and the socio-political orientations of the reform.

"In society, there is a very subtle tendency, inspired by a desire for equality and an outgrowth of certain ideologies of recent centuries, but all the more dangerous because it is based in appearance on highly humanitarian sentiments. We refer here to the search for equality in respect to fortune." [76]

158

The Commission went on to quote François Bregha:

"... a growing number of people, especially young people, see poverty as the worst kind of inequality. The logical outcome of thus confusing poverty and inequality is the vision of a controlled utopian society, where equality is imposed by an all-powerful state. To avoid any misunderstanding, I would hasten to add that I am in favour of doing away with socio-economic inequalities, but primarily of *those below the level deemed acceptable by society. Above that level, towards the top, I prefer an open, diversified and therefore unequal society*, in which there is no need to sacrifice liberty for the sake of equality."[77]

In a later chapter, it wrote:

"An overly great inequality [of income] may offend but it must be admitted that a perfectly egalitarian distribution of income in a society is unthinkable. There will always be people poorer and richer than oneself."[78]

"It is not a question of establishing the equality of all..."[79]

Once this concept of inequality in society had been spelled out, the next step was to identify how the hierarchy of classes — or the levels of the social pyramid, if one prefers — could be defined and implemented. The key concept here is related to the notion of a *vital minimum*, namely what society considers to be the minimal living conditions necessary for a "decent" standard of living. Below this level, one merely *survives*; above it, *personal development* is possible. This paired notion of *survival-development* was at the heart of the social philosophy governing the CIHSW's reforms.

"At the vital minimum level, one merely survives; personal development or proper functioning depend on achieving optimal levels.... In industrial countries on the verge of the affluent society... personal development comes to the fore as what should be the general rule for all citizens. Survival is then an essential prerequisite that becomes the inalienable right of every citizen."[80]

In this approach, the idea of *social development* sums up all the social measures designed to allow the poor — the individuals living at a mere subsistence level — to acquire the *minimum* standard of living at which they can then be expected to take charge of their own personal development, on the basis of their own capacities and resources. "Social development may be defined as the implementation of a series of policy measures designed to provide each member of the society with the means to realize his potential. This definition

159

emphasizes... that man is the principal agent of his well-being... and that development... is limited for each individual."[81] Thus society must see that everyone has the possibility of personal development. "The individuals forming society are very different from one another but all of them need this society to develop. Development does not bear the same significance for all individuals."[82]

This was the social philosophy underlying the discourse on *equality/inequality* to be found throughout the work of the CIHSW. "Social development," "social rights" and "universally accessible services" were the key terms and themes of the Commission, but the intent behind them was actually the perpetuation of a ruling system based on the preservation of a fundamentally non-egalitarian society.

This was so true that the CIHSW carefully pointed out that in discussing equality, it was not referring solely to economic "catch up" measures to bring people suffering from blatant socio-economic inequalities up to some minimum acceptable threshold. Instead, the basic tool for upgrading their standard of living was to be the provision of support *services*, rather than a redistribution of income. "The scope of non-satisfaction of its needs, more than the sum total of its income, determines if a family is poor or not."[83] "It is an error to relate poverty to low-income earners."[84] A coordinated strategy of services for the inhabitants of the survival zone should enable society to ensure that these "second-class citizens"[85] enjoy the necessary conditions for personal development, which, the author notes, would be in accordance with the "Universal Declaration of Human Rights"[86] since this proclamation amounted to "the solemn affirmation that since all men are equal, all must benefit from the same advantages for development."[87] These *services* might even be extended to include income security, but it was clearly specified that this was a *service* intended to achieve "a more coherent distribution of resources among citizens so that society, without seeking equality of income, may enable its members as a whole to lead a more decent life."[88]

Appendix 25 even evoked the possibility of a full-fledged "society of services" for the sake of "development":

160

"A society of development requires the establishment of a coherent set of services for the individual, the family and groups. Needless to say, these services must be broken down into sub-systems of services in order to be efficient.... The following are the main services: an open-ended educational system (that will instill... basic general knowledge and provide occupational training and an introduction to political and cultural life); a health system designed to protect the public's physical and mental health; a system of guaranteed income combining welfare, insurance and other kinds of payments; a system of housing and planning and development; a manpower retraining and employment system; a system of community organizing; a system of information adequate for participation in the democratic process; a cultural system divided into many sub-systems ranging from sports to arts centres; a system of personal counselling to help individuals achieve autonomy and regain a general psychological equilibrium or to treat abnormal behaviour; a system of legal protection designed to protect a person's individual and collective rights.

The first principle of all these systems is that they must provide universal coverage. This means that all these services should be available to all people in Québec without discrimination. It also entails abolishing means tests, along with the idea of welfare recipients and second-class citizens.... [However,] while seeking to make services truly accessible and available to everyone, the priority is to ensure that all these services are available in the under-privileged communities in rural and urban areas....

To be of real benefit to individuals and small groups, the various services have to be coordinated locally so that the individual only has to contact one office. This central agency could make a general diagnosis. It could guide the individual through all the various channels and processes and evaluate his progress regularly.... Any such regular evaluation would require the compilation of a single, cumulative file for each individual and each family.... It is essential that the different services belong to a genuinely integrated and coordinated network.... This coordination has to go beyond coordinating the different services. It is absolutely essential that the institutions responsible for providing the population with universal services be coordinated with the institutions for economic growth and planning production."[89]

This all-embracing society of services was well-suited to reproducing a non-egalitarian structure of social relations; at the same time, it spelled out the predominant role of the technocratic class as intermediaries in managing dependence. Indeed, this class thought solely in terms of enlarging the role of the state as a provider of services, thus affirming its political role in defining the new functions of the monopoly capitalist state. The purpose of the ideology of the "society of services" (or "development") was to conceal the conflictual nature of social relations and the economic causes of social inequality, rooted in the class structure. In fact, it portrayed the economic sphere as entirely separate, mentioned only in the concluding lines of the description of the future society: all the services had to be coordinated, that is to say, surbordinated to the logic of economic production.

This ideology, which postulates as an organizational response to social problems, also uses the rhetoric of universal coverage. Paradoxically, it was this insistence on universality that revealed its real function in the reproduction of social relations. This ideology was part and parcel of the concept of a hierarchical society divided into "second-class citizens" and the rest: those who survive and those who develop. The whole strategy of social development was aimed at "eliminating poverty" or, more precisely, "managing" poverty. For as we have already seen, the "services strategy," presented as part of a broader approach to the definition of poverty ("Real poverty in developed societies is primarily social and political poverty, rather than economic poverty"[90]), led in practice to an attempt to deny the social relations of production and the economic dependence of entire social groups. The emphasis on universal coverage (means tests were to be abolished) tended to mask the fact that the specific purpose of many of these services was the ideological control of the poor and the administrative control of "high-risk" groups; hence, for example, the guaranteed income plans, housing programmes, retraining or manpower programmes, community organizing, education, adequate information for participation in the democratic process, personal psychological services, legal aid, etc..

To be effective, services have to be coordinated: "although problems are interdependent in all situations, this holds especially true for the disadvantaged. Currently, the average citizen does not make regular use of all the universally available services."[91] Ultimately, their effectiveness was linked to the establishment of a single, cumulative file for each family and each individual.

162

Although the Report insisted on the universality of services, it recommended that priority be given to disadvantaged areas in establishing coordinated services. In fact, the list of suggested services corresponded to the list of deprivations suffered by the poor: "... lack of education, poor physical and mental health, lack of individual and collective economic activities, lack of political understanding, unemployment, lack of cultural activities, inadequate housing, etc."[92] It was noted that these negative factors had mutually reinforcing effects and were transmitted from generation to generation. "Poverty, like epidemics, has a cumulative and multiplier effect."[93] Poverty was thus defined and circumscribed. There was ample justification for taking strong steps to deal with it.

"Disadvantaged urban and rural communities are in greater need than any others of an integrated system that takes a comprehensive approach to the problems of the individual and the community. It is therefore important that the first multi-purpose agencies be located in these disadvantaged communities.... Similarly, it is of fundamental importance that we break the pattern in these communities of conditions passed on from one generation to the next. For this reason, special treatment for children from disadvantaged environments is a very urgent priority."[94]

In the end, the Report acknowledged that the universality of services was more a principle than a concrete necessity for action:

"If the economic situation of Québec were to require that a choice be made between universal coverage of all services and concentrated action for disadvantaged communities... it is our opinion that the disadvantaged groups should get priority, even if this means violating the principle of universal access for a certain period of time."[95]

In the fifth chapter of this book, we will see that the principles set forth in Appendix 25 were identical to those that governed the development and implementation of the Local Community Service Centres model. Both this ideology and the specific institution developed to implement it have played a critical role in the vision of society held by the new technocratic class. They are key tools for perpetuating the established social order, despite the accompanying references to the democratic notion of "universal social rights":

"All citizens, regardless of who or what they are or their standard of living, have a right to a certain quantity of goods and services

163

defined as the vital minimum in their society. This vital minimum is distributed to all on a universal basis without the individual having to prove anything whatsoever. The concept of the 'socially assisted' disappears, to be replaced by that of 'citizen'." [96]

In this context, "social rights" became the modern version of traditional liberal teachings on class inequality.

"The 'Welfare State' thus becomes the 'Social Security State' demanded in the name of justice by the consumers with lower incomes. The liberal mass society is thus slowly transformed into a technocratic mass society." [97]

Talking about "social rights" had the added advantage of paving the way for introducing the complementary topic of social *obligations*—the duty of those benefitting from the right to cooperate with the ruling class in its plans for society: "If social rights oblige society to do everything possible to reach a certain level of development, they, in turn, oblige each citizen to cooperate in this social action." [98] The same applied in the field of health care:

"Affirmation of the right to health constitutes an act of faith in modern medicine and in scientific research. Today, man further enjoys his right to health because medicine tends to preoccupy itself with both his physical health and his psychological behaviour. This right also represents a very important social value because of the advantages derived by society from improvements in human capital.

As medical services and the health benefits plan develop, the obligations of citizens increase. The obligation to health becomes an inseparable complement of the right to health, a correlated objective of this right." [99]

There was a systematic attempt to mask class relations. Any reference to the economic sphere was carefully avoided, as were any attacks on economic structures or mechanisms. Instead, emphasis was put on a "philosophy of services" that became the cure-all for dealing with all forms of inequality. The domination of the ruling class was clearly revealed when the Commission admitted that a *majority* of the population needed the services it proposed as a "treatment" for inequality. "In practice, it is known that more than 50 per cent of the population does not enjoy a reasonable level of income. It may therefore be stated that the majority of the population is poor: this is the great paradox of the affluent society." [100] Further on, the Commission added: "In general, Québec accepts the

164

fundamental values of Western democracies... Western society believes that capitalism, despite its weaknesses, promotes individual and social development more effectively than any other system."[101]

The ideology of the "society of development" elaborated by the technocratic class implied an expanded role and responsibilities for the state that corresponded perfectly to the specific position of this new ruling class in general social relations. In defining the new state, it defined its institutional basis for exercising its newly acquired power.

Taken as a whole, Appendix 25 portrayed a society undergoing a gradual process of rationalization and planning, a process that required working out prospective models of future development:

"As Western societies realize the necessity of rationally organizing their own economic and social growth, they also realize the necessity of knowing or at least predicting the future."[102]

This reasoning depends on a linear perception of time: decisions made in the past determine the present; a lot of energy is spent correcting the results of bad decisions; if we improve and above all make the present more rational, we are shaping the future, we are "building a desirable future." The underlying assumption is that society is stable, or at least can be stabilized (an unquestioned goal), and capable of surmounting the irrationality of diverging interests and making rational decisions. It can do so because it is subject to an authority above and beyond individual or particular interests that guarantees a reasoned course of action, namely the technocratic experts vested with state authority. Such a vision of society ignores the dynamics of concrete social relations. Social struggles are seen in negative terms because the planners see in them the failure of their social planning. They disrupt the planners' attempts to achieve orderly social relations, which is a prerequisite condition of "progress." This is why special attention is paid to identifying potential sources of social unrest. The poor are a potential threat to the plan to stabilize society. The solution is therefore to guarantee them the vital minimum and to ensure their organized participation in the decision-making process.

The experts turned to state authority as an agent of

social cohesion. The state was thus associated with the traditional idea of the Common Good, and the experts became the servants and guardians of the ideal. Implicit, however, was the major assumption that the economic and social spheres, the private and public sectors, were strictly separated and that the former had unquestioned primacy over the latter.

It is already obvious that a reform based on such assumptions would rapidly be vulnerable to the various pressures and resistance that came once reforms began to be implemented in health and welfare.

The traditional petite-bourgeoisie believed the state should act in favour of social rights: "The State... must also provide citizens with an environment favourable to their development."[103] State intervention was therefore legitimate in all the increasingly important fields that helped guarantee adequate conditions for personal development to all "citizens". Besides being the key entrepreneur in a society of constantly expanding services, the state was to act as the guardian of personal and collective development against the abuses of organized groups or special interests. The traditional faction saw the state's new role as one of responsibility for development, rationalization and integration of social support services. This was not in contradiction with the role envisaged by the technocratic faction. It simply did not go as far as the latter since it did not reflect the social position of a class faction that could affirm its class leadership by developing the state machinery in which it had technocratic expertise. Both views recognized and accepted the dominant social order and were in fundamental agreement on the need to actively cooperate in preserving and developing it, as well as perpetuating hierarchical social relations nuanced by the universality of the "society of services":

"There may be disparities in income and material resources but they must not exist in services.... Any policy which truly tends to reduce these disparities [in services] is incorporated within a context of social development."[104]

"The functions of the State are that, and that alone: to be an agent of social development."[105]

Thus (since economic development was basically a matter for private enterprise), state intervention should be

166

limited to what the CIHSW called *social* development, which in fact means taking responsibility for those who are living at bare subsistence levels through a strategy of sectorially integrated services. In this light, the Commission's section on development can be seen as a rhetorical exercise intended to modernize its approach to the issue of poverty. At the same time, it proposes a comprehensive realignment of local social relations without challenging—in fact while reaffirming— the legitimacy of class domination. As Claude Castonguay, cabinet minister at the time, put it:

"Social development has a positive role to play in economic development. It has to see that the social climate does not deteriorate, that the changes resulting from technological progress do not lead to excessive social tensions, that human resources are adequate for contributing to economic development."[106]

In this respect, the volume on development is perfectly compatible with the ideological framework of the volumes on income security and health insurance. The Commission's perspective on development places the same emphasis on the "poor"—those who "survive" rather than develop, and these people, the Commission admitted, account for a majority of the population of Québec. The volume on development was thus an integral and indispensable part of the CIHSW's general project. It was the specific job of social services to deal with these sectors of the population; and as we will see, one of the primary roles of the CLSC was to provide the institutional framework for this work.

One view of poverty and how to eliminate it says that, apart from making systematic use of various services to bridge the gap between subsistence and conditions allowing personal development, what has to be done is to help the poor organize in pressure groups to defend their own interests as disadvantaged social groups. In short, the poor should mimic the way the élites and middle classes operate in liberal society. The poor are not individually to blame for the fact they are poor; it is their collective failure. They are not organized and do not know how to promote their interests in a society that functions by responding to special interest groups. It is therefore not surprising that society ignores them, since they are neither present nor represented when decisions are made.

This kind of analysis is why the Commission developed the model of "community organizers" (people with university training in social work or social sciences), assigned mainly to the CLSC. Their job was in part to convince the institutions in a given territory to use their resources to meet specific needs of the "survival" sectors of the population and to coordinate those services, and in part to enable the poor to articulate their needs and organize into pressure groups to promote their interests in the "right way," at the "right place," and at the "right time."

Obviously, the CIHSW's ideal society was a society neatly organized into interest groups for all social classes, at all levels, all properly respecting their place in the reorganized and newly legitimized hierarchy, so as to allow an ongoing process of consultation, negotiations and *concertation*. This was the ideal of the "participatory society" or the "democratic development society" advocated by the sociologist Gérald Fortin. [107] It also represented the Utopia of a ruling class, a vast project to integrate Québec society through the state, which would play its political role by organizing the distribution of services. Potential instability inherent in class domination could be neutralized by modernizing the service delivery system designed to deal with the negative effects of Québec's dependent status within the framework of world capitalism.

The CIHSW Report: ideology as action—the organization of health care, social services and the professions

The CIHSW outlined the underlying principles of a thorough reorganization of health care, social services and the professions. The proposed reforms in services were basically bureaucratic, aimed at rationalizing and coordinating existing services into one comprehensive, integrated system. It would be characterized by planning, a hierarchical organization of establishments, services and decisions, and the coordination of work at the various levels. Rationalizing and systematizing health and welfare required a greater concentration of power in the hands of the state and called for changes in the role of the professions and their professional organizations.

This vast institutional reorganization is the topic of this section. Here again my approach will be to examine the political changes in the relations between the various authorities active in the field of health and social services. The three volumes on health, social services and the professions were each the work of specific groups that controlled their given field within the Commission. As has already been mentioned, there certainly do not seem to have been fundamental differences of opinion in the written reports. All of them strongly criticized the existing organization of the particular field dealt with. All stressed that state intervention was urgently required and that jurisdiction should be centralized in the hands of the state. In short, all seemed to agree on the general characteristics of the bureaucratic reform described above. The issues defining and dividing the various factions in the CIHSW can be traced in the volumes written by the different groups, but are really clearly identified only in retrospect, in light of subsequent developments in the proposed reforms, the struggles arising from their implementation, and later political decisions. In addition, several major reforms commonly associated with the Commission's work were in fact introduced only late in 1971 with the act on health and social services, a piece of legislation decisively influenced by the technocratic faction surrounding the Commission's chairman, by then minister. This is true, for example, of the merger of the ministries of "health" and "family and welfare"; the creation of Local Community Service Centres (CLSC); the refusal to implement regionalization policies; etc..

The volume on health was produced by what I have termed the "techno-professional" faction—an alliance of public health physicians and health economists. This group was strongly influenced by U.S. experiments in the functional reorganization of health care establishments on a regional basis (for instance, the Kaiser Foundation in California) as well as by community health care centre experiments undertaken as part of the "War on Poverty" and the programmes of the Office for Economic Opportunity, particularly in the Boston area, where they received backing from Harvard University's Department of Community Health. The volume

169

on the professions was written by legal experts whose own profession put them in close proximity to state power; they represented the technocratic faction. The volume on social services, we have already explained, was a compromise between the traditional clerical faction and academics in social sciences associated with the technocratic group.

a) Health

One of the main organizational themes of the volume on health was the development of a new model of community social medicine that involved expanding the concept of health care through programmes of complete and continuous general care ranging from prevention to rehabilitation. The state's basic goal here was to correct the abuses of liberal medicine, which tends to focus exclusively on curing individuals through the use of costly and specialized treatments and personnel. The new concept of health care was expanded to include hygiene, nutrition, physical education, early screening for disease, as well as environmental protection and measures dealing with the social and medically related problems of disadvantaged groups such as the aged, the chronically ill and the handicapped.[108] Community social medicine seeks to correct the inequalities engendered by the practice of liberal medicine both geographically (between urban and rural areas) and socially (between well-off and disadvantaged social groups). Its priority is to eliminate disparities.[109] In other words, while health insurance established the principle of universal access to health care, the projected reform of the delivery system for health care gave priority (despite the general formulations about its comprehensiveness) to reorganizing services for "disadvantaged groups." In doing so, it betrayed the real social function of the reform in health care, namely the modernization of the instruments of social control over the working classes. This clarifies one of the major roles of the CIHSW's work: above and beyond the rhetoric about universal access, the goal was less to reform the entire health and welfare system than to reform the part dealing specifically with the working classes and disadvantaged groups; these services would enable the new technocratic class to manage and control the social relations of domination.

The Report determined three priorities in implementing

170

its recommendation: the elimination of disparities; broadening the concept of care; and cleaning up the environment.

Eliminating disparities:

"The health of certain disadvantaged groups as well as treatment facilities in certain isolated urban and rural areas leave so much to be desired that they must be the prime concern of public authorities."[110]

"Disadvantaged communities and groups must benefit not only from equal and universal access to services but also from more complete and better adapted services... the following groups must be cared for, on a priority basis...
— the newly-born, particularly those in areas where mortality is highest;
— children, from infancy to adolescence, with a view to building a sound, strong and well-developed generation...
— the physically and mentally handicapped so that they may return to their families and working environments;
— the aged, so that they may be maintained within a human and social framework."[111]

It is striking to note how these target groups were actually or potentially marginal socially or, to use the technocratic jargon, "high-risk" groups. Indeed, the groups were identified through the use of social indicators based on a sophisticated use of statistics.

Above all, however, it is striking to see how objective health criteria, supposedly the decisive factors, overlapped in practice with social criteria. For these target groups, it is quite appropriate to talk about the medicalization of social relations: their social relations are defined as medical problems.

These groups had already been identified as target populations by the federal royal commissions on health. They would be designated as priorities for CLSCs by the provincial ministry of social affairs in 1975, and since 1978, the ministry of social affairs has been preparing and implementing general legislation for the protection and defence of the rights of youth, the handicapped and the aged that in practice facilitates the social management of each of these groups.

The report's statement of priorities reiterated that

"The health plan must incorporate special measures for these population groups and the first is the creation of LHCs [local health centres] and the formation of multi-disciplinary service teams in regions and sections where the needs are most pressing. Studies on

171

the population's state of health and statistics available to the Department of Health make it possible to determine the most disadvantaged areas and existing disparities with respect to care."[112]

As will be seen in Chapter Five, this recommendation was followed to the letter in creating the CLSCs. As a result, they were identified right from the start with the special role of looking after the health and welfare of "disadvantaged" groups.

Broadening the concept of care:

Here the Report basically emphasized that organizing the delivery of general health care, ranging from prevention to rehabilitation, was to take priority over what it called specialized and highly specialized care.[113] Nine categories of general health care and services were listed: public health services, nutrition, physical education, school health services, personal counselling services (in particular for students with drug problems), screening and general examination services, mental health services, rehabilitation, and programmes for the aged. Again, this expansion of the concept of health care directly evoked the social dimension of health and disease. Clearly the social groups most directly concerned were the so-called "disadvantaged" groups—those whose health was most directly influenced by their material and social living conditions. It should be noted that these priorities corresponded precisely to those set out by the federal royal commissions.

Cleaning up to environment:

"If living conditions frequently determine people's health, special attention must be paid to those of the poor, whose poor health reflects the deterioration of the environment and the economic and social restrictions against which they struggle."[114]

Thus all three of the Commission's priorities clearly referred to the most dominated segments of the population. Above and beyond the general organization of the health care system, the Commission was especially interested in the social repercussions of how health care is organized.

There were three fundamental elements in the model of social medicine proposed by the Commission.[115]

1) The definition of complementary levels of care, based on the needs of the population and the technical requirements of

172

medicine, rather than on categories of illness, particular population groups or sectors of medical activity. The three basic levels of care were:
— *General care* (80% to 90% of the care provided), focusing on maintaining and improving the individual's state of health, preventive medicine and rehabilitation. This care would be provided by interdisciplinary health teams (composed of three to five doctors, four to ten nurses, and a social worker). It was primarily at this level that the goal of comprehensive community medicine would be reached;
— *Specialized care,* namely comprehensive medicine providing personal contact, continuous and coordinated care to supplement general care;
— *Highly specialized care.*

2) The establishment of complementary health care services based on three fundamental principles: the definition and creation of a health care delivery system; the coordination of medical work at the local and regional levels; and regional planning of health care services. To implement all this, the Report called for three categories of health care centres.
— The *local health centre* would be the core of the health care system. It would ensure full and continuous care and be an ideal setting for teaching comprehensive medicine and thus changing medical practices. It would also provide home care.
— The *community health centres* (hospitals) would provide specialized general care. This would mean that hospitals would no longer be at the heart of health care organization. They would become treatment centres responsive to the community and its needs.
— The *university hospital centre* for highly specialized care would round out the health care structure and make each region fully autonomous for all its health care.

3) The regionalization of the health care system within the framework of a comprehensive approach to and planning of health. This would require that powers be decentralized and that users of the services participate in advisory and decision-making roles. The various agencies and institutions involved would be autonomous but should coordinate their work. Regional Health Offices (RHOs), reporting to the ministry of

health, would be responsible for regional services and structures. The Commission proposed three major health care regions for Québec, based on the three cities with university hospitals (Montréal, Québec City and Sherbrooke).

In its call for comprehensive medicine, the Commission's report on health emphasized the expansion of general health care, fewer and shorter hospital stays for the ill, greater flexibility in the division of labour, the creation of interdisciplinary health care teams, and the development of health care centres. However, the "core of the entire reorganization of the health system... rests with the creation of RHOs which enjoy broad powers delegated by the National Assembly... "[116]

It was chiefly in this emphasis on very strong regional health care structures that the techno-professional interests of the group behind the volume on health were to be seen.

In terms of specific programmes, the Report concentrated on recommendations for changes in the way health care was provided and "consumed." It was considered particularly important to encourage disadvantaged groups to make more use of health services by making the services more accessible to them and by trying to overcome psychological barriers to their use. Changes were also to be made in costly medical habits, such as the excessive use of acute care facilities. Attempts should be made to avoid hospitalization and general medical care for what were often psychological rather than medical problems.

The changes called for in health care delivery included: 1) An expansion of general care with the emphasis on comprehensive medicine to meet the most common needs when and where those needs arose. [117] The local health centres (what were to become CLSCs) were the most adequate structure for providing general care. They were to concentrate on increasing the "proportion of preventive visits, health and screening examinations... in relation to those for the purpose of diagnosis and treatment. This at least is the principal objective of creating LHCs.... The goal of LHCs is to render general care more accessible and to raise its quality..."[118] 2) Reduced hospitalization as a result of the establishment of a network of general care. "In the context of the social cost-effectiveness of care, raising the general level of health is in

174

our view much less related to an increase in the number of beds than it is to the availability of care for those who need it most and who do not resort to it."[119] There should be a trend away from hospitals towards general care in the use of health care resources. Home care, out-patient services and long-term care were all to be developed at the expense of acute care.

3) Delegation of medical tasks. Traditionally qualified personnel would be supplemented with auxiliary personnel who would be less highly trained and probably more adaptable to a system of simple care. The LHCs, because of their specific role, could employ this less-qualified personnel, with an assistant for each doctor. The paramedical personnel could carry out all the screening, preventive work and educational activities. The doctors would continue to diagnose and treat. At the root of this approach was the concept of care teams.

4) Formation of care teams. A care team would include general practitioners, nurses and social workers. It would work with consultants and refer patients to specialists when necessary. The interdisciplinary teams would be at the heart of a health service oriented towards a comprehensive approach to health problems rather than the diagnosis and treatment of acute illness.[120]

5) Salaried doctors.

"The method of payment... must not harm mechanisms which make it possible to attain the objectives of the health policy."[121]

"There is, in payment for service, an incentive contrary to the objectives of health policy since this method of payment tends to place the accent on medical activity related to sickness.... The method of payment for service constitutes a direct incentive to increase the volume of medical care, particularly the most complex and most profitable care.... Conversely, comprehensive care is based not on the number of services but rather on the full responsibility for the health of a given group of people."[122]

Consequently, the Commission recommended that doctors be paid "on the basis of a salary, as seems logical..."[123] although, it emphasized, "salary levels must be related to the payment assured the physician, on the average, by fee for service."[124]

These kinds of changes in medical practices had been recommended by the federal royal commissions on health care as well. They can be traced back to the absolute

175

necessity for the state, with its growing responsibility for the population's collective health, to achieve significant breakthroughs in the productivity of health care establishments and workers so as to improve the general performance of the health care system and thus the public's general level of health. Hence the attempt on the one hand to identify the groups in the community responsible for lowering the average level of health—the poor, the newborn (infant mortality), etc.; and on the other hand, to identify the relatively more costly and less efficient aspects of the health care system—those involving acute care, namely hospitals and specialist doctors. By promoting LHCs as a way of providing simple care, using paramedical personnel, in decentralized structures as accessible as possible to the target populations, and focusing on prevention, education and rehabilitation, the government reports defined an organizational approach to health care that was to play a key role in the state's strategy for administering the health care system. This theoretical approach to the organization of health care was based on a number of pilot projects in community health in the United States in the 1960s, all of which were aimed at enabling the technocratic state to fulfill its overall role of regulating social relations ("human resources" management), be it through health, social or educational policies.

The CIHSW developed a very coherent vision of community social medicine in its volume on health. It clearly illustrated how this theoretical model related the need for a new approach concerning health to new relations between government, health care personnel, the institutions involved, and the population. Highlighted in this approach was the role of the community, participation, regionalization and decentralization.

b) **Social services**

Similar principles governed the reorganization of social services: organizational integration; a hierarchy of functions; participation; regionalization and decentralization. [125]

By their very nature, social services are primarily directed at "disadvantaged" or "excluded" groups. They thus have a primordial role to play in the overall management of

176

social relations, and the authors of the volume on social services had no qualms about adopting a definition of social services that emphasized their role as a factor in social integration. Indeed, they subscribed to the objectives assigned to social services in 1967 by the Economic and Social Council of the United Nations: 1) "Contribute to the achievement of objectives of the other sectors of development"; 2) "promote development by encouraging individuals and groups to participate in defined projects so as to give rise to personal efforts aimed at modifying, by this very fact, the attitudes of persons and groups"; and 3) "help the most vulnerable sectors of the population to attain a minimum level of development... migrant workers, groups... or inhabitants of disadvantaged areas... the handicapped, the chronically ill, the elderly, etc...."[126]

In organizational terms, this orientation in social services corresponded to two levels of services structuring the "survival" zone referred to earlier. Thus, "the ultimate objectives of social services action are governed by the necessities of social organization for the maintenance of the coherent balance and development of society as a whole. Social services must then be placed in a political perspective of social development."[127] The ultimate objectives, corresponding to the two levels of services, were the integration and advancement of persons and groups. "The objective of integration is common to income security and social services"[128] inasmuch as social problems were defined in terms of a deficiency or deprivation in the individual or community. Social problems might have economic roots (hence the reference to income security), but they occurred among people who were psychologically disadvantaged or who lived in "disorganized" communities. The solution was therefore to implement a "process" of integration and advancement through the "maintenance, formation or re-creation of a basic personality [or basic community]..." and the creation and maintenance of a "conscious capacity and motivation in a person..." to enable him or her to achieve social reintegration. [129]

Hence two systems of social services. The first, directed at maladjusted and handicapped individuals, "aimed at allowing these persons a functional re-education and social re-

177

adjustment which renders them apt to eventually integrate into the community as active members."[130] The second, for communities, "includes services for adjustment, organization and technical assistance for disintegrated communities, technical support services for unorganized communities and, finally, mass education services, certain community services and technical counselling for other community services in the organized communities."[131] There was thus an acknowledged "pedagogical" hierarchy in the social reinsertion of communities. Concerning community organizing for disintegrated or disorganized communities, the Commission observed that "the nature of these interventions confers upon them a political significance whose responsibility cannot be assumed by the apolitical services of the administration";[132] consequently, they were to be the direct responsibility of the minister of social affairs.

The report recommended the establishment of a "Regional Social Services Office" (RSSO) comparable to the regional health offices recommended in the report on health. The RSSO was to be a distinct legal entity responsible to both the population and the government for all regional activities. The goal here was to create a strong regional structure: the office would be in charge of regional planning and programmes, administer the regional budget, approve the budgets of local institutions and have the power to contract loans. In addition, this regional structure would be closely linked to the population so as to maximize the public's participation in and responsibility for social management, with seven of the fifteen seats on the RSSO's board of directors set aside for public representatives. A Regional Social Services Council would be created to oversee and supervise the work of the RSSO. Its role:

"to restore... the sovereignty of citizens over the fields of collective action...

to provide a channel of expression for those who are voiceless in modern society, that is, for those citizens whose lack of sociopolitical organization deprives them of institutional spokesmen...

to palliate the inconveniences inherent in bureaucratic organization...

to finally constitute... the "conscience" (rather than the watchdog)

178

outside the Administration, even a sort of "counter-administration" whose vocation, through the structure of consultation parallel to the politico-administrative structure of conception and execution, consists in introducing into the latter the ideas and reactions of the social environment, thereby preventing the evolution of policies, programmes and operations of social services from being neglected."[133]

The Regional Social Services Council was an innovation added to the organizational structures borrowed from the volume on health. It reflected the authors' concern with offsetting the bureaucratic tendencies of the complex system they proposed. As they pointed out:

"Institutionalized, factionalized into specialized organs and channelled into determined processes, the sector's activity, spontaneous and mobile in the model, will, it must be admitted, be somewhat systematized, bureaucratized and asepticized by the proposed administrative plan. In effect, it did not appear possible, in our view, to avoid a period of functional specialization of the organs of the plan: in other words, a period of "bureaucratic" organization in the Weber style is necessary in order to establish the new tasks and to train the agents of the administration for their respective roles before it becomes possible to consider a more spontaneous administrative model."[134]

The social service establishments, formerly autonomous to a large extent, were to be subjected to a process of integration that would accentuate their bureaucratic tendencies and heighten the social and technical division of labour. The authors of the report tried to forestall the tendency towards bureaucratization that they themselves were actively helping to instill by insisting on the importance of public participation, and simple professional practices that would be accessible to the population (hence their virulent critique of professionalism).

"Because we prefer, above all, for reasons both of realism and of efficiency, to take into account necessities stemming from the popular will, we must give precedence to the feeling of regional belonging and the population's will, expressed with increasing vigour in view of the slowness and inertia of administrative bureaucracy, to have the decision-making centres which influence its collective life brought closer to it."[135]

Further on, they stressed "the citizens' desire for collective control of their own affairs... [which] will find increasing expression in contemporary Québec region-

179

alism."[136]

At the local level, they recognized "the will to participate clearly expressed by the population" which revealed "the deep dissatisfaction of social groups... the immense majority of Québec workers, in respect to present mechanisms for the expression of the popular will... the loss of confidence of this same population in respect to the 'professional politicians'... the exasperation... of clients in respect to an administration whose operation appears more concerned with bureaucratic requirements than with services to be rendered to the population."[137]

The authors' emphasis on the public's strong demands for participation allowed them to highlight the importance of their own techno-professional position which, in social services, was directly derived from the traditional petite-bourgeoisie. Their populist rhetoric also allowed them to pose as defenders of the dominated classes and justify their virulent critique of the professionalization of services and bureaucratization of service organizations whose basic function was to mask the major implications of the new division of labour and the process of integration of the new system of social services into the technocratic logic of the state.

Despite its championing of people's participation, the new ruling class set strict limits concerning the possible consequences of any such participation:

"Interest in such participation, however, rests rather in its educational value. In effect, the exercising of responsibility contributes to political apprenticeship: it makes requests more reasonable, the participants more patient in respect to answers which do not give full satisfaction and replaces negative ideological contestation by more constructive and more detailed criticism."[138]

This is why they proposed that local "community centres"—the counterparts of the local health centres—be established at "the request of a community which suggests the territorial area to be covered by the projected centre, based on its own feeling of belonging."[139] Using a community's "feeling of belonging" as the reference point ran counter to the rational technocratic approach, which tended to divide the territory into districts with relatively similar sizes of population. It was a good illustration of an approach to social services based on "grassroots solidarities" rather than predefined vertical models. Thus the report recommended that community centres in Montréal be based on the "large cultural communities of the metropolis (French-Canadians, Canadians of English or Irish origin, Italians, Jews and others)... and the homogeneous communities constituted in different points of the territory (district, parish or suburb)."[140] As we will see with the CLSC, this orientation derived from the humanist ideology characterizing social services was to conflict with the technical approach associated with medicine, which defined communities as administrative units.

The report on social services proposed that all members of the boards of directors of community centres be elected by the population of the territory served and that the people choose and organize the activities offered. These were to be aimed at improving the social environment and protecting the family nucleus.[141] The centres would organize four kinds of community services: day-care centres; day centres for adolescents or adults; family homemakers; and cooperative stores.[142] Generally speaking, they were not to offer psycho-social services; these were the responsibility of more specialized centres.

The activities to be organized by the community centres corresponded exactly to the kinds of services established by the "citizens' committees" in working-class and disadvantaged neighbourhoods. The state would now take charge of them. The overriding role of the community centres was social and political, the report implied, in contrast to the conceptual model of health care delivery that lay behind the proposal for local health centres.

Social control of the dominated classes required an approach that was both clinical and community-oriented, in which heavy reliance on participation was seen as a strategy and indeed a prime therapeutic tool for integrating them into the dominant society. Here again the technocratic class used the defence of the poor, their exasperation and the danger of revolt to force through sweeping reforms in the organization of social services and bring the professionals working in these services into line.

181

c) The professions

In formulating the fundamental principles of a complete reorganization of health and social services, the CIHSW was inevitably confronted with the question of reform of the professional organization of the producers of these services. This subject was tackled in the volume entitled *The Professions and Society*, definitely the clearest statement of the goals, strategy and ideological tactics of the new technocratic class in its political undertaking of rationalizing the organization of services. Once again the technocrats sought to achieve a fuller integration of the organization of services—in this case professional services—and the functions of the state, by eliminating the organizational aspects that tended to hinder the process of integration, such as professional autonomy and professional powers and prerogatives. Their strategy: to modify the legal status of the professional orders by defining them as emanations of the state; to distinguish between the role of the orders in "protecting the public" and their role in "defending the interests of their members" (to be assumed henceforth by union-style organizations), thus institutionalizing the social division of work within many professional groups and weakening their unity; and to introduce various outside controls on how the orders functioned. The ideological tactics chiefly involved invoking the interests of the public and the need to defend them against those of the professional orders. The interests of the professional orders or corporations, it was suggested, were in conflict with those of the public that made use of professional services. Therefore the "neutral" state should oversee matters and surmount the conflicting interests of the parties involved for the sake of the common good. Finally, the report condemned the anachronistic and perhaps even corrupt nature of corporatist organization. This ideological line of argument led to a single conclusion: it was legitimate and necessary to curb the existing powers of the professional orders and subordinate them to state authority.

The proposed reform of the profession was grounded in a highly critical analysis of contemporary legislation concerning the professions in Québec. Said the report: "It must be concluded that the law governing professions was more an expression of the professional groups' strength than of a

182

transcription of social and political needs into law." [143] Existing professional organization was rooted in a liberal society that profoundly rejected state intervention and in which the state had consequently delegated its own powers to professional orders to an extent that was both exceptional and excessive, given society's current needs.

"The notion of professions which guided the edification of our professional law owes less to the survival of Middle Ages corporatism than to the ideas of liberal society on State intervention, to the fearful attitudes of Québec's population with respect to the State and to the legislative function in Québec. At least, it is difficult to explain in any other way the sometimes exaggerated tendency of the Québec state to entrust its own roles to corporations." [144]

The Commission pointed out "this peculiarity of Québec corporatism," which delegated more powers to the professional corporations than any other country. In Québec the corporations could be administered exclusively by their own members and control entire sectors of services without any formal responsibility to the state.

"From society's viewpoint, this was an alienation of its natural power of orienting development and participating in the evolution and the inclusion of professions within its framework." [145]

By defining an unconscionable historical situation in which the professional orders had appropriated extensive state power — alienated society's powers — the new technocratic class justified its political intention of bringing the professional corporations under control; all it was suggesting was that the state, or society, reappropriate the powers that were its own by right, powers that had been usurped by the corporations for too long already.

The Commission was interested in more than merely reasserting state authority over the profession in order to give the community greater control over professional services. It believed the state had to intervene because society had "evolved" and the professions had new roles to play in the framework of a new political logic. The Commission clearly acknowledged that this evolution, namely the penetration of monopoly capitalist relations in the organization of work, had resulted in the disappearance of "certain of the characteristics which formerly served to define the 'professional'—such as the fact of being an autonomous worker, of having been freely

183

chosen by the client and of having received a remuneration mutually agreed upon..."[146] Many professionals were becoming salaried workers, working "in conditions often identical to those of other workers"[147] and losing the autonomy traditionally associated with their professional status.

"The recent development of unionization, even among professions already incorporated and often despite the resistance of their own professional bodies, shows clearly, by the conduct of professionals themselves, that the notion of professions, with its liberal character-istics, no longer holds for them its original juridical meaning."[148]

The existing structure of corporations was thus no longer adequate, as proven by "the conduct of professionals themselves," and "the reform proposed in regard to health and the social services would be compromised if the disorder in professional organization were to continue."[149]

In other words, the trend towards unionization of professionals was a sign of the social division of labour that had already penetrated the state organization of services and that would be accelerated by the proposed reform. This division of labour required a transformation of the role and powers of the professional orders because the existing struc-tures perpetuated professional control of services that hindered organizational changes.[150]

The reform proposed by the Commission was thus aimed at redefining relations between the professional cor-porations and the state. To begin with, the two roles of the corporations—that of "protecting the public" and that of "defending the interests of their members"—had to be distin-guished and separated. As the state assumed the costs of social and health care, it put an end to the free market in care and thus transformed the traditional liberal framework of economic relations in this area. "Corporations must be viewed exclusively as specialist (possession of the discipline) and specialized (administration of the profession) public agents.... On the other hand, the law must recognize the legitimacy of protecting economic interests of professional groups and institutionalize it in an appropriate union organization."[151]

If the corporations were to be "public agents," this meant they would become "part of the public authorities." The corporations thus became part of a single professional orga-

184

nization accountable to the state. As "mandatories of society," the professional orders should have representatives of the community and of public authorities on their boards of directors; "delegation of public powers obviously postulates such a broadening of their composition." [152] The existence of professional orders was henceforth dependent on the National Assembly, which delegated to them the authority to regulate their members and control the quality of services. [153] Legislative provisions for the professions were to be combined in a *Code for the Professions* that would amount to a new law of the professions. Since the corporations became in an integral part of public administration, public funding would be provided to cover the costs of various aspects of supervising services and protecting the public delegated to them by the state.

The professional orders were to become "real arms of the State" [154] but were nonetheless subordinate to it. The state deprived them of their chief means of self-protection: "Anything resembling limitation of competition should be eliminated." [155] Consequently, the orders lost the right to set conditions for admission to the study or exercise of professions. The state would use "state diplomas" to control general conditions of access to the professions. "Academic standards, programme of studies, organization of probation, requirements of control (exams, etc.) would be consigned in an order-in-council adopted by the government" and revised periodically. [156] Uniform standards could thus be set for all of Québec and all state diplomas would be equally valid.

"We believe such a system of State diplomas would be singularly fruitful, particularly for the new disciplines of health and the social services. Recognition by the State of diplomas, certificates or technical certificates... would guarantee the competence of candidates..." [157]

Union organization of professionals would henceforth be entirely separate from the professional orders. Their sole purpose would be to defend the economic and social interests of their members.

Although the reform of the professions called for a clear separation between the new orders and professional's unions, it left both forms of organization under the jurisdiction of a single ministry. The ministry of financial institutions, com-

185

panies and cooperatives, responsible for regulating companies, was to be "empowered to require from all professional orders the reports which it deems necessary, including the communications of records, and to inquire into their activity." It was also to be "charged with the strict supervision of non-profit associations... to see to it that they be organized and administered according to democratic criteria..." [158] It was to compile registers of voluntary associations and professional unions, not only in the fields of health and social services, but in all other sectors of activity.

> "This would allow the State and the bodies involved to keep count of the manpower strength in the various sectors and to call upon their associations or unions, either in an advisory capacity or for the implementation of numerous tasks of the administration." [159]

Thus, in addition to proposing that the professional orders become part of the state, a means of decentralizing its authority in the professional field, the Commission said the state should supervise the professionals' voluntary associations and unions, within the framework of the same *administrative* structures. Its recommendation to give the same structure jurisdiction over both professional orders and professional union groups was aimed at perpetuating a close association between the two and thus "controlling" the consequences of the state-provoked breakdown of professional corporatism in terms of class relations. The new professional unions were not covered by the Labour Code, as workers' unions were, and were not the jurisdiction of the ministry of labour. They were administered by *ad hoc* professional representatives. The new petite-bourgeoisie, now incorporated into the monopoly capitalist organization of services and thus subject to the division of labour, was to ally its class interests with those of the technocratic class in power — even though, as the Commission itself conceded, for some professionals the changes in the organization of work meant their "proletarianization":

> "The civil servant jurist of a public administration or employee of an industrial company and the practitioner of a medical speciality working under the salaried system [may work] in conditions often identical to those of other workers." [160]

Here again we find the prerogatives that the CIHSW Report on health insurance conceded to doctors to offset the social effects of their inclusion in the organization of services.

186

It was less a concession than an indispensable class alliance, for although the new bourgeoisie severely criticized the traditional petite bourgeoisie and the latter's organization, its criticisms were nonetheless an expression of a struggle between factions of the same ruling class. The professional union favoured by the Report reflected the alliance that the new ruling class had to establish with the traditional faction in order to guarantee its class rule and the reproduction of the social relations of domination.

The technocrats' proposed realignment of powers within the ruling class was not restricted to the fields of health and social services. It could be effective only if it was extended to cover "professions generally in Québec."[161]

"The professional organization, not only of health and the social services but of all sectors of organized activity, is of considerable importance.... Professional laws governing the activity of hundreds of thousands of practitioners involve the rights of society as a whole....

In short, the *Code* [for the professions] should contain all laws governing all professions in every field."[162]

The CIHSW rounded out its reorganization of services by establishing the professional orders that would on behalf of the state guarantee the social order resulting from the policy on services. Thus their creation confirmed the profoundly political role of the Commission's strategy, described in this chapter, for developing services as tools for the management of social relations.

Footnotes

1. *Report of the Commission of Inquiry on Health and Social Welfare, Social Services*, Vol. VI, tome 1, pp. 148-149. The translations that are used are those of the translators of this book.
2. Fortin, Gérald, *La Société de demain: ses impératifs et son organisation*, CIHSW, Appendix 25, 1970.
3. Conseil des œuvres, *Une politique sociale pour le Québec*, brief presented to the CIHSW, 1967; written under the direction of Auger Ouellet.

4. *CIHSW, Social Services*, Vol. VI, tome 1, p. 272.

5. Maheu, Louis, *Enseignement supérieur et structure sociale: les fonctions sociales de l'université québécoise francophone*, doctoral dissertation, Paris, École Pratique des Hautes Études, 1974, pp. 271-272.

6. Comité de recherches sur l'assurance-santé, Vol. I, *L'Assurance-Maladie*, Québec, 1966, p. 34.

7. *Ibid.*

8. *Ibid.*

9. *Ibid.*, p. 36.

10. *Ibid.*

11. College of Physicians and Surgeons of the province of Québec, working paper presented to the provincial government and the public. Montréal, September 1964, p. 16, cited in *L'Assurance-Maladie*, p. 37.

12. *L'Assurance-Maladie, op. cit.*, p. 38.

13. *Ibid.*, p. 39.

14. Boudreau, Thomas, "Assurance-maladie et planification de la santé" in *Maintenant*, Montréal, March 1967, p. 95.

15. *CIHSW, Health Insurance*, Vol. IV, tome 1, pp. 33-35.

16. *Ibid.*, p. 49.

17. *Ibid.*, pp. 38-39 (my emphasis).

18. *Ibid.*, p. 110.

19. *Ibid.*, p. 111.

20. *Ibid.*

21. *Ibid.*, pp. 19-20, 22-23.

22. *Ibid.*, p. 5.

23. *Ibid.*, p. 22.

24. *Ibid.*, pp. 111, 112.

25. *CIHSW, Development*, Vol. III, tome 3, p. 175.

26. Fortin, Gérald, *op. cit.* p. 45.

27. *CIHSW, Development, op. cit.*, p. 214.

28. *CIHSW, Health*, Vol. IV, tome 1, p. 69.

29. *CIHSW, Health Insurance, op. cit.*, p. 246, p. 257 and ff.

30. *Ibid.*, p. 261.

31. *Health, op. cit.* p. 70.

32. *Health Insurance, op. cit.*, p. 115.

33. *Ibid.*, p. 156.

34. *Ibid.*

35. *Ibid.*, pp. 157-58.

36. *Ibid.*, p. 156, p. 133, note 1.

37. *Ibid.*, p. 145, note 1.

38. *Ibid.*, p. 148.
39. *Ibid.*, p. 147.
40. Cf. Piotte, Jean-Marc, *Le Syndicalisme de combat*, Montréal, Éditions Albert Saint-Martin, 1977, pp. 103-108.
41. *Health Insurance, op. cit.*, p. 117.
42. *Ibid.*, pp. 117-118 (my emphasis).
43. *Ibid.*, pp. 200, 202, 204.
44. *Ibid.*, p. 206.
45. *Ibid.*, p. 210.
46. *Ibid.*, p. 224.
47. *Ibid.*, p. 225.
48. *Income Security*, Vol. V, tome 1, p. 210.
49. *Ibid.*, p. 33.
50. *Ibid.*
51. *Ibid.*, p. 51.
52. *Ibid.*, p. 55.
53. *Ibid.*, p. 41.
54. *Ibid.*, p. 55.
55. *Ibid.*, p. 91.
56. *Ibid.*, p. 11.
57. *Ibid.*, p. 32.
58. *Ibid.*, p. 83.
59. *Ibid.*, p. 87.
60. *Ibid.*
61. *Ibid.*, p. 269.
62. *Ibid.*, p. 271.
63. *Ibid.*, p. 226.
64. *Ibid.*, p. 205.
65. *Ibid.*, p. 210.
66. *Ibid.*, p. 220.
67. *Ibid.*, pp. 210-211.
68. *Income Security*, tome 2, pp. 13-14, section 415.
69. *Income Security*, tome 1, pp. 209-213.
70. *Ibid.*, p. 226, section 276.
71. See Thibault, Pierre, *Savoir et pouvoir: philosophie thomiste et politique cléricale au XIXe siècle* (Québec City, 1972).
72. Fortin, Gérald, Appendix 25, *op. cit.*, Foreword, p. vii.
73. *Ibid.*, p. vii.
74. On this aspect of ideology, see Bourdieu, Pierre, "La production de l'économie dominante," *Actes de la recherche en sciences sociales*, no. 2-3 (June 1976).

75. *Development, op. cit.*, tome 1, p. 199, section 385; our translation.
76. *Ibid.*, p. 34, section 17.
77. *Ibid.*; my emphasis; our translation.
78. *Ibid.*, p. 111, section 152; see also section 373.
79. *Ibid.*, p. 201, section 394; see also section 397, as well as Fortin, Gérald, *op. cit.*, p. 43, and *Health Insurance, op. cit.*, p. 22.
80. Fortin, Gérald, *op. cit.*, pp. 8-9.
81. *Development, op. cit.*, tome 1, p. 212, section 436.
82. *Ibid.*, p. 201, section 393.
83. *Ibid.*, p. 111, section 153.
84. *Ibid.*, p. 118, section 167.
85. *Ibid.*, p. 165, section 303.
86. *Ibid.*, p. 170, section 321.
87. *Ibid.*
88. *Ibid.*, pp. 182-183, section 373.
89. Fortin, Gérald, *op. cit.*, pp. 77-78.
90. *Ibid.*, p. 44; see also *Development, op. cit.*, tome 1, pp. 224-225.
91. *Ibid.*, p. 80.
92. *Ibid.*
93. *Ibid.*
94. *Ibid.*, pp. 80-81.
95. *Ibid.*, p. 81.
96. *Ibid.*
97. *Ibid.*, p. 21.
98. *Development, op. cit.*, tome 1, p. 173, section 328.
99. *Ibid.*, p. 178, sections 347-348.
100. *Ibid.*, p, 116, section 164.
101. *Ibid.*, p. 167, section 311.
102. Fortin, Gérald, *op. cit.*, p. 13.
103. *Development, op. cit.*, tome 1, p. 182, section 369.
104. *Development, op. cit.*, tome 2, p. 154, section 1052.
105. *Development, op. cit.*, tome 1.
106. Castonguay, Claude, speech to the Saint-Laurent Kiwanis Club, November 1970.
107. Fortin, Gérald, *op. cit.*, pp. 43 and ff., as well as other publications by the same author.
108. *Health, op. cit.*, tome 4, pp. 219-220, sections 1888-1889.
109. *Ibid.*, pp. 217-219, sections 1882 and ff.
110. *Ibid.*, p. 218, section 1883.
111. *Ibid.*, pp. 218-219, section 1884.
112. *Ibid.*, p. 219, section 1885; also p. 200, section 1815.

113. *Ibid.*, p. 219, section 1887.
114. *Ibid.*, p. 221, section 1889.
115. *Health, op. cit.*, tome 2, pp. 28-124, section 538-748.
116. *Health, op. cit.*, tome 4, p. 210, section 1863.
117. *Ibid.*, p. 162, section 1707.
118. *Ibid.*, p. 166, section 1716.
119. *Ibid.*, p. 167, section 1723.
120. *Ibid.*, pp. 175-176 ff, sections 1742, 1751 and ff.
121. *Ibid.*, p. 207, section 1849.
122. *Ibid.*, p. 207, sections 1851-1852.
123. *Ibid.*, p. 209, section 1859.
124. *Ibid.*, p. 209, note 2.
125. *Social Services, op. cit.*, tome 1, pp. 219 ff, section 682 ff.
126. *Ibid.*, p. 21, section 43.
127. *Ibid.*, p. 181, section 583.
128. *Ibid.*, p. 183, section 585.
129. *Ibid.*, p. 183, section 587.
130. *Social Services, op. cit.*, tome 2, p. 14, section 756.
131. *Ibid.*, p. 15, section 761.
132. *Ibid.*, p. 46, section 852.
133. *Ibid.*, pp. 67-68, section 927.
134. *Ibid.*, p. 19, note 1.
135. *Social Services, op. cit.*, tome 1, p. 219, section 684.
136. *Ibid.*, p. 221, section 688.
137. *Social Services, op. cit.*, tome 2, p. 58, section 896.
138. *Ibid.*, p. 58, section 898.
139. *Ibid.*, p. 56, section 886.
140. *Social Services, op. cit.*, tome 1, p. 228, section 715.
141. *Ibid.*, p. 228, section 712.
142. *Social Services, op. cit.*, tome 2, p. 56, section 887.
143. CIHSW, *The Professions and Society*, Government of Québec, 1970, p. 26, section 36.
144. *Ibid.*, p. 24, section 26.
145. *Ibid.*, p. 25, section 30.
146. *Ibid.*, pp. 26-27, section 37.
147. *Ibid.*, p. 27, section 37.
148. *Ibid.*, p. 27, section 39.
149. *Ibid.*, p. 30, section 53.
150. Renaud, Gilbert, *op. cit.*, pp. 277 and 280.
151. *The Professions and society, op. cit.*, p. 32, sections 62-63.

152. *Ibid.*, p. 35, section 74.
153. *Ibid.*, p. 41, section 93.
154. *Ibid.*, p. 70, section 213.
155. *Ibid.*, p. 50, section 127.
156. *Ibid.*, p. 51, section 132.
157. *Ibid.*, p. 52, section 136.
158. *Ibid.*, p. 68, section 202.
159. *Ibid.*, p. 69, section 206.
160. *Ibid.*, p. 27, section 37.
161. *Ibid.*, p. 10, foreword.
162. *Ibid.*, p. 74, sections 228 and 231.

CHAPTER 4
The Reform in Practice: The Issues Involved in Centralization, Regionalization, Reform of the Professions, and Participation

This chapter is an analysis of how the reforms in health and welfare were put into practice, and some of the main issues involved. The new ruling class established its power on the basis of a greatly accentuated centralization and concentration of state powers, which were transferred from the professional groups and institutions to the ministry in Québec City. The regionalization of health and social services became a major political issue between the new state technocracy and the representatives of the petite bourgeoisie coming from the institutions and professions, who saw their institutional power bases undermined. A similar issue arose with the implementation of the reform of the professions. Furthermore, the new ruling class included public participation as part of the organizational changes it instigated. This overture to the public illustrated its strategy of allying with the "grassroots" to win control over the intermediate authorities entrenched in the institutions and the professions. I will therefore take the themes of centralization, regionalization and the reform of the professions in the application of the reforms as three lines of analysis for examining the new social relations at play in the field of health and social services. In each case public participation is discussed as an integral part of the strategy for concentrating powers at the top of the new integrated system of services.

Using the same approach, the fifth and last chapter will look at the evolution of the Local Community Service Centres (CLSCs), a new institution that embodied all the issues at stake in the reform. The CLSCs were more than mere complements to the existing health and social services network; they were the "cutting edge" of the fundamental principles underlying the transformation of the network, the technocrats' chosen tool for implementing the reform. It is thus legitimate to see their short history, with all its ins and outs, as a concentrated expression of the dynamics of the social relations developing in the field of health and social services. Thus, while Chapter Four tries to take an overall look at the issues at stake in the reforms by theme, Chapter Five seeks to understand them dynamically, over time, by looking at the CLSC as a case study. For the CLSC should be seen as an instrument for reform, rather than simply as one more element in the chain of health and welfare institutions.

The constitution, concentration and integration of new powers

The technocrats' rise to power signalled the beginning of a full-scale reorganization of health and social services. There was no doubt about the diagnosis: the existing organization had very serious flaws, beginning with a very low level of productivity. There were no objective data on the effectiveness of the services in terms of improving the collective state of health. The structure of health and social services had been determined by the relative strength of the interest groups involved; and if there was any logic to how they were organized, it reflected more the interests of the professional groups and directors of institutions than any political will to promote the collective health of the population.

This extremely negative diagnosis was to justify drastic reform—at least in principle—of the health and social services system. Consequently, a group of "experts" from the academic world and the private sector, most of whom had already participated in the CIHSW's research teams, were moved into central positions of authority. The vast majority of these experts did not come from health or welfare institutions. At the upper levels, most were economists, legal experts or management specialists, along with a sizeable contingent of accountants. Their arrival heralded the introduction of a new administrative logic in the management of the ministry, which lost its old roles of supporting and coordinating institutions and directly dispensing certain public health services. With the former roles, "professional" interests had predominated, and most of the administrative positions had been held by physicians or, later, by social workers. But now the physicians were replaced by accountants: the proportion of physicians dropped from 32.9% to 7.4% of all administrators, while that of accountants grew from 13.9% to 32.6%[1]. The accountants were supervised by "experts" and senior civil servants, the new élites who had joined the ministry with the reform. Old management was shunted aside: of the forty members of senior management in the ministries of health and social welfare, only five carried on with similar or higher-ranking roles in the new organization.

The former internal organization, based on administering specific programmes that had accumulated gradually one after the other as the state took charge of more and more social and health care services, gave way to a functional division of labour, encouraged by the funding policies of the federal government (with funds allotted for health units, hospital insurance, laboratory services, mental health and placement). From the conception of major policies through to their implementation at the local level, everything was to be organized and flow in an orderly, coherent fashion, as part of a single integrated system. At each organizational level there was to be a rational decision-making process. Six functional departments in each of the three fields covered by the ministry (health, social services and income security) ensured the general coherence of the new administrative system: planning, programmes, financing, professional relations, social assistance and administration.

Such a structure meant that specific programmes implementing ministerial priorities were theoretically accountable to all six departments, each of which administered

195

the aspect of a given programme that fell under its jurisdiction. Unless the decision-making process was decentralized, allowing the programmes to be reassembled at a lower level in the structure, local institutions were faced with dispersed decision-making powers that in practice tended to cancel each other out. Responsibility was effectively divided along functional lines, but this could work efficiently only if the decision-making structures were really decentralized. As we will see later, this was not the case.

The entire operations of the ministry were reorganized on the model of the Public Programming Budgeting System (PPBS). The ministry created a service of operational research, designed in part to produce economic, social and health indicators for identifying the state of health and social development of the population, following its evolution and making rational and "objective" decisions on ministry programmes and then evaluating them. The ministry also set up a complete data-processing system and a public information service. Research, data processing and public relations are all hallmarks of the management of large and highly centralized businesses.

The ministry's internal reorganization was more than the "modernization" of a specific administrative system. It represented a transition from the administration of supplementary programmes, from a service controlled by representatives of the liberal professions and institutions and shaped by lobbying by these interest groups, to an approach based on the integration of health and social services as part of the new functions of the monopoly capitalist state. The representatives of the former centres of power, ousted at a later date and in a more gradual fashion from the sector of health and social services than they had been from education, had to give way once and for all to the agents of a new technocratic rationality.

The new organizational model seemed extremely centralized, authoritarian and bureaucratic right from the start. Local institutions had to give up many of the responsibilities that guaranteed their local or regional power, and the first to go was a certain financial autonomy. The structure of functional administration, and the resulting compartmentalization of the management of specific programmes, obliged local institutions to overhaul their entire system of management and relations with the ministry, broke up the old lobbies, and diluted ministerial responsibility by dividing it along functional lines. It thus added a layer of bureaucratic insulation and gave the minister an appearance of objectivity, removed as he was from the details of the various departments.

Henceforth, it was the ministry that was running things, and not local or regional authorities like the regional councils, local institutions, the professions, counties or municipalities. Furthermore, it was the ministry that defined the issues and set the rules—the most important at the outset being the internal organization of the new ministry, its plans and bureaucratic concepts.

The introduction of the administrative technique of a *global budget* for local institutions has often been presented as an example of the ministry's intention to decentralize powers. It in fact became a method for controlling additional spending by local institutions, and hospitals in particular. This technique had already been recommended by the *Reports on the Cost of Health Services in Canada*,[2] which suggested applying the techniques and standards of industrial management to hospitals. It consists in determining in advance the operating budget of an institution on the basis of the anticipated volume of services to be provided, and then handing over the total amount to local management, which is free to use it as it deems best and dispose of any eventual surplus. Although this technique gives the local establishment some internal administrative autonomy, it also allows the ministry to centralize and compare the management of various institutions and then standardize it by defining rates and allowances that are easily controlled by the ministry. For the ministry the global budget corresponded to the new relations it sought to establish with local institutions and constituted the main technical innovation in the management of health and social services. But it was also the prime administrative mechanism for subjecting local

197

establishments to the new technocratic rationality and integrating them into a system of complementary functions. The small or medium-sized institutions, and the powers attached to them, were definitely a thing of the past; if such institutions persisted, they simply took the form of functional branch offices of the central ministry.

A complete reorganization of the ministry depended on the prior merger of the old ministries of health and of family and social welfare, which was the first thing the new minister did when he took office. Since the merger ignored the recommendations of the CIHSW reports on health and social services, it is worth clarifying the political reasons for this decision, especially since its long-term social impact included Bill 65 on the organization of health and social services, which gave rise to the CLSC offering both kinds of services—something else that was not foreseen by either report.

The most common reason given for the merger was that a single ministry was more functional and therefore more efficient in administrative terms; this was consistent with the concentration and maximum integration of powers and resources. In addition, it should be noted that the previous government had in practice already begun to set the merger in process: a single minister had already been responsible for the two ministries for several years and their official integration was already under study. Lastly, the total disorganization reigning in both administrations— according to the CIHSW—provided an opportunity for completely and systematically redefining a new comprehensive organization, a task that was part of the CIHSW's original mandate. But all these reasons reflect the perspectives of the individuals and organizations involved, and thus seem only partially satisfying.

Indeed, I think the minister in charge himself acknowledged that administrative efficiency was not the sole reason for integrating health and social services when he said that the merger of the two ministries had to "facilitate indispensable changes in orientation"[3] and that "the decision resulted more from the need to provide services required by the population than from any drive for administrative efficiency."[4] The minister was actually articulating a specific political project, of which the merger of the two ministries was the first result and the CLSC model the symbol.

In my opinion, the integration of the fields of health and social services corresponds to the new global functions of the neo-liberal state. The description in Chapter Two of federal initiatives in these fields clearly illustrates the need for the state to play a growing role in the social management of the increasingly numerous and diversified categories of people excluded — temporarily or permanently — from production as a direct result of the industrial and financial concentration that characterizes the current stage of capitalist development. At the same time, however, the state is called upon to sustain the accumulation of capital and simultaneously reduce the cost of its social intervention. Since the state does not have unlimited financial resources, its dual role of supporting capital accumulation and dealing with the consequences of that accumulation is inevitably contradictory and ultimately leads to a full-blown fiscal crisis of the state.[5]

An analysis of the federal studies and reports indicates two separate phases and orientations in the strategies developed by the health and welfare experts for dealing with this contradiction. During the first phase, until about 1973, the state's only means of reconciling its conflicting obligations was to organize services in a more productive and rational way, to find less expensive and more productive organizational models, a strategy that proved ineffective. Consequently, although it was not abandoned during the second phase, after 1973 the state opted increasingly for a strategy of influencing the consumers of services directly, inviting them to reduce their use of services, stressing instead preventive measures and individual responsibility for maintaining satisfactory health.

Social and health services in Québec were integrated against the background of the first period. By directly funding services, the state in effect instigated the transition from a liberal economy in the field of health, governed

199

basically by market forces, to a planned and integrated economy under state authority. As we have seen, the reason for this was the state's need, as manager of social relations, to broaden access to services, making them available to social groups that had previously gone without because they were unable to pay for them. Since then, the state has sought to ensure its efficiency of intervention, both in terms of real access to and use of services by the formerly excluded groups, and in terms of containing rising costs and improving productivity and organization. The roles of the two kinds of services were to be directly complementary, leading to their administrative integration. Simply put, social services would socialize medicine, and health services would "medicalize" social relations. The state's economic role in encouraging capital accumulation implied corresponding political and ideological roles in the management of social relations, and a fundamental mechanism of the integration of health and social services. The reasons for this integration were not really organizational or administrative; they are to be found in the imperatives of the management of social relations.

Economic rationality was the overriding factor in the general process leading up to the decision to merge. As we saw in the analysis of the CIHSW's reports, the problem of how to deal with the poor, the "disadvantaged," was the predominant concern, a concern that stemmed from the realization that the economic and social costs of poverty were a dead loss for the state and consequently an economic aberration. The state has three main ways of "resolving" the economic and social marginality of these groups, for getting them back into the labour market: education, health care and social services. After the education reform of the early years of the Quiet Revolution, the state undertook health and social service reform. Health care was portrayed as dominated by doctors and hospital structures, and social services by social workers and institutional care, while this domination was in turn defined as economically irrational, since most professional tasks performed by doctors and social workers could be done just as well by lower-ranked personnel (nurses or social work technicians) and institutional care was often useless, or at least

200

unnecessarily prolonged. Patients and clients were instead to be sent home as soon as possible with back-up care through auxiliary services such as home care, assistance with family and housework, psychological services, and so on. The move to deprofessionalize and de-institutionalize services was rooted in the search for a system of services that would be more productive in economic terms, supplemented by an attempt to focus services on target populations presenting a higher risk of social or health problems; by channelling services to these populations, a satisfactory level of general performance could be achieved—both economically and socially—in the system of care and services.

Besides reorganizing the health and welfare system, the state reoriented it towards the management of social groups whose very existence threatened its rationality and therefore its economic and social domination. Elitist and specialized medicine was no longer appropriate. Medicine had to become social and comprehensive. Care was to be geographically and socially accessible, economically and socially simple, continuous, preventive, and comprehensive. The common thread in all of this was the move to connect the economic and social roles as a necessary condition for resolving the fundamental contradiction underlying intervention by the monopoly capitalist state. Health and social welfare minister Claude Castonguay told doctors that it was necessary "to go from a traditionally closed system to an open system... social openness will be seen in the system's sensitivity and adjustment to social influences and surrounding conditions... in a better balance between the purely scientific concerns and the social concerns of medicine."[6]

This political move to interrelate health and social services indicated a social policy to orient health care not only towards solving the problems of working people and in particular the socially marginal, but towards the management of social problems as well, helped along by modernizing the ideological terms used to control socially marginal people. Terms that had once been moral or psychological became medical as the frontier between the medical and the social became increasingly vague. The concept of "stress" is perhaps one of the clearest examples of the use of a medical approach to social conditions, but others include preventive, industrial and environmental medicine, community health, etc.

The CLSCs were a focus for the political dimensions of this dual role of health and social services. They were designed by economic strategists to reorient the organization of health services to fulfill its social role. The history of these centres bears this out: they can be traced back to two different models in the CIHSW reports on health and social services. The report on health called for local health centres that would provide comprehensive care throughout a given geographic territory as part of the state's plan to guarantee equal access to health care resources. The model was seen by its planners as both a complement to the existing network and a tool for reforming the network as a whole by promoting and serving as an example of the new approach to health care organization. It was thus a model proposed by specialists in the technocratic management of health care who emphasized the technology of health care and the model's openness to the other components of the system. But the CLSCs were also heir to the tradition of the community social centres, which had been reactivated in the poor neighbourhoods of large American cities during the 1960s as part of the war on poverty. Far from being models of an abstract theory dreamed up by experts, these community centres were the fruit of a compromise between the ruling classes and the ruled in the management of social relations. In this sense, they were the organizational reflection of a pragmatic political concession, which is why these centres relied heavily on public participation and during their early years took an open attitude towards their surroundings, fostering user control of their economic and social development rather than turning towards an integrated institutional system of services.

In deciding to combine these two models in one centre, the minister gave a clear indication of the ultimate significance of the merger of health and social services. The consequences of this merger will be examined in detail in Chapter Five, when we take a closer look at the CLSCs.

Finally, the integration of services must be seen as part of the new ruling class's strategy for taking the offensive, imposing a realignment of powers.

202

The professional groups had foreseen this, and in the CIHSW reports tried to preserve their full autonomy *vis-à-vis* each other and the state, which threatened to include them in its projected reorganization of services, endangering their prerogatives by undermining their institutional foundations. The volume on social services illustrates this unequivocally: months after the government had introduced legislation to integrate the two fields and bring them under state authority, the report reiterated the specificity of social services in relation to medicine and called for their relative autonomy from the state.

This analysis is borne out by the debates on regionalization and the reorganization of the professions.

The issues at stake in regionalization, decentralization and public participation

The issue of regionalization was undoubtedly one of the most controversial aspects of the reform. It challenged the power and interests of various established groups in the fields of health and social services, upsetting the relative equilibrium by introducing a new factor. This issue takes us to the very heart of the reform, for the debates and struggles over regionalization, decentralization and public participation brought to the surface the underlying power relations in health and social services. These conflicts also revealed the profoundly political nature of this reform, which was in fact a class intervention aimed at changing class relations at the institutional level. They highlighted the real issues at stake, namely the conflicting goals of the different classes involved.

Regionalization and decentralization were specifically concerned with the division of powers between the central ministry, the regions and the various institutions providing services. They were therefore directly related to the concept of the functional, hierarchical organization of the new system and the underlying chain of authority. Participation, however, was an issue at all levels of reorganization since it defined the relations that the technocratic class hoped to have with the local administrative, political and professional factions. Above

203

all, it introduced the "public" into the system as a new variable, defined as a new and active source of power. The theme of public partipation thus runs through all discussion of decentralization, regionalization, the professions and the CLSCs.

As was pointed out in Chapter One, regional coordination of social services and health care institutions was begun in the 1960s when people first started looking at a genuine integration of resources, as a result of the growing influence of the state's new monopoly capitalist orientation in health and social services. The new petite bourgeoisie of managers and professionals fell back on the regions, defined as an administrative level of coordination and integration of resources, both as a way of adjusting to the new rationality in services and as a means of retaining control of the new organizational model that was gradually being imposed on the institutions and eventually the professions. The trend began in the early 1960s in the mental hospitals and was later extended to the general hospitals. It was also present in the social service agencies and the regional welfare councils, already structured on a diocesan basis. As for the professions, the new union of general practitioners (the Fédération des médecins omnipraticiens — FMOQ), as well as the professional corporations of social workers and psychologists and the association of social counsellors, were all organized on a regional basis. The regionalization of the interest groups in health and social services started with existing local resources which then coordinated them regionally in an intermediate level of authority in response to the vague but real threats of state intervention. Regionalization was also based on existing divisions between the institutions and the professions, divisions that were to be aggravated by the reform. There were, of course, experiments like the Eastern Townships Planning Committee (referred to earlier) which innovated horizontal integration of the resources of various institutions; but all in all, the sectorial corporatist kinds of groups remained predominant in the structures in health and social services throughout the 1960s.

The Castonguay-Nepveu Commission reports also saw the regions as key building blocks in organizing the new health and social services system. The Commission considered that it

204

was at this level that resources could best be integrated and coordinated, based on a recognition of established relations at this level. The experience of the Eastern Townships Planning Committee, whose founder helped write the report on health, is a good example of the techno-professional conception of regionalization. A similar view was being pushed at the same time by the federal government's experts, who said:

"The concept of area-wide or regional planning for health facilities and services has been accepted as a viable, effective approach, and is required if integrated and balanced health care systems are to be achieved ...Only at the regional level can sufficient perspective be gained to effectively organize and integrate the various health resources...

This requires that regional planning organizations become health planning groups as rapidly as possible, rather than remaining simply hospital planning groups...

The organization of regional health planning boards should be encouraged. Boards should be composed of representatives of hospitals, other health and welfare agencies, medical profession and other appropriate groups."[7]

The technocratic view of regionalization could thus be reconciled with the regionally organized interest groups. This was the view of one Canadian expert in particular, Thomas Boudreau, whose paper on the regionalization of health services was part of the summary of the experts' research for the federal task force on the cost of health care[8]. Thus the region became a strategic negotiating point between the new technocratic models for organizing services and the management of the institutions and the professions.

Just when a new regional organization of health and social services seemed to be under way, the representatives of the new technocracy took power and made significant changes to the regional power structure being established. They imposed greater centralization and ministerial authority as they tried to break up the institution-based interest groups by introducing a programme oriented system based on a functionally integrated hierarchy of institutions. At the same time, new institutions were created and public participation was introduced in advisory or decision-making roles at all levels of the new system. As we will see, all these elements contradicted the strategy of regionalization and the recommendations contained in the CIHSW's reports on health and social services. The report on health recommended regional health offices with genuine regional authority over planning, integration and programmes and full authority for the administration of regional budgets set by the ministry, which could amount to as much as 35% or 40% of the total budget for social affairs. The report on social services called for regional social services offices with similar powers, supervised by a regional social services council with advisory powers.[9] The role of the regional council was to see that the interests of the public predominated, to ensure that the voice of the "disadvantaged" was heard, and to act as a check on any trend towards bureaucratic introversion—in short, to act as the outside "conscience" of the administration.[10]

In contrast to the report on health, which called for only marginal public participation, the new ruling élite introduced intensive public participation in the operations of the social services and health care systems. Participation was to have three main roles. First, the inclusion of formal public participation lent legitimacy to the reforms initiated by the ruling class, adding substance to its social democratic rhetoric and its claim to being the defender of the "public good." Second, introducing the public as a new "partner" in social services and health care paved the way for changes in the dynamics of the existing power relations. It was part of "opening up" services as called for by the minister, but above all it symbolized the end of the reign of the professionals and the institutions, with their promotion and defence of their own special interests rather than the collective good or universal interests. It also signalled the ministry's determination to overcome corporatist resistance to changes in power relations in health and social services. It was thus the symbol of the "deprivatization" of health and social service institutions and professions, which became accountable to society for services rendered. Third, as we will see with the CLSCs, public participation was introduced with the "disadvantaged" particularly in mind, and corresponded to the technocratic goal of institutional control of all the variables involved in the production of services. It was thus entirely consistent with the monopoly capitalist state's new role in exercising greater social control.

These last remarks call for two further comments. Keeping in mind that the powers of the petite bourgeoisie and the institutions were structured regionally, and that in contrast public participation was primarily an initiative of the state to modify existing power relations, it is easy to understand that organized public participation was by and large not part of the experiments in regionalizing services. Nor was there much mention of it in the CIHSW's reports, except in the specific context of "disadvantaged" groups. Second, it should be clearly pointed out that although public participation is discussed here solely as a strategy of the ruling class or as a result of the functions of the neo-liberal state, it was also in large part a response to various demands for greater participation raised by working-class people in Québec during the 1960's. This aspect of participation will be discussed when we look at the CLSCs.

There were three stages to the debate on regionalizing health and social services between the time when the Liberal Party took charge of social affairs in 1970 and the adoption of Bill 65 by the Québec National Assembly in December 1971. To start with, during the year before Bill 65 was introduced for first reading, the Parliamentary Committee on Social Affairs held a number of hearings to scrutinize and debate the cabinet's proposals. The proposed bill, which called for the creation of Regional Social Affairs Offices to help implement regionalization, gave rise to a great many briefs submitted by various concerned special interest groups. Regionalization emerged as a major political issue and the parties involved took stands on it. Then in December 1971, the government introduced a second draft of Bill 65 with substantial modifications in the strategy for regionalization, replacing the Regional Social Affairs Offices with Regional Health and Social Service Councils (CRSSSs). It was this second version that was ultimately adopted at the end of 1971.

Less than three months after joining the cabinet, Claude Castonguay gave a very straightforward reply when asked about applying the recommendations of the CIHSW report on regional offices and decentralization: "I do not consider myself bound by this report... Government responsibilities may mean we have to make decisions that are somewhat different."[11] He then added: "We want to regionalize and even decentralize so that decisions can be made at the local level... so that the ministry's work is really suited to the needs of the population."[12] He was quite clear about the strategy he intended to follow, talking about decentralization rather than regionalization. He replaced the dynamic of established regional authorities with administrative rationality. Decentralization ignored the regional level, referring directly to the institutions at the local level, and pitting regional interests against the public and its needs.

Even more significantly, the minister in charge upheld the necessity of strong centralization in the debates on the orientation of the ministry:

"There is a need for planning, not on the basis of local institutions and their lobbying, but on a more general level... to provide a basis for evaluating the needs and resources of a region... this planning role will have to be taken away from the hospitals and done at top levels... The ministry must provide services for the entire population."[13]

Local institutions were thus to lose their authority to plan services on a territorial basis. The reasons invoked were always the same: centralization would guarantee objectivity and a better distribution of resources. There was a persistent underlying assumption that for institutions, as for the professions, their own interests, their internal dynamics and the interests of their component groups outweighed the real needs of the population when the time came for decisions about the direction of future development. The ministry's technical expertise would ensure that services were allocated on a more rational basis. The concentration of power was justified by invoking the "common good":

"Needs can only be seen by taking a more general look at them. What are perceived at the individual or grassroots level are particular needs. That is why we have to pull back a bit and take a larger view."[14]

The "overall picture" possible from a "central position" was opposed to special, individual views at the local level. The new ruling class identified with state power as a central and centralizing power; institutions and professions were threatened and undermined inasmuch as local autonomy became dysfunctional for the new central authorities. Local levels of authority were consigned to peripheral roles, obliged to abandon their initiatives, autonomy and prerogatives. The rhetoric of the new ruling class was built around a simple system of contrasting notions describing the concentration of powers and seeking to legitimate it by presenting it as a defence of the public and consumer interests against producers, of the masses against the élite: thus the global was opposed to the particular, central to local, public to private, general to specialized, new to old, open to closed, objective to subjective, the observable to the experienced. By polarizing the issues into a rhetorical series of opposed pairs, with an implicit hierarchy, they hoped to camouflage the class nature of the new ruling technocracy's efforts to incorporate health care producers into the new organization of health and social services.

Given this situation, the promotion of the *regional* level became a fundamental issue as the local élites drawn into the new rationality fought to preserve their autonomy. The region became their ideological, political and administrative power base as they sought to preserve their relative autonomy at this level by developing strong regional institutions to protect their position. Although subscribing to the idea of rationalizing resources and improving productivity, they demanded respect for the established authorities in health and social services (the institutions and professions). In their opinion, only the experienced representatives of the existing authorities could modernize institutions and integrate resources and facilities in the context of a new logic of regionalization. The process should proceed from the bottom up, acknowledging the power of the administrators, who, organized at the regional level, would deal with central authorities as equals.

This was the approach advocated in the two volumes of the CIHSW on health and social services. These volumes recommended that local institutions lose their unofficial lobbying power with the ministry and certain administrative powers, such as the authority to borrow or expropriate. But in return, the Regional Health Offices and Regional Social Services Offices with their corresponding positions and jurisdictions would give them new institutional channels for lobbying that they had previously lacked.[15] In the Regional Health Offices, local institutions would hold nine out of twenty

209

positions, while the ministry would hold three, the universities two and the public six; in the Regional Social Services Offices, they would have six out of fifteen, the ministry two and the public seven. In the all-important field of health, the administrative and professional groups would have a good chance of controlling the regional offices, especially given the combined strength of the institutions and the universities. In social services, the institutions would obviously seek an alliance with the public (six plus seven out of fifteen positions), especially since the report on social services also recommended the creation of regional councils to supervise the offices and offset their inevitable tendency towards bureaucratization. In both cases, the ministry would be very much in the minority.

Both CIHSW volumes recommended the creation of a strong regional level, adequately equipped for exercising its authority over institutions in the region but also for dealing with the ministry as a valid intermediary.

Castonguay, however, rejected the strategy of regional powers and put an abrupt halt to the initiatives of this petite bourgeoisie, whose model remained the Eastern Townships Planning Committee. He commented on that committee in these terms:

"The Eastern Townships Planning Committee has drawn up a plan [to reorganize services] that does not seem to meet with the acceptance of the population. People are not at all interested in it, as the plan is too limited in the range of services offered."[16]

Since there were already planning committees in some other regions, the minister intended to incorporate them into the new structures. This centralizing approach was confirmed by his decision to impose a general legislative framework on the regional planning committees rather than authorizing their independent legal existence. He concluded, "In any case, I do not feel bound by these committees."[17]

In the debate on Bill 65 one year later, he definitively rejected the regional committees, reproaching them chiefly with their failure to solicit public participation[18]—in other words, with once again identifying more with the interests of the administrators and professionals than with the reorganizational model proposed by the centralizing technocrats. The Regional Health and Social Service Councils (CRSSSs) created by Bill 65 were set up in early 1973 as structures independent of and parallel to the existing planning committees. The personnel attached to the planning committees were not transferred to the new councils and the government grants that kept the committees going were cut off.

But let's go back to the second stage, the period of debate on the first draft of the act to organize health and social services (Bill 65), introduced in July 1971. The first draft provided for Regional Social Affairs Offices (RSAOs) that, as a result of the merger of the two ministries, would combine work in health and social services. The proposed structure, however, only partially implemented the recommendations of the Castonguay-Nepveu Commission.

The Offices were tied much more closely to the central authorities than to local authorities, since the ministry reserved the right to appoint all the administrators; there was no provision for the public to elect any of them. Although the draft bill seemed to respect the fundamental premise of the Commission's report to the effect that the reorganization of health and social services required the creation of strong regional structures, the Offices proposed came directly from central political circles that retained effective control of the powers assigned to the regions by using their right to appoint administrators. The RSAOs were less representative of existing regional and local interests than an example of the devolution of central power to the regional level; and for this reason they were in contradiction with the CIHSW recommendations. In addition, the bill made no reference at all to the regional councils proposed as a supervisory structure in the report on social services. The net effect was to further weaken regional influence.

The RSAOs were given powers to supervise, regulate and investigate institutions. They were not, however, given responsibility for the financial management of the regions as a whole nor authority to approve the decisions of local institutions and allocate monetary resources. They could make recommendations to the ministry and maintain systematic communication with it, but that was all. The lack of financial authority was decisive for the RSAOs, for it allowed the institutions and their associations to continue their old lobbying

211

with the ministry, despite the formal recommendations to the contrary by the CIHSW.

"What the Offices lose in control over material resources, the establishments gain in official lobbying with the ministry."[19]

Not only did the ministry ensure its control of the Regional Offices, it also retained and in fact strengthened its right to intervene directly with local institutions. On both these essential points, the Commission's recommendations— and thus the aspirations of the institutions and professions that lay behind the recommendations—were clearly overridden. It was thus not surprising that their representatives protested strongly at the hearings of the more than one hundred briefs submitted to the parliamentary committee by various interest groups. The vast majority of the briefs called for more decentralization of powers, challenged the principle of having RSAO administrators appointed by the ministry, and expressed concern about the possibility of direct ministerial intervention in local institutions.

When the minister presented his bill at the parliamentary hearings, he emphasized that in his opinion it stressed "the decentralization of services, citizen participation in their administration and clarification of the responsibilities of the government, the ministry of social affairs and the institutions."[20] He added, however, that "we are very conscious of the fact that the Commission recommended more decentralization than is proposed in this bill."[21] Why the change? Four kinds of reasons were given by the minister during the parliamentary hearings:

— genuine decentralization must be accompanied by local taxation powers and the election of those responsible for administering public funds in social affairs; but there was no tradition of separate taxation for this sector as there has been for schools and "there is currently no question of establishing such powers";

— there was a lack of competent personnel at the regional level to carry out all the work in planning and management;

— the performance of the hospitals was at the time too

212

poor to leave control of their spending solely in the hands of the regions;

— the need to control rising costs required central integrated planning of resources.[22]

The minister clearly articulated the imperative need for the technocrats in power to control taxation and spending. At the same time, he once again questioned the competence of regional administrators and professionals. His arguments confirmed the centralizing strategy of the new ruling class which, unable to impose a decentralization that corresponded to its class interests which would, at least theoretically, ensure a reduction in costs, opted instead for much stronger centralization of planning and management.

The local institutions and professional groups condemned the minister's strategy. They demanded more autonomy, denounced the severe limitations to be imposed on them, demanded the right to choose the members of the RSAO boards of directors and rejected the idea of giving the RSAOs authority to investigate institutional and professional activity. What they wanted above all was to block the chain of authority that flowed in one direction only from the ministry to the Office (administrative bodies) to the institutional or professional practices.[23] To do so, they basically asked for RSAOs that would be more closely linked to regional authorities, be they in the institutions or the professions, so as to be able to exert direct influence on the ministry, through the RSAOs, protecting themselves against the threat of ministerial control.

The main opposition party at the time, the Parti Québécois, assumed the stance of unconditional defender of regional powers and consequently of strong regional offices. It condemned the centralizing nature of Bill 65, the radical departures from the spirit of the CIHSW recommendations, and the "non-approval of one of the Commission's essential recommendations."[24]

"We are disappointed to see that Bill 65 is a clear setback in terms of the firm and explicit recommendations made by the CIHSW... We consider decentralization and regional planning to be absolutely essential and this requires strong and representative regional offices... The bill should make it possible to expand the role and powers of the regional offices in the future."[25]

213

The PQ approved submissions on this made by the representatives of the hospitals (AAHPQ), doctors (FMOQ), social workers (FSSF), the Eastern Townships Planning Committee, and others. The PQ also recommended that the public be closely involved in the operations of the RSAOs, as the major labour bodies (QFL, CNTU, CEQ) had demanded.

Castonguay, the minister in charge, then presented two fundamental alternatives. One possibility was a genuine decentralization, giving more powers to the RSAOs in planning, programmes and allocation of financial resources. The other possibility was to confine the RSAOs to helping identify needs, developing research and advisory services and promoting participation.

"These are the two choices, and I think the whole balance of the bill depends on which choice is made."[26]

"If there is regional decentralization, it is not necessary to have as much decentralization at the local level; if the second possibility is chosen, it will then be necessary to clarify the roles of the ministry and the many different institutions with more autonomy... This is... one of the most delicate, most difficult questions in this bill."[27]

Thus, above and beyond the administrative arguments the minister used so well, the question of decentralization was eminently political. By presenting decentralization to the *regions* or to *institutions* as mutually exclusive choices, the minister was in fact betraying where his final choice would lie. He would opt for extremely limited powers at the regional level and present growing administrative control over the institutions combined with semi-elected forms of public participation as a process of genuine decentralization:

"Decentralization can be seen not only as the delegation of powers by the ministry to regional offices, but also as more flexible powers for the institutions themselves to take action."[28]

He referred to the example of the global budget, a technique that, as we saw earlier, gives the ministry greater control over the management of individual institutions.

There were two conflicting models of how powers should be organized. The first called for a weak regional level and, in theory, a strong local level, although the latter was in theory only, since the central authorities would do their best to exercise direct control over local institutions by using the global budget technique, by training administrators in modern

214

management techniques and by ministerial supervision of local management. There was room in this kind of decentralization for strong public participation in the administration of institutions. The second model advocated a strong regional structure with power to negotiate with the ministry, institutions controlled by the professionals and administrators, and only limited participation by the public.

The third stage of the debate dealt with the final version of the bill, in which the RSAOs were replaced by Regional Health and Social Service Councils (CRSSSs). The ministry had modified its entire strategy on both the regional offices and local institutions. Rather than turning over rather broad powers to them, compensated by strictly controlling who got the administrative jobs—a tactic that had provoked almost unanimous complaints from the various groups concerned—the ministry decided to give the interest groups and the public substantially stronger representation on the boards of directors of the CRSSSs; in return, however, it whittled down even more the already limited powers of the councils.

In the final draft of the legislation, the role of the CRSSSs was much more marginal than that of the RSAOs had been in the previous version. Their role was basically one of support for the operation of the institutions with a view to making them more open and responsive to the surrounding environment. Since they had no real authority over institutions, their role was more that of facilitating operations than directing them. They were supposed to encourage public participation, hear complaints, facilitate the integration of resources and creation of new services, and identify needs. "The CRSSSs have no more power over the public than the public has over them."[29] They lost the power to investigate institutional and professional activity, while administrators and professionals were given administrative positions in the CRSSSs. This dual concession to the institutions and professions remained largely insignificant, however, for the CRSSSs were no longer clearly part of the chain of authority. As for the institutions, they lost several prerogatives: the ministry appropriated some of their internal management rights and the legislation consecrated the primacy of ministerial authority over them.

Basically, the idea of decentralization was dead. The lengthy debate had given the various interest groups a chance to speak out publicly, which allowed the minister to evaluate the institutional strength of the institutions and professions sufficiently to convince him that no major powers should be conceded. In the end, the Regional Councils bore a strange resemblance to the advisory councils proposed in the Castonguay-Nepveu report on social services. Their supervisory role toward the regional offices helped mask the unprecedented concentration of powers in the hands of the ministry. The systematic inclusion of representatives of the public and interest groups on the boards of directors of the various institutions served to distract attention from the introduction of a very authoritarian system of management.

Thomas Boudreau, who had been involved in the work of the CIHSW over a long period of time, opposed the new minister's choices and methods of operation. In an article for the journal of the federation of general practitioners (FMOQ) entitled "The Conditions for Successful Social Development" he launched a thinly veiled attack on the offensive under way by the new ruling class:

"It is difficult to find striking examples o f 'practitioners' of change who have gone against the tide of long-term trends... At certain points in history when conditions are extremely favourable... an individual endowed with great talents of perception and expression can achieve the status of superman or prophet... This is undoubtedly how many of our 'practitioners' of change would like to be seen... But ignorance of the heritage of the past... and an overly narrow identification with classes or very limited sects that prevent one from grasping the common values of the community are handicaps to a fruitful career as an agent of social change... By its very nature, social change is a process that is not subject to authority... Our cultural heritage, still very strong, of a society oriented towards the notion of authority... encourages us to identify with established authorities; or, if we believe we have 'become Authority,' to widen as much as possible the gap that marks the 'essential' difference between those who govern and those who are governed."[30]

The techno-professional petite bourgeoisie might voice its disapproval of the manoeuvres of the centralizing techno-cratic class, but that was about all it could do. The technocratic class did not acknowledge the importance of history; without "roots" it was not "national," much less "nationalist"; instead, it was "internationalist," actively involved in the monopolization of capital.

The CRSSSs were created in Québec's twelve administrative regions in 1972 and early 1973. They paralleled the existing Health Planning Councils, the Regional Welfare Councils and the Social Development Councils, all of which they ignored and with which they in fact directly competed, leading to the rapid elimination of the older bodies. Only a tiny handful of management personnel from the former committees and councils found meaningful administrative jobs with the CRSSSs. In contrast, many of them already held office at the regional level in the Desjardins cooperative movement (credit unions) that has traditionally been a regional bastion of power for the petite bourgeoisie in Québec. In their creation and operation, the CRSSSs remained marginal institutions in the new "social affairs network." Although the minister had promised to pay them very careful attention, they were still at a loss as to what their role should be. One possibility was to play a greater role in the ministry's chain of authority, in terms of management and the creation of new programmes and services. Another was to act as a pressure group,[31] the path chosen by some CRSSSs that sought to develop regional power through the analysis and expression of regional needs and an effort to endow institutions with an ideology of regional "consciousness" and "sense of belonging." The choice of orientation was made for them with the "decentralization" policies developed by the ministry under the Liberal government in the summer of 1976 and implemented by the PQ when it took power in November 1976. This policy of decentralization, which we will discuss later in analyzing the evolution of the CLSCs, installed the CRSSSs in the ministry's chain of authority once and for all.

Although the large institutions in the network had previously been able to bypass the CRSSSs and deal directly with the ministry, this had not been the case for the smaller establishments, which tended to see the CRSSSs as a protective intermediary between them and the ministry. This was especially true in the regions where the CRSSSs acted as a pressure group to defend small local institutions, the CLSCs in particular. And it was this group of institutions that was the

217

primary target of the decentralization policy in 1976.

The issues at stake in reforming the professions

In the fall of 1971, the Liberal government introduced Bill 250. *The Professional Code*, as it was called, was directly inspired by the main recommendations of the CIHSW report *The Professions and Society*, in particular the suggestion that the reorganization of the professions in health and the social services be extended to cover all professions. Like Bill 65, the legislation was discussed by a parliamentary committee for more than a year, hearing more than 150 briefs. The act was finally adopted in July 1973 and implemented in February 1974. It decisively sanctioned state intervention in governing and controlling professional activities, thus putting an end to the very substantial autonomy previously enjoyed by the professional orders.

The primary purpose of the new legislation was of course to subordinate the producers of services to the new logic of the social services system. But since the changes in the status of professionals went beyond the field of health and social services to apply to all professions, we can conclude that the new ruling class used the reform in health and welfare as an opportunity to tackle professionals in general, as representatives of a specific class, namely a petite bourgeoise "in transition" from a traditional status of autonomy to a status in which they would be integrated into the big new organizational entities being established.

The professional petite bourgeoisie was pushed into the technocratic organization using three specific techniques that reflect a ruling class ideology for managing professional groups. Only a brief summary of the three is needed because the arguments are found in the Commission's report on the professions, analyzed in Chapter Three.

The first step was a severe critique of professional social and political conduct, severe enough to necessitate and justify the intervention of a superior authority — namely the state — in professional matters. For example, the generally poor state of health of the population was blithely associated with the

218

alleged disorganization of the health care delivery system, implicitly blamed on the lack of social conscience among those who produced and administered services.

The second technique was an appeal to the "public" as a third party in the conflict between the professional petite bourgeoisie and the technocrats. The technocrats painted the public as victims of the professionals' abusive control and proposed an alliance to free it. The strategy used by the new ruling class to realign powers was the same used to organize services: it argued that the reforms would defend and protect the "public," which became a pretext to impose and justify the submission now required from professionals. Thus the sole role of each professional association was henceforth to be "the protection of the public,"[32] while the job of defending the interests of its members now fell to the unions.

To make sure the professional associations properly fulfilled their mission of protecting the public, the state gave the public a role:

"Charged with giving expression to the needs of their fellow citizens and acting as their spokesperson in the professional world, the public representatives in the decision-making spheres of the professional corporations are some of the main agents in adapting professionalism to better serve the needs of the users. Through their constant vigilance and vigorous and constructive criticism, they can help make professionals more aware of the need to listen to the public. The public must not leave it up to the professionals alone to proect the interests of the public. It is the role of the public representatives on the professional corporations' boards of directors to make sure that the work of the corporations meets the real needs of the clients... Oriented towards carrying out sophisticated technical acts... professionals have too often tried to define their clients' needs in terms of their own techniques and knowledge instead of adapting that knowledge and technique to serve the expressed needs of the clients... It must be admitted that professionals have all too often kept the public in ignorance and reinforced the myth of the specialist's exclusive competence."[33]

Public involvement was more or less a way of putting into practice a model of open, non-specialized professional practice that we have already seen evoked in the organization of health care delivery and the critique of local and regional powers.

Ruling class rhetoric about the "public" was mainly

aimed at legitimizing state intrusion in professional affairs in the name of the higher interests of democracy. When the Office des Professions (the board set up to oversee all the professions) said that public participation would "open the corporations to public scrutiny,"[34] it was confirming, in euphemistic terms, the state's new prerogatives concerning the professional associations.

The third technique affirmed the state's new authority over professional organization, defining professional services henceforth as a public service.[35] The state, of course, did not do away with the associations, but it revoked their autonomy, redefining them as "instruments for administering the professions"[36] with the mandate of supervising their members. The associations became an instrument for quality control.[37] The state created a supervisory agency, the Office des Professions du Québec, that governed the general functioning of all professional associations which were in turn to establish professional inspection committees which would encourage members to update their professional and scientific education, would retrain them and eventually limit the right to practise; the license to practise would be valid for a defined period of time, subject to renewal on a regular basis.

In addition, the associations were to establish disciplinary committees chaired by a government appointed lawyer, paid by the ministry. A professionals' tribunal was established, with hearings open to the public.

"The Professionals' Code manifests the legislator's firm resolve to see the professions' disciplinary system tied into the legal system."[38]

The Office also had considerable regulatory authority with regard to the two main responsibilities of the associations: professional inspection and discipline. It could replace the professional associations in tightening up their codes of ethics or determining how their professional surveillance committees would operate.[39] Concerning training, the state assumed the right to approve university professional education. Although it could not set the curriculum for academic programmes, it could evaluate the level of degrees granted and the quality of the degree-granting institutions.

As a final step, the state used its authority to separate

220

the associations into two new categories: those with reserve of title, and those with both reserve of title and exclusive right to practise. Professions were placed in one category or the other, less on the basis of the training required than on the context in which the profession was practised, which pushed for professions to be more and more frequently practised on a salaried basis, in organizations with a high degree of division of labour. Where this was the case, the institutional framework for professional practice was judged to be adequate and the profession was given reserve of title.

Exclusive right to practise, in contrast, was something the government tried to avoid granting very often. It applied to professions requiring a substantial degree of autonomy in their practice, because of the specific nature of their work or the highly specialized technology used. In fields involving a broad range of knowledge, "professional self-regulation is... frequently the only mechanism for controlling people in private practice, who have a clientele composed of individuals."[40] The government was loath to grant exclusive right to practise, for in doing so it consolidated monopolies—hardly the best way to ensure greater integration of the professions into the new organization of services. Not having exclusive right to practise was a source of tension among professions, needlessly dividing them and making it difficult to see professions as complementary to each other and creating an obstacle to delegating work (by doctors to nurses in particular) and constituting one of the fundamental reasons for the rationalization of care delivery and improved productivity.

The Office reserved the right to create, combine or dissolve professional associations. It proposed fee structures for private practice and compiled a complete information bank on about 125,000 members of the professional associations in Québec. The information fed into the data-processing system was to enable

"... the main agencies responsible for applying the legislation to keep track of the evolution of the professional world in Québec and assist them in making the decisions required to protect the public."[41]

The sombre portrait drawn by the ruling class of the state of the professions in Québec; the appeal for public

221

participation; and the state's intervention with its strategies of centralizing decisions and affirming its authority over professionals: all this reflected the technocratic class's resolve to develop a new kind of management specific to the professional petite bourgeoisie, its institutions (associations, universities) and their integration into the new modes of production of services. Government texts are quite explicit about its general goals.

Two substantial texts by René Dussault,[42] a key figure in the reform of the professions in Québec and president of the Office des professions du Québec, explicitly place the reform in the context of transition of traditional Québec society towards new social relations of production characterized by the growing political and ideological role of the state. The same texts made clear the strategy of the new ruling class in its plan to redefine the social functions of professionals.

Dussault distinguishes two major phases of professional development in Québec, "corresponding the two historical periods in the evolution of work."[43] On the one hand, there were the professional associations created more than fifty years ago: "most of their members are engaged in private practice, hold exclusive right to practise, enjoy higher incomes and are very active in the protection of the public."[44] Basically, these included lawyers, notaries, architects, engineers, doctors, dentists and pharmacists. These professional associations had been founded in

"... an economy based on free enterprise. Most professionals were engaged in private practice, working alone, autonomously and in isolation. More often than not, the members of the corporations established at that time worked in broad, general fields of knowledge. Skilled manpower was rare and the division of labour less advanced... In this situation... establishing a corporation was a means of standardizing the distribution of professional services in a given sector while still respecting the prevailing system of free enterprise."[45]

The second group of associations were founded more recently and were "usually composed of workers who are not self-employed, do not hold exclusive right to practise, have lower incomes and are relatively inactive in protecting the public."[46] These newer associations included management consultants, specialists in labour relations, agronomists, urban

222

planners, and a whole series of professions focusing on human relations or health: guidance counselllors, psychologists, social workers, nurses, dietitians, physiotherapists, occupational therapists, and a dozen more paramedical occupations requiring community college training. Dussault associated the emergence of this second wave of assocations with

"... the rapid industrialization of Québec society and the technological revolution brought about by World War Two [that] greatly changed both working conditions and the characteristics of the labour force. Three phenomena are particularly striking: the shift to salaried status for employees, the fragmentation of work processes due to the sharp expansion of fields of knowledge, and state intervention in providing essential services... In recent years... many members of the professional corporations have become salaried workers. As such, they are less isolated, less autonomous, subject to regular, hierarchical control by their employers. They also often belong to unions... Their work is often specialized, fragmented. These workers are more easily supervised, for they are increasingly called upon to perform specific tasks, using tried and proven methods and in clearly defined circumstances... [As well, the state is] directly or indirectly... the main employer of professionals or else the main client of professional services provided in private practice... [It] can pass legislation authorizing it to directly regulate a given sector of work and itself license those doing that work."[47]

The situation described corresponds directly to the transformation of social relations that we have identified as an inherent part of the transition from a competitive capitalist mode of production to a monopoly capitalist mode. The concentration of resources and powers that gives rise to the social and technical division of labour penetrates the field of production of services, where the trend towards the socialization of the costs of production requires more state intervention. Most of the associations in the second group were in fact established in the early 1960s, the period when the superstructures of Québec society were "modernized" and when the service organizations experienced spectacular expansion. Nine of them in the field of health were direct creations of the 1973 Professional Code, which marked the implementation of the new organization and division of labour produced by the first pieces of reform legislation. We will look at the political reasons for these associations later on. Thus when Dussault says that the transformation of working conditions "modifies

the role of professional corporations for salaried employees...
definitely reducing the foreseeable role of professional corporatism in new sectors of activity,"[48] he does more than state the
obvious; he is in fact announcing a new kind of manpower
policy—Dussault himself uses the term "workers" (travail-
leurs) rather than "professionals"—run by the state, in which
a redefined concept of professionalism will be an essential
instrument for the new ruling class in power.

A look at the debates that accompanied the drafting of
Bill 250 on the professions as well as the recent strategies of
the leading professional associations would seem to suggest
that despite the official stance of the Office des professions on
the need for uniform treatment of professions, there are in fact
three very different kinds of relations between the state and
the various associations. For instance, the distinction between
old and new associations, with their different characteristics,
corresponds in practice to very different kinds of treatment,
while the older associations were themselves divided into at
least two groups. In the professions directly affected by state
intervention, notably medicine (including dentists and
pharmacists) and law (lawyers, notaries and jurists), a large
proportion of the membership is being incorporated into the
state organization of services. A second group, more closely
related to private enterprise, seems to be less affected by the
drastic professional control established by the state; this is
especially true in administration and business, engineering,
planning and development.

Therefore analysis in this chapter deals only with the
new associations in the fields of human relations and health
and the older ones directly incorporated into the organization
of services. These are, it should be noted, two very different
situations, stemming from the new hierarchy of social relations,
or, to put it another way, the modernization of the forms of
domination.

For the newer associations, the state had two main goals
in its reorganization. The first was to enhance the associations
of the new rising professions practising increasingly specialized
services, tied to the new functions of the monopoly capitalist
state. These associations already had less autonomy, were
more directly controlled by the state, and were limited to a

224

more narrowly defined field of work, requiring more specialized tasks (part of the increased division of labour). As well, their situation was more contingent on immediate circumstances, since their fields of work depended directly on a specific model of social organization that was always liable to change. Because of their dependence on the organization of production and therefore on the state, these newer associations were strategic tools in the hands of the new ruling class in its struggle against the traditional petite bourgeoisie, represented by the old associations. Thus in the field of health, for instance, the growing number of new associations for paramedical technicians was to help the technocratic class achieve its fundamental goal of cutting health costs by delegating medical practice and diluting the power of the doctors. This was in fact one of the avowed goals of the Office des professions, consistent with the vision of all the Commissions of inquiry into the costs of health and social services, as we have seen:

"Provided for in the Professional Code, the delegation of acts is designed to render certain fields with exclusive right to practise more flexible and thus make professional services more accessible to the public. The Office will see... that this mechanism... is effectively applied. Thus professional acts will normally be delegated by doctors to nurses... [and by nurses] to nursing assistants."[49]

The same was to apply to dentists and pharmacists, "allowing a notable improvement in the distribution of certain professional services throughout Québec."[50] This is why the Office itself created nine paramedical associations in 1973, and why it had full authority to create, dissolve or combine associations.

The younger associations that emerged with the reorganization of services were thus used to undermine the power of the older associations, and we come to the state's second purpose in creating these new associations: they were part of its strategy for the management of the technical professionals reduced to a status of performing circumscribed tasks in the new organization of services. The Office des professions, in *The Evolution of Professionalism in Québec*, gave this description of the process by which an increasing proportion of the personnel involved became salaried workers:

"The increasing takeover of work activities by large organizations, private or public companies, has gradually led to a more salaried

225

labour force... a great many qualified people possessing specialized knowledge have become salaried employees. This process... has greatly lessened the role of the professional corporations in controlling the distribution of professional services. For, as salaried employees, working people are at the same time less isolated and less autonomous. They usually express their solidarity within unions expressly formed to defend their own interests, and they are subjected to a formal hierarchical control which is more structured and precise than that exercised by the professional corporations over their members in private practice.

Indeed, very often the employer... carries out the functions of discipline, competence assessment and continuing education in a more direct and sustained way than could be done by a professional corporation. In this context, the professional corporation mechanism only serves to complement other mechanisms aimed at defending consumer interests... the greater number of salaried workers has stabilized both the production and distribution of these services as, in earlier times, did the professional corporation mechanism with regard to services offered in private practice."[51]

The technical division of labour and the professional associations duplicated supervision and control. To all intents and purposes, there was no longer any need for the professional associations. Scientific organization of work outweighed the importance of professional training, identity and ethics. In acknowledging this evolution of professionalism in its 1976 report, the Office shed some light on the recommendations the same authors had drafted six years earlier for the CIHSW, which established a sharp distinction between the role and responsibilities of a professional association and those of a union. A presumed conflict of interest and the need for better protection of the public were invoked to justify the real goal of integrating the old corporatist organization of professional work into the new relations of production. Control was to be taken away from members of the profession who function as peers, and given to the managers of the organization. It was the organization itself, the hierarchy of roles, rather than any professional knowledge, that would guarantee production in the new socio-professional order.

Thus the very existence of all the newer associations was directly threatened.

"What is 'reserve of title' worth if employers do not require that their employees belong to the corporation?... How can the corporations with reserve of title be economically viable if part of their

226

membership withdraws and no longer pays their annual dues ?"[52]

These questions raised by the Office were echoed by the members of the endangered associations who, worried about their professional survival, vainly tried to obtain exclusive right to practise for their professions. They wanted to overlay the new division and control of work with a new corporatism whose sole purpose would be to perpetuate the old corporatist structures, now meaningless, through legal constraints on members. This is how a psychologist, former president of his association, saw the problem in 1978:

"Professionalism as it currently exists should normally gradually wither away. People cannot be asked to pay more and more for the privilege of being controlled more and more tightly... I am not convinced that people feel like organizing in a structure that exists to regulate them... Generally speaking, the corporations with reserve of title are going to pieces. The debate on the exclusive right to practise boils down to one thing: professions that do not get it will cease to exist as professions. It's sort of a matter of life and death... and even for the professions with exclusive right to practise, those that have a long history aren't facing this crisis yet... They aren't worried about it yet, but it's coming there too..."[53]

Although the associations were objectively threatened, the state seemed nonetheless intent on preserving them. But the contradiction was only superficial. It was as if the ruling class had first sought to limit the professional associations' powers as much as possible only to discover later on, around 1976, that there was another role for them to play. This new role corresponded to the state's second goal in its policy on the professional associations. By reducing professionals to the status of salaried employees after installing them in the centralized organization of services, the state provoked the breakdown of their professional bodies.[54] They were henceforth divided into two class factions, caught in new relations of domination. The supervisory faction can be described as the technocratic petite bourgeoisie, and those carrying out tasks as the technical petite bourgeoisie, or the petit-bourgeois technicians.

A theoretical comment is called for here. This petite bourgeoisie in state services can be defined as "those who ensure certain conditions for the production and reproduction of social relations through the maintenance of labour-power

227

and its ideological subjugation."[55] These include economists, public administrators, doctors and medical technicians, lawyers and legal technicians, teachers, researchers and journalists. It should be noted that "it is the chain of command that divides this petite bourgeoisie"[56] and differentiates it in class terms. On the one hand, there are the agents who plan, programme, organize, supervise—in short, control and administer—the production and reproduction of social relations at various levels in the social structure; these are the managers, or the *technocrats*, including the intellectuals, or "experts", whose functional knowledge in the apparatus transmits the production-reproduction of social relations. On the other hand, there are those who are managed, the subordinate workers, the *technicians*, who, with the increasing social and technical division of labour, find themselves simple performers of tasks, with no control over the conditions of production of their services, and with technical or professional knowledge that either goes largely unused because of the overriding importance of the division of labour or is completely integrated into the goals of the organization. This is the case with teachers, nurses, and social workers, for example. With their inclusion in the new technocratic organization of state services, they have lost the professional autonomy they once enjoyed that made them members of the traditional petite bourgeoisie. They now constitute a new petite bourgeoisie of technicians (or subordinates) whose new status of simple performers of tasks in the division of labour pits them against the "upper" reaches of the petite bourgeoisie charged with supervising them. This explains the recent trend towards unionization among these "deskilled" segments of the petite bourgeoisie, who have been joining the ranks of the unions representing other public service employees. The political influence of these unions is considerable, especially when they join together as they did in 1972, 1976, and 1979-80 in powerful "common fronts" of public employees.

The state thus finds itself in the position of an employer faced with the problem of managing his salaried labour force. This is why it turned to the professional associations for help. By resuscitating professional ideology with strongly corporatist overtones, it hoped to attentuate the exacerbation of labour

228

relations with its professional employees. In the language of the Office, this was known as "the adaptation of professional corporatism to companies and institutions"[57]:

"The Office... will do all that is in its power to help professional corporatism adapt to the salaried environments."[58]

Thus the Office intended to see that employers respected professional titles, prosecuting them if necessary when corporatist privileges were ignored. As well, it would undertake a study

"... which has the objective of determining the significance and effectiveness of the principles of professional ethics... [and] the role of the corporations with regard to professional ethics when labour conflicts occur... The Office intends to recommend, if need be, legislative amendments aimed at allowing the corporations to assume an effective role in salaried environments, taking into account the respective jurisdictions of employers and unions...

Such interventions by professional corporations in the salaried environments will be more likely to succeed if a degree of cooperation is obtained from the employers and the unions. This is the greatest challenge facing professionalism, and the greatest obstacle to its adaptation to present working conditions."[59]

One could hardly be more explicit about the new role the professional associations were to play in the harmonious management of labour relations. The Office was quick to back up its initiative with a promise, followed immediately by a threat, to the professional associations:

"If the efforts to adapt professional corporatism to the salaried environments prove successful and if real progress were seen in this direction, the Office could then re-assess, on behalf of the groups seeking professional self-regulation, whether the condition relating to private practice [i.e. the exclusive right to practise — F.L.] was still essential. However, should the opposite occur, the Office would be led to retain this requirement and even to re-examine the principle of self-regulation for some existing corporations, for those with reserve of title as well as for those with exclusive right to practise."[60]

In other words, if the professional associations cooperated effectively with the technocratic class in dealing with the conflictive labour relations the state had introduced in the field of services, they would be granted privileges that had previously been considered exorbitant or dysfunctional in establishing new social relations. If they did not cooperate,

229

they were explicitly warned they would be eliminated.

In concluding this analysis of the strategy of the ruling class for handling the professional petite bourgeoisie, it is worth recalling that the criticisms directed at the professional associations for the poor job they had done in protecting the public cited the overly specialized and dehumanized, fragmented nature of services, and the professionals' excessive concern for the defence of their immediate interests. Now that we see how the ruling class intervened against the newer associations whose members suffered more from the social division of labour, it becomes obvious that criticism of professionals was in fact criticism of the consequence of their new position in the labour process. By couching its criticism in moral terms ("the lack of a sense of social responsibility" among professionals) and giving it credibility by parachuting an alleged victim, the "public," into the heart of the conflict, the ruling class tried to saddle the professionals with "responsibility" for the results of the structural changes it had itself introduced in the production of services.

The older associations that health and social service reform threatened to incorporate into the organization of services were vigorous and well organized in their resistance to change. This was especially true of the general practitioners, who succeeded in thwarting the new technocrats' plans for them. The doctors not only preserved their acquired rights but won some new ones, including the establishment of Professional Surveillance Committees in all institutions. They were also successful in refusing to delegate medical tasks; in retaining the system of remuneration on a fees-for-service basis; and in undermining the CLSCs by refusing to work in them and by opening private group-practice clinics on a massive scale.

At the present time, all the evidence would seem to indicate that, having failed to bring these older professional associations under control as it did with the newly created ones, the ruling class will have to develop strategies for collaborating with them.

An examination of the evolution of the CLSCs and recent developments in the organization of health and social services illustrates the issues at stake in this process of incorporating the professional associations into the health and social services system.

Footnotes

1. Renaud, Marc, *The Political Economy of the Québec State. Interventions in Health: Reform or Revolution?*, PhD thesis, Madison, University of Wisconsin, 1976, p. 190.
2. *Task Force Reports on the Cost of Health Services in Canada*, Vol. 1, Ottawa, Government of Canada, 1970, pp. 51-52.
3. Quebec National Assembly, *Journal des Débats*, Québec City, Commission permanente des Affaires sociales, July 14, 1970, B—867.
4. *Ibid.*, B—867.
5. O'Connor, James, *The Fiscal Crisis of the State*, New York, 1973.
6. Speech by Claude Castonguay to the professional unions of surgeons, gynecologists and obstetricians of Québec, Montréal, April 14, 1972 (our translation).
7. *Task Force Reports on the Cost of Health Services in Canada*, op. cit., Vol. 1, pp. 19-20.
8. *Ibid.*, Vol. 2, Appendix 1, pp. 31-41.
9. CIHSW, *Social Services*, tome II, pp. 66-67.
10. *Ibid.*, tome II, section 927, pp. 67-68.
11. *Journal des Débats*, op. cit., July 14, 1970, B—891.
12. *Ibid.*, July 14, 1970, B—874.
13. *Ibid.*, July 15, 1970, B—936-938.
14. *Ibid.*, July 15, 1970, B—952.
15. Lemieux, Vincent, *Les C.R.S.S.S.: une analyse politique*, Québec City, Université Laval, department of political science, June 1974, p. 20.
16. *Journal des Débats*, op. cit., July 15, 1970, B—940.
17. *Ibid.*, July 15, 1970, B—954.
18. *Ibid.*, June 30, 1971, B—3006.
19. Lemieux, Vincent, op. cit., p. 24.
20. *Journal des Débats*, op. cit., Aug. 24, 1971, B—3598.
21. *Ibid.*, Aug. 24, 1971, B—4047, and Dec. 2, 1971, B—5443.
22. *Ibid.*, Aug. 24, 1971, B—4047, and Dec. 2, 1971, B— 5443.
23. See Lemieux, Vincent, op. cit., p. 28.
24. *Journal des Débats*, op. cit., Aug. 24, 1971, B—3605.
25. *Ibid.*, Dec. 2, 1971, B—5443-44.

26. *Ibid.*, Dec. 2, 1971, B—5435.
27. *Ibid.*
28. *Ibid.*, Dec. 2, 1971, B-5445.
29. Lemieux, Vincent, *op. cit.*, p. 34.
30. *Le Médecin du Québec*, Dec. 1972, pp. 23-30.
31. Lemieux, Vincent, *op. cit.*, p. 98.
32. Québec National Assembly, Act 250, *Professional Code*, art. 12, July 6, 1973.
33. Office des professions du Québec, *3e rapport d'activités*, 1975-76, Québec City, pp. 15-16.
34. Dussault, René, "La Participation des citoyens à l'administration publique," speech given Feb. 11, 1975, p. 1.
35. Dussault, René, "La Protection du public exige du professionnel compétence et intégrité," speech given Oct. 15, 1974, p. 7.
36. Dussault, René, speech given March 21, 1975, p. 2 (our translation).
37. Dussault, René, "La Protection du public... " *op. cit.*, p. 1.
38. *Ibid.*, p. 5.
39. *Ibid.*
40. Office des professions, *The Evolution of Professionalism in Québec*, Québec Government, Sept. 1976, p. 61.
41. Office des professions du Québec, *3e rapport d'activités*, *op. cit.*, p. 22.
42. *The Evolution of Professionalism in Québec*, *op. cit.*; and René Dussault, "L'évolution du professionalisme au Québec" in *Administration publique du Canada*, Vol. 20, no. 2 (Summer 1977), pp. 275-290.
43. Dussault, René, "L'évolution du professionalisme au Québec," *op. cit.*, p. 281.
44. *Ibid.*
45. *Ibid.*, p. 282.
46. *Ibid.*, p. 281.
47. *Ibid.*, pp. 282-283.
48. *Ibid.*, p. 283.
49. Office des professions, *3e rapport d'activités*, *op. cit.*
50. Office des professions, *2e rapport d'activités*, 1974-75, Québec City, p. 15.
51. *The Evolution of Professionalism...*, *op. cit.*, p. 52.
52. Office des professions, *2e rapport d'activités*, *op. cit.*, pp. 14-15.
53. Gendreau, Pierre, former president of the Professional Corporation of Psychologists of Québec, in an interview in *Les Cahiers du psychologue québécois*, 3 (June 1978), p. 20-24.
54. Renaud, Gilbert, *L'éclatement de la profession*, M.A. thesis, Ecole de service social, Université de Montréal, 1978; published by Éditions coopératives Albert Saint-Martin, Montréal, 1978.

55. Saint-Pierre, Céline, "De l'analyse marxiste des classes sociales dans le mode de production capitaliste," *Socialisme québécois*, no. 24, 1974, pp. 9-33.

56. Piotte, Jean-Marc, "Le monstre bicéphale," *Chroniques*, no. 29-32, 1977, p. 22.

57. *The Evolution of Professionalism...*, *op. cit.*, p. 67.

58. *Ibid.*

59. *Ibid.*, p. 68.

60. *Ibid.*, pp. 69-70.

CHAPTER 5
The Reform in Practice:
The Issues Involved in the CLSCs

The Centres locaux de services communautaires (local community service centres), commonly referred to as CLSCs, was the vehicle chosen to implement the main elements of the technocratic vision of health and social services reform. Because they were part of the first phase offensive to establish new forms of social and political control, they provide an excellent opportunity for observing and analyzing the main social issues at stake.

"The CLSCs are of strategic importance today. They give us a firsthand... exemplary... look at the basic conflict between the social affairs ministry, doctors, other medical and social service professionals and the community groups."[1]

In developing the concept of the CLSC as a concentrated and integrated solution to rising costs in the now universally accessible system, the technocratic experts were circumventing a basic principle embedded in the heart of the capitalist system which holds that "good health depends almost solely on the production, distribution and consumption of goods..."[2] The idea of a model based on social, preventive, comprehensive medicine and incorporating community participation and responsibility was in contradiction with "the equation between healing and consumption of medical care...

by which health problems are transformed into specific problems of consumption in a specific economic market."[3] Government experts thus came into conflict with dominant economic interests as well as the existing organizations and professionals providing services when they intervened, in the name of the "disadvantaged," to promote a fairer distribution of resources—or to put it another way, when they tried to control the social consequences of growing economic accumulation and concentration.

The CLSCs in their early years must be analyzed not as simply another health care establishment but as part of an overall strategy within the context of existing power relations in the field of health and social services. The issues raised by their very existence went well beyond the technical questions of how they were organized, how they operated, and how their performance should be evaluated. They pointed to the social interests at stake in the established system of social services and health care. Ultimately, the social roles of the CLSCs were related to the two main roles previously identified here as characteristic of the technocratic state's intervention in health and social services: the search for the greatest possible productivity in the organization of services; and the attempt to extend and intensify the use of the organization of health and social services as an instrument for the social and political control of the population groups excluded from production. Corresponding to these two roles were two different kinds of organization—the local health centre and the community service centre.

The local health centre was the product of a theoretical model defined by experts in health economics. It reflected changes in the philosophy of health care aimed at overcoming the dominant logic of providing care only after a person had become ill, and promoting in its place a preventive, comprehensive, continuous approach that took the surrounding environment into account. Such an approach implied major changes in medical methods of practice along with changes in the patient's or "client's" expectations of the health care system.

The community service centre was identified with strategies for dealing with poverty and the need for a coordinated and integrated approach to this problem by all service organizations. As I explained earlier, this kind of centre was first and foremost a form of recognition on the part of the ruling class that there were indeed poor people and that it was necessary to deal with the problem of poverty. This was why such centres relied heavily on public participation as a strategy for the social integration and organization of the people whose disintegration and disorganization constituted a danger. The ruling class sought in fact to "reach out" to the people, to bridge the gap of antagonistic class relations by designating community social workers and community organizers to mediate these relations. The function of these intermediaries was to "locate" the poor, make them visible and identifiable and to encourage them to participate in the institutional system defined by the dominant classes.

In the final analysis, both kinds of centre responded to the same economic logic. Both were aimed at changing the way services were dispensed and received with a view to make them less expensive. Both tried to limit the various forms of social exclusion so as to reduce the social cost of controlling these groups by reinserting them into productive activity and by making institutional practices more efficient.

But the two kinds of centre also belonged to two different institutional traditions, and the attempt to combine them—in the CLSCs, for instance—seriously distorted and even undermined their evolution and development. In some cases, depending on the socio-geographic conditions in which they were established, their role in dealing with poverty took precedence over their role in changing health care practices and *vice versa*. Delivery of services and public participation rapidly appeared antithetical; planning and programmes conflicted with people's articulation of their own needs; medicine and community action soon became poles that were often diametrically opposed. At least, this was what happened in many CLSCs in Québec.

In this last chapter, I will try to analyze the evolution of the CLSCs and the issues and conflicts played out within them by relating them ultimately to these two basic roles of transforming medical practices on the one hand, and dealing with poverty and potential or real social exclusion on the other,

237

and the different management models and social dynamics in which each was rooted.

Strategies for making CLSCs a reality: "disadvantaged" urban neighbourhoods and rural areas

The early debates among government technocrats on the practical details of CLSCs and strategies for developing them were characterized by their association of these new institutions with, on the one hand, the social and health care management of disadvantaged urban environments, and on the other, the more specifically medical needs of certain isolated rural regions lacking adequate health care facilities — a reflection of their generalized social and economic under-development.

Once the new Liberal cabinet took office in 1970, discussions of the CLSCs were largely shaped by the concern with finding efficient institutional responses to the problems of poverty and regional shortcomings in health facilities. The CLSCs seemed to be the ideal solution inasmuch as they combined a specifically social approach to poverty with a decentralized and relatively inexpensive form of health care centre.

This analysis concentrates on the establishment of CLSCs in disadvantaged urban areas because in my opinion they more clearly combine the two roles of a new approach to dealing with poverty and the promotion of a new kind of health care. Furthermore, although only a minority of CLSCs were located in disadvantaged areas, these have occupied a pre-dominant place in discussions of CLSCs, which can be seen as an indication of their strategic political importance. In other words, even though some, and eventually a majority, of CLSCs were not established in poor neighbourhoods, it is nonetheless true that in their early years the role of CLSCs in dealing with poverty and social exclusion took precedence over the reor-ganization of health care delivery, both in terms of the official political rhetoric and in practice. Even in affluent neighbour-

238

hoods, the CLSCs assumed responsibility for the most under-privileged social groups. This was so true that the minister felt compelled to clarify:

"We want to establish CLSCs in the regions where the needs are greatest, and often these are the disadvantaged regions. However, we want to be careful that CLSCs are not identified with second-class centres... This corresponds to a very essential concept of a level of basic care in comparison with another level of specialized care and also of continuity... We want to avoid this at all costs. But the problem is that, given that the most disadvantaged areas in Montréal and Québec City, for instance, are also those where health services are most inaccessible, if we establish the CLSCs on the basis of priorities the conclusion that will be drawn is that they offer second-class services. And that is not at all what we want."[4]

I referred earlier to the emergence of community groups and citizens' committees in urban areas during the 1960s. Most of these groups were similar to movements that developed in the United States after World War Two, where community social workers helped to organize the poor into pressure groups capable of making their demands heard by the appropriate decision-making bodies. In our analysis of the work of the Castonguay-Nepveu Commission, we saw how often the new state technocracy used the theme of poverty and the political organization of the poor to justify its plans for reform. There is a central political ambiguity here, with the élites both encouraging and fearing the development of organized mass opposition. Consequently, they seek to intervene directly to manage and control the movement.

"In the context of the Quiet Revolution and the reorganization of the Québec government's administrative apparatus to adapt it to new realities, some technocrats saw the community groups as key stepping-stones in developing working relations between the Québec State and certain social groups left out of this 'revolution.' These technocrats sought to map out ways to include these citizens in the various stages of the decision-making and administrative process."[5]

This helps explain why the technocrats from the ministry of social affairs systematically linked the CLSCs to under-privileged areas when preparing the implementation of the reform and in the wording of the pertinent legislation.

The CLSCs were partly modelled on the Neighbourhood Community Centers developed by the Office for Economic

Opportunity in the United States in the 1960s,[6] and it was certainly true that in theory these community centres were not to be limited solely to disadvantaged areas since the programme and philosophy underlying the services offered were designed to meet the needs of the population as a whole. In addition, they incorporated principles of reform in social services similar to those to be promoted by the local health centres. In practice, however, the centres were always identified with poor and mainly urban communities (although some were established in poor rural areas) and with approaches specifically adapted to these groups, particularly for everything affecting the integration and participation of the target groups in the operation of the centres.

When he announced the creation of the CLSCs, the minister stated that the centres would be an integral part

"... of the ministry's social policy, whose main purpose is to make services better adapted to the needs of the population... [They become] a method... of achieving the major social objectives set by the ministry, namely improving the health of the population, the social conditions of individuals and groups, and the environment... [They will be] the point of entry, an individual's first contact with services... Consequently, these will be basic services..."

After giving this general definition of CLSCs, the minister explained the development role he hoped to see them play. In his speech, he clearly associated the CLSCs with the management and control of disadvantaged groups.

"The network of CLSCs will become a major instrument of development for the community... The public will be called upon to make a positive and desirable contribution in terms of the services offered... The creation of local centres requires citizen participation at various levels. They must not be seen... as passive consumers or recipients, but as resources called to play a positive and dynamic role in the establishment, functioning, development and administration of their centres. It is increasingly urgent that we try to discern the positive trends in different communities and identify them as objectives and then programmes of action."[7]

The ministry hoped to associate the "positive" initiatives of the citizens with its own, thus allowing it to describe CLSCs as "their" centres. Indeed, the ministry decided to launch its pilot project in the Hochelaga-Maisonneuve neighbourhood of Montréal, where the workers and welfare recipients who made up most of the residents had some of the most active and

240

organized community groups in the city.

But the ministry's strategy of cooperation was not supported by all community groups. Some of them had already created their own community health services and condemned the ministry's strategy in briefs to the parliamentary committee on Bill 65 (to reform health and social services). The Pointe Saint-Charles community clinic in Montréal stated:

"Bill 65 is a blow to citizen participation... an anti-participation act... the bill deprives citizens of all control over health and social services... If the citizens are not consulted, things will proceed as usual; they'll be given some nice little houses, with some food in the fridge, but the same thing will happen as happened to the Eskimos. They'll kill us. We are afraid of your bill... "[8]

The Regroupement des comités de citoyens de Québec (Québec City coalition of citizens' committees) stressed that

"... nothing in the bill mentions providing ordinary citizens with the means of organizing on their own... We detest the attitude of our governments; with this bill they want to set themselves up as judge, jury and sole standard of what is good or bad. We definitely don't want Bill 65... You give a little bit of your power back to the people, but we don't want your power. It is phoney and worn out... The main question we would like to see such a law answer is not 'What do you plan to do to solve our problems?' but rather 'What do you plan to do to help us build what we need ourselves?'"[9]

Despite the minister's denial that he intended to "co-opt the citizens' committees in the CLSCs,"[10] eleven of the first twenty-five CLSCs created were explicitly allocated to the major disadvantaged neighbourhoods in Montréal and Québec City and certain other underprivileged towns or rural areas. In most of these areas there were already active citizens' groups. The other fourteen were set up as part of the reorganization of health care to replace the hospitals and other health facilities that were lacking, especially in isolated areas. The list of planned CLSCs was in fact drawn up on the basis of studies of public health and social indicators using mortality and morbidity rates to identify the most well-off areas and the areas with the most serious shortcomings in care. "This is what justified the creation of more centres in the most disadvantaged areas of Montréal and Québec City in the beginning."[11]

A few months after the first series of CLSCs was

241

officially launched, the minister reiterated his flexible and pragmatic approach to developing the centres:

"We will let people themselves define which programmes are priorities, although we may give them some help... These people are organizing and using the centre to meet the needs they perceive in the community."[12]

If the ministry is to be believed, cooperation with citizens was successful. This is how it described the situation of the Hochelaga-Maisonneuve CLSC in the October 1972 issue of its official magazine:

"The citizens see the CLSC as theirs, as something that belongs to them... The Hochelaga-Maisonneuve CLSC is the fruit of people's work in the neighbourhood who have analyzed their problems over the last several years and come up with this solution. It is proof that the grassroots can find its own solutions, with technical and financial support from the outside."[13]

Although the ministry implied that its involvement was limited to providing support for community initiatives, it in fact drew them into a process of gradual integration into the social logic established by the technocratic powers and ratified by the legislation they had passed. The appeal to the "citizens," the valorization of their initiatives, lent legitimacy to the state's political and social control of the working classes. The same official publication was very straightforward about this in its discussion of participation, which it defined as a process for integrating working people and the disadvantaged:

"Popular participation is one of the major goals of Bill 65... The citizens of Hochelaga-Maisonneuve set up their own CLSC and created a board of directors. This board respects... the spirit of Bill 65... All that has to be done subsequently is to make some changes to conform with the modalities of Bill 65."[14]

In the parliamentary debates, the question of integrating community initiatives into the technocratic organization of services provided an opportunity to reiterate the main positions already articulated in the confrontation over regionalization.

To try and offset the relations the ministerial technocracy had established with community groups, the representative of the Parti Québécois, who defended the interests of the techno-professionals, declared his sympathy for the community groups' demands for autonomy and argued for human and professional values that he implicitly defined in opposition to the values of the organization and its structures. "If society is to avoid depersonalization, the citizen must be rendered 'responsible'."[15] He insisted on

"... the importance of the CLSC being an integral part of the life of the neighbourhood... Everything possible must be done to ensure that all citizens, and not just those who are ill or on welfare, feel at home in the CLSC and that they can administer it to serve their interests and needs... The CLSC must belong to the citizens, not the 'others' or the state... We propose that citizens constitute a majority on the board of directors."[16]

Thus the representative of the techno-professional factions advocated participatory structures and people's control in an attempt to offset the technocrats' concentration of powers that threatened their traditional power base. The minister countered with arguments in favour of integration and the subordination of existing powers to the organization he was promoting.

"When it comes time to organize services, I think our draft legislation has to apply... It has to be the basis, the framework for ensuring that the services established by citizens work out and that all interested parties have a say at the appropriate time and place... If the CLSCs fail to meet needs to such an extent that the population is ready to establish another, parallel centre, it will be an indication that the model has failed. We will have to correct it, not create another one next door... "[17]

In the end, the legislation gave the public a minority of seats on the CLSC boards of directors (albeit, proportionately more than the public had received in other institutions). Significantly, the public in this case was defined as CLSC users, and not citizens in general. In other words, "citizen," with its connotations of political relations, had been replaced with wording that evoked consumer relations. The minister presented this as a minor change, designed to avoid having to draw up lists of residents of a given territory.[18] The PQ spokesperson insisted that "the entire population of an area served by a CLSC take part in the election" and deplored that "community groups are not given sufficient opportunity;... the population is ripe for participation."[19]

The debate on regionalization was repeated, with two visions of participation and therefore of the CLSCs shaping up. Both sides agreed that powers should be concentrated at the top and accepted the goal of integrating the community

243

groups, but they differed on the degree and methods. For the ministerial technocrats, the "participation" of these groups was to be seen in terms of the logic of efficient organization and as an extension of its role in managing social relations:

"It is basically a mechanism for making the system more efficient by adapting it to suit the demand, the needs, more closely. The need for a mechanism for participation... stems from the bureaucratization of the organizations that insulates them from users and necessitates new channels of feedback. These mechanisms do not alter the distribution of power prevailing before their introduction. They can be compared to a kind of permanent opinion poll of users."[20]

The shift from the concept of citizen to that of user is indicative of the technocratic nature of the ruling class that presided over the definition of the CLSCs. This class is dominant precisely because it couches its political management of the dominated classes entirely in a "neutral" language of organization. All choices are presumably governed by the search for organizational rationality. The duplication of services in a given sector is irrational, and therefore not to be tolerated. Furthermore, the pursuit of efficiency calls for recognition of a central authority to which existing institutions and agencies agree to submit. Participation means focussing all the scattered, disparate elements into a systemic whole.

For the techno-professionals, on the other hand, participation is not primarily an organizational mechanism. Rather, it involves the creation of a political actor in the system that can alter the distribution of powers. They see participation as political; they are sympathetic to the "citizens," whom they see as potential allies in offsetting the governmental centralization of powers that inevitably threatens their institutional power bases in the regions.

The conflict between the organizational and the political visions was to be fundamental in shaping the evolution of the CLSCs. It involved the relations of domination developing in the organization of health and welfare and the various related symbols affecting professional practices, personnel, ideologies and the client groups. The technocratic faction was in conflict with the techno-professional faction.

The technocrats saw the CLSCs as models of a new kind of health organization and a new way of managing poverty.

The techno-professionals saw them as a potential threat to their autonomy. They thus sought to control the CLSCs and build alliances—more symbolic than real—with the community groups that attempted to oppose the technocrats' strategies for their one-way integration into the organization.

As René Loureau has put it:

"'Participation' refers to and does not distinguish between two kinds of social demands, one of which emanates from the dominant ideology and powers and the other from the social groups in search of power. In the guise of a single strategy for the whole of society taken as a 'community,' it actually contains two strategies. One consists of preserving and improving the established order of things, while the other demands that social groups excluded from power share in or conquer that power."[21]

This, then, was the conflict that shaped the CLSCs right from the start. It underscores their importance as an active instrument for transforming traditional powers and establishing comprehensive social and political control.

Opposition movements to technocratic power

During the first two years of the CLSCs, the ministry attached great importance to the preliminary phases involved in setting up these new establishments. It encouraged public participation and gave "start-up grants" to local groups that assumed responsibility for establishing CLSCs.

Generally speaking, the first steps included a systematic study of the needs in the assigned territory, done by researchers reporting to a provisional board of directors. The board then hired a general director and preliminary working team. It should be noted here that institutions provided for under Bill 65 on health and social service reform (CLSC, CSS, CRSSS, etc.) enjoyed a status of legal autonomy. The institutions were basically governed by an *ad hoc* legislative framework, and by their budgets set by the ministry of social affairs. Thus there were no predetermined hierarchical relations between different levels of establishments; only horizontal contractual relations were acknowledged in the legislation.[22] The institutions had full autonomy in their choice of personnel and in the relations they chose to have with other establishments in the network. This autonomous status encouraged CLSCs to identify and become part of their surrounding community: it also encouraged decision-making by local representatives in the CLSCs. Thus public participation became a reality, for the first two years at least. Responsibility for the development and orientation of these early CLSCs was left in the hands of expert advisers—the "project officers"—from the ministry who had no formal authority over them since at that stage the decisions on orientation and functioning tended to be influenced more by lobbying than by the formal chain of authority.

Using this approach, the ministry launched several pilot projects in disadvantaged urban and rural areas. It decided to give the Outaouais region "saturation" coverage because, in addition to studying how the population took charge of these institutions and adapted to the new facilities, it wanted to evaluate the regional impact of an optimal number of CLSCs on the functioning of all institutions in an integrated network. After all, the CLSCs were supposed to have an impact at two levels: socially, through public participation, especially in "disadvantaged" settings; and organizationally, by adding a new resource to the network—"its only purpose is to relieve overcrowding in the hospital emergency wards."[23]

Thus the first two years of the CLSCs were characterized by their experimental status, the emphasis on participation and local roots for the centres, and the ministry's "hands-off" attitude ("in an effort to not direct, the ministry has gone to extraordinary lengths to refrain from spelling out minimal orientation and content so as to allow the centres to adjust to local realities and needs"[24]). This orientation confirmed that their social impact took precedence over organizational effect. In other words, the problems of social management of the "disadvantaged" and access to health care facilities were a greater priority for the ministry than was the transformation of social and health care production and delivery. The installation of the CLSCs into the general network was of only secondary concern, despite the ministerial statement to the effect that the CLSCs were destined to become the sole point of entry for the new health and social services system.

At this point, one could hypothesize that although the emphasis on disadvantaged areas and under-equipped regions was certainly related to the monopoly capitalist state's function of regulating social inequalities, it also undoubtedly stemmed from its political incapacity to impose its model of social medicine, given the existing balance of power between the new state technocracy and the professionals, particularly doctors—backed, as we will see, by financial and industrial interests. The CLSCs were the symbol and expression of an attempt to break out of an approach to medicine that equated the preservation or recovery of health with receiving health care and medication. In this situation, the state had no real authority; it was itself part of and ultimately dependent on the lobbying game. The fact that, despite what might have been expected from the technocratic reorganization of health, Bill 65 did not institute compulsory interdependence between institutions or a hierarchy of resources based on the level of care, illustrates in my opinion the state's dependence on the professional and economic groups tied to medicine.

Indeed, the medical profession began attacking the CLSCs before they were even set up. It saw them—rightly—as a symbol of what the future might hold for doctors: their integration into the general state-sponsored organization of health services and the loss of their status as professionals and independent entrepreneurs. Although they had objectively benefitted from the establishment of universal health insurance, which had guaranteed them more regular and higher incomes, they were determined to win control of medical services, the key to their continued control of their own working conditions.

As soon as Bill 65 was introduced, the federation of general practitioners (FMOQ) demanded that it include a mechanism to give doctors a way of "influencing the operation of institutions and participating in decisions affecting their organization."[25] Concretely, it proposed the creation of a council of physicians and dentists within the CLSCs and representation for physicians on the boards of directors. If these conditions were met, the FMOQ was "ready to participate actively in the reorganization of health and welfare services."[26] But the specialists' federation (FMSQ—Fédération des médecins spécialistes du Québec) rejected CLSCs outright:

"Our federation believes that these institutions... are not and

247

cannot be the basis for an adequate medical care delivery system in Québec... We strongly state that we believe them to be necessary in disadvantaged urban areas... and in rural areas, on a temporary basis. The kind of medical care we advocate is not the medicine of a local centre, which in our opinion is a mini-medicine—convenient, useful, utilitarian..."[27]

However, it was the FMOQ that was more affected by the proposed CLSCs, because of the general kind of care they would offer. And starting in 1973, the FMOQ opted for a strategy of trying to compete with or forestall the government initiative, asserting that it would itself solve the problems of access and continuous, readily available health care that the CLSCs were to provide. In the fall of 1973, the FMOQ developed a detailed plan for organizing health care delivery by general practitioners in a given region so as to ensure that care was available on a continuous basis around the clock. It began a systematic boycott of the CLSCs, recommending to its members that they refuse to work for them. In February 1974, it launched a major public campaign to strengthen its hand in negotiations with the ministry: "The CLSCs: an adventure to be avoided!" declared the federation's president.

"We will continue to advise physicians to avoid the preposterous situation of becoming institutional employees... the doctor must retain his freedom to treat as he sees fit and a degree of authority that corresponds to his responsibilities."[28]

The president berated the "irresponsibility of a policy that encourages citizens to participate in the administration of CLSCs and to identify their needs."[29] Such remarks reflected the doctors' determination to preserve their prerogatives in matters of medical organization. They combatted the state's attempt to impose a salaried status and conditions of medical practice that might violate their professional autonomy. They also fell back on trade-union unity to oppose the divide-and-conquer tactics of the state, which tried to negotiate individual agreements with doctors to work for CLSCs without recognizing the "union" (i.e. the federation) as the sole bargaining agent in the negotiations.

The FMOQ's attacks were accompanied by a systematic campaign urging its members to set up group practices and private clinics to compete with the public network of CLSCs. With this in mind, the FMOQ took the initiative of drawing up a guide for identifying sectors favourable to the establishment of private clinics throughout Québec. It hired a firm of organizational and development consultants. It also received financial backing from major Canadian banks which, in collaboration with drug companies in the United States and Ontario, declared themselves ready to encourage the development of private medical facilities. The kind of clinic promoted by the FMOQ usually consisted of a single centre offering as wide a range of medical specialties as possible on an outpatient basis. Certain paramedical services (physiotherapy, occupational therapy, nutritional counselling) were often included to parallel the services normally offered by CLSCs and justify the claim that private clinics could provide full integrated services.

The strategy was apparently successful. Private medical clinics sprang up everywhere and by 1977 there were more than 350 of them throughout Québec. The 1500 general practitioners participating in these clinics accounted for more than half of all the general practitioners in the province. By the same date, there were still only 72 CLSCs, not all of them yet in operation, employing a total of 111 doctors and 600 paramedical workers. In the space of just a few years, an entire parallel system of first-line care (basic general care and emergency services) had been developed in Québec. Private clinics were regularly and systematically established in the immediate neighbourhood of most CLSCs.

"The network of private clinics and group practices was developed by borrowing attributes from the CLSCs with regard to first-line care and continues to consolidate its position based on the following modus vivendi: protecting private practice against state infringement of freedom to practise or medical independence."[30]

The confrontation between the state and the doctors signalled the beginning of a new phase for the CLSCs, the doctors' prime target. The state technocracy began to play a much more direct role in determining the orientation of the CLSCs. Although in early 1974 the state still envisaged a gradual integration of doctors into the public organization of health services, when the showdown with them came in the spring of 1974 it was forced to back off and take a much more conciliatory attitude. The FMOQ's strategy had been successful: the federation was recognized as the sole bargaining agent in negotiations with the state and, most important of all, private clinics were implicitly recognized as a basic and valid component of the network of health services. In May 1974 the new Liberal minister, Claude Forget, said:

"I have said on several occasions that... we have no objections to the creation of medical clinics ... It is a development that I have always warmly welcomed... On the other hand, these clinics are not the appropriate solution to all health problems; in particular, it has never been suggested that they can solve the problems of preventive medicine and public health, both major questions... Even if all of Québec were covered by CLSCs, they would only employ part of the medical profession... It is important that medical services be organized as well as possible, in conjunction with or parallel to the CLSCs... If the concept of CLSCs has helped stimulate the organization of medical services in Québec, I think it is to their credit..."[31]

A few days later, he added:

"It is obvious that it takes much longer to set up CLSCs. The private clinics will open before the CLSCs are established, so how are we going to live with them? We will do our best to avoid duplicating services, and perhaps we will try to cooperate with them, or to offer complementary services."[32]

In other words, the Liberal minister had definitively abandoned the original idea of the CLSCs as a tool for reforming the organization of health care and social services. The economic and professional interests of the groups involved had won out over the theoretical models of social medicine and the technocratic goals of rationalizing the organization of services. The state offered very little resistance to private initiatives. On the contrary, it endorsed them with its pragmatic approach, which amounted to agreeing to take a backseat role to the private clinics that were, after all, funded by the state through the health insurance plan. The state was financing its competitors. Seen from a slightly different angle, the reform in health care had succumbed to the liberal logic of the market economy: the most profitable sectors of medical care were to be left in private hands, while the state, through public establishments and in particular the CLSCs, took charge of the unprofitable parts: health care for the disadvantaged and in isolated regions, preventive medicine, public health services.

Once this new power structure in medical care had been

250

confirmed, the FMOQ no longer had any objections to some of its members individually deciding to work for CLSCs, even on a salaried basis.

The medical profession's attack on the CLSCs was paralleled by a political campaign against them. Starting in early 1974, the CLSCs became the target of public criticism by the daily press and some Liberal members of the National Assembly — i.e. from within the very party that had instigated the reform in health and welfare.

Criticism was directed chiefly at the two new kinds of practices promoted by the CLSCs: social medicine, with its consequences for the medical establishment; and community organizing, aimed both at changing the power structures within the organization of health and social services and at creating a new dynamic between the local establishment and the surrounding community.

The press published a number of analyses questioning the validity of the participatory structures and the power struggles that occurred in them between different groups of professionals, particularly doctors and community organizers, as well as between "citizens" and professionals. Most of the articles concluded that the responsibilities of the various partners in these experiments were poorly defined and called for government action to restore order. Others were more alarmist, pointing to the potentially subversive nature of community organizing in the CLSCs. Many of the early CLSCs established in disadvantaged neighbourhoods seemed to be more involved in ideological confrontations than in the delivery of concrete services. Doctors declined to work in them because, they said, they would be the target of steady ideological criticism by the representatives of the "community" sector in particular, more interested in "participating against" than in contributing to the integration of different disciplines. During the same period, the ministry's pilot project in Hochelaga-Maisonneuve was seriously shaken by repeated internal crises: the doctors resigned, accusing the community organizers of systematic manipulation, including manipulation of the board of directors. In the CLSC in the poor lower-town area in Québec City (CLSC de la Basse-Ville), the crisis came when the ministry ignored the recommendations of the board of directors and refused to fund the services provided by "people's lawyers."

In short, each article came to much the same conclusions: the CLSCs were more like a free-for-all among the various interest groups than establishments providing real services. The ministry should intervene to restore order by neutralizing the participation and influence of the political groups that it authorized and by being "realistic"—i.e., toning down the ideology and goals of its medical programmes, which no longer corresponded to the reality of the doctors' organized interests. The ministry should set clear and specific objectives for the CLSCs if they were to provide the public with concrete and identifiable services. The press repeated the line of the organized groups that, led by the doctors, each developed a strategy for the CLSCs consistent with its own narrow interests. They all agreed on a negative assessment of the early experiences with CLSCs and argued that it was therefore necessary to supervise continuing or future experiments with them. They also all made similar criticisms of the participatory structures, denouncing the subversive role of community organizing. Doctors and community organizers became the symbols of antagonistic social interests. Their debates and rhetoric occupied the forefront in the CLSCs, overshadowing the health care and social services provided by the nurses and social workers. All called for state intervention to settle their differences.

In the crisis atmosphere that followed the health and welfare establishment's counter-attack against the technocrats' initiatives, the ruling class developed a new strategy for the CLSCs. This new approach ratified the realignment of powers stemming from legislative decisions but, for lack of political will, failed to impose the thorough changes in social relations in health and welfare that the new ruling class had proudly proclaimed earlier. Its new policy on the CLSCs recognized that it could not control the medical establishment, abandoned the model of social medicine and paved the way for gradually discarding participation and neutralizing community action. Having recognized the powers of medical free enterprise, it confined the CLSCs, as public institutions, to the unprofitable sectors of health care. The ambivalence about the political role of the CLSCs was ended; it became possible to plan their functional integration into the network. The situation in the CLSCs would be normalized and goals defined for them that would complement those of the established network.

This was precisely what the civil servants who had taken charge of the CLSCs had begun to do when the federal health minister formulated his new orientation for health and social service organization. Developed in a context of economic crisis, the new orientation was aimed at improving productivity, thereby finally reducing costs. As we saw earlier, it stressed de-institutionalization, de-specialization and the identification of target groups. As the CLSCs had lost their ideological coherence and their *raison d'être* had been forgotten, they became the choice institutional candidates for implementing the new priorities in health and social service organization.

The major debate on the new role of the CLSCs can be reconstituted and followed thanks to a particularly rich source of information: the minutes of the regular meetings between the top political and administrative officials in the ministry of social affairs and the "project officers," the young civil servants hired by the ministry to help the population "take charge" of the first CLSCs.

The minutes of the regular meetings between these civil servants and the deputy minister detail the main difficulties arising from the establishment of the CLSCs. Invariably, the debate came back in one way or another to the question of the CLSCs' dual orientation: were they an instrument of social development that should encourage participation? or were they an integral part of the network whose main job was to deliver services to the population? or were they both? For most of the project officers, there seemed to be no doubt that it was the first orientation that should be encouraged and that should take precedence over the organization of services. But for the ministry, this orientation might lead the project officers to "identify" with causes that logically result in ideological conflicts and general protests and opposition."[33] Furthermore, "participation should not involve just the disadvantaged; businessmen and professionals should also be involved."[34] At one meeting the minister himself declared that "participation comes after services, not before. Participation

253

is one aspect of the administration of the institutions."[35]

Everyone on the ministry's side insisted that the preliminary work of defining the needs of the local population should be shortened and the delivery of concrete services to the population speeded up. It was the ministry's job to define programmes. The public could be consulted on priorities in implementing different aspects of the programmes, but "more intensive participation is an illusion."[36]

As for the doctors, the deputy minister insisted on the importance of developing "an attitude that encourages doctors to join. People must not always be against doctors and constantly blame them for all the ills of capitalism."[37] On the contrary, efforts had to be made to attract doctors, "by offering them the system of remuneration they prefer" and "avoiding the ideological conflicts that drive them away."[38]

CLSC general directors could be divided into two main tendencies, with some oriented towards community organizing and the others towards an administrative role. The ministry judged that most of them were not suitably qualified for the job they held. It therefore announced that it would be represented on selection committees in the future so as to encourage a "better choice" of candidates. As well, better trained personnel would be attracted by improving the salaries offered to make them competitive with other management positions.

The ministry was increasingly inclined to view the rural CLSCs, which provided services, more favourably than the CLSCs is disadvantaged urban areas, which tended to be characterized by policies of community organizing and participation. "The population wants services, not protests."[39] In the future, CLSCs were to rapidly reach the stage of offering services, so as to ensure a normal size and range of clientele in health and social services. As well, new programmes specifically designed for target groups of clients would be added.

Powers were further centralized in the fall of 1974 with the appointment of a new person in charge of CLSCs for the ministry. The ministry resumed direct responsibility for "special programmes." These became programmes for the major "high-risk" groups and the groups for which the state wanted to develop special techniques to reduce the cost of looking after them (residential care for the aged, for example)—

groups that had been pinpointed by the federal as well as the provincial levels. With the appointment of the new official, relations between the project officers and the ministry changed. The project officers lost their role as privileged spokespersons for experimental CLSCs and became subordinate performers of local tasks for the ministerial decision-makers. The ministry developed a number of technical tools for standardizing the process of establishing CLSCs. CLSCs were more and more clearly identified with a "service" orientation and the project officers lost both their power and their influence.

With the creation of a department of community services in the ministry of social affairs, a standard process for establishing CLSCs was defined, based on the rapid choice of a local director and the immediate delivery of services. There was reduced emphasis on public consultation and participation. Priority programmes were defined. Methods for evaluating the performance of local institutions were designed and implemented. Budgets and the number and kinds of jobs were strictly controlled. Jobs in community organizing were curtailed drastically. The ministry took control of the process for choosing general directors and encouraged the selection of candidates with degrees in administration. Their salaries were raised substantially to correspond to those normally offered elsewhere, thus offering them mobility and attractive career plans. Special training in administration was offered to directors already hired and members of the boards of directors. Certain CLSCs disrupted by internal conflicts were put into trusteeship. The development of new CLSCs was frozen to allow for the implementation of these control mechanisms. And a team of analysts was formed with the mandate of evaluating the existing CLSCs. All these measures were definite signs that the ministry had taken the CLSCs firmly in hand.

The standardization of the CLSCs meant their functional integration into the social affairs network as a complementary resource. The established policies and authorities remained untouched, while the CLSCs became responsible for promoting the new ministerial priorities in the production of services. The development of policies for universal coverage under special programmes placed severe restrictions on the autonomy

255

of local groups of users. At the same time, future growth in the number of CLSCs and their operating costs would tend to encourage more and more detailed planning by the ministry. The local general directors became the key figures in applying programmes, to the detriment of the boards of directors which saw their role reduced to approving orientation determined at higher levels in the ministry or else dealing with strictly internal management problems—more often than not, questions of material resources. Participation was reduced to a question of administrative support and the local level became one of several levels in an integrated system that used a devolution of roles to respond more adequately to certain "basic" needs.

The decision to give integration into the network precedence over community participation sparked internal resistance, giving rise to a generally informal alliance between the different members of the CLSCs. By 1975, many members of the boards of directors, along with general directors initially attracted by the dynamic structure of a relatively unbureaucratic model, community organizers as well as representatives of other professional sectors in the CLSCs and many project officers were all trying to resist the movement towards standardization, fighting to defend the "community" ideal that became the new banner of opposition to the technocratic offensive.

The members of this opposition represented a specific fraction of the new petite bourgeoisie. With backgrounds in social sciences or religious structures, they found themselves in a middle ground between the traditional world of the professionals and liberal capitalist institutions, which they criticized (hence their opposition to both doctors, symbol of the professions, and the bureaucracy), and the new world of the technocratic organization of monopoly capitalism which, as it penetrated the fields of health and welfare, threatened to displace and de-skill them.

Educated in humanist and ethical values to fulfill a specific ideological role in the fields of religion, education, social services and cultural activities, this portion of the petite bourgeoisie was torn. Integration into the technocratic organization was necessary if this group was to survive as a sub-class whose status was linked to its role as a relay of the ruling class and benefit from that status as intermediaries. But the new values promoted by technocratic organization—functional integration, efficiency, rationality—obliged it to modify its ideology. The prospect of subordinate status with which this group was faced prompted it to seek closer ties with the working classes and the disadvantaged and try to establish alliances based on the consensual and integrating ideology of the *community*, defined as a place where "basic solidarities" are built. Thus when a reform designated the local level and disadvantaged social groups as the focus of intervention and created a kind of establishment whose essential role was to mediate social relations between the ruling classes and the dominated classes, it was hardly surprising to find this group within the petite bourgeoisie trying to use this institutional framework as a basis for promoting its autonomous class interests.

For a while the transitional or marginal position of the local institutional level represented by the CLSCs allowed them to reconcile the humanist values of community and participation with technocratic orientations that defined them as "input" in a system of services. But when the larger technocratic organization began to override the relative autonomy of the local level and include it in its overall logic, this class element was directly threatened and had to develop strategies to defend its own positions and interests. This is what happened in May 1975 with the creation of the Fédération des CLSC du Québec (Québec Federation of CLSCs), whose evolution illustrates the initial resistance and then the gradual elimination of this techno-professional group of "community organizers." This is what is analyzed in the next section.

From community resistance to employer: the Fédération des CLSC du Québec

The founding of the Fédération des CLSC du Québec was a direct result of the ministry's decision to take control of CLSC orientation in 1974, a move symbolized by the creation of a "department of community services." The two developments were linked in two contradictory ways. On the one hand,

257

ministerial intervention came at the expense of the community orientation and participatory aspects of the CLSCs. The class element behind these orientations found itself directly threatened and sought to organize its own defence. On the other hand, and more importantly, the ministry wanted greater control over the growing number of CLSCs that were offering more and more services. But since each establishment was an independent legal entity, it could not act directly. The solution was the creation of a federation, representing all CLSCs and defending their interests, that would act as their duly authorized intermediary between the ministry and the CLSCs. A further decisive factor in all this was the centralized negotiations between the government and the unions representing public sector workers. The highly centralized nature of these negotiations required a concerted strategy on the part of all the health and social service establishments funded by the ministry.

The head of "community services" in the ministry decided to encourage the creation of such a federation as part of the process of taking control of the CLSCs. He was ready to finance it by authorizing contributions from each CLSC:

"In the ministry, we count on a federation of CLSCs. We need a channel, we can't communicate with 800 different people... We count on the federation to help us project a new image of the CLSCs... It is essential that the federation be involved throughout this entire process. We will encourage each CLSC to contribute financially to its development. What we want to see above all is everybody working together, cooperating on a common strategy."[40]

When the Federation was officially founded in May 1975, the "participatory" element won a majority of executive positions—a victory that reflected its predominant influence in the CLSCs at the time. In subsequent years, this representation did its best to use the Federation to promote and defend a community orientation. The ministry had hoped the Federation would help integrate the CLSCs into the social affairs network and manage their employees; instead, it found itself confronted with a federation that reopened the debates—and for the ministry, the problems—concerning integration that it wanted to eliminate in the institutions. In developing its strategy of resistance to the technocratic offensive, the Federation counted on a consensual ideology of

258

participation: it tried to bring together the different participants likely to share this ideology around a common project of "community development," regardless of their position in the organization of services. It refused to define itself solely as a federation of general directors or boards of directors. Instead, it encouraged cooperation among everyone involved sharing a common ideology. This strategy ran into a major stumbling block when the ministry confronted the Federation with its role as a representative of employer interests in the centralized negotiations on working conditions for the salaried employees of the CLSCs. At the same time, the Federation was faced with a drive to unionize CLSC workers, initiated in many cases by community groups. The Federation was forced to face up to the structural evidence of the social and technical division of labour that it had previously chosen to overlook but that was nonetheless built into the structures of the CLSCs. It was a hard and probably fatal blow to the participatory strategy.

At its founding convention, the Federation adopted bylaws concerning the membership of its general meeting and board of directors that unmistakably reflected the principles of community participation it intended to defend against the ministry. The emphasis was on user participation, and the new federation did what the ministry had always refused to do: it gave the users majority control. Furthermore, it strove for cooperation between the boards of directors, general directors and employees. The president elected by the first convention was a general director clearly identified with the "participatory" tendency.

The minister of social affairs gave a speech at the founding convention which he began by emphasizing that the creation of the CLSCs was part of the "normal evolution of the social services and health care delivery system."[41] He reiterated the importance of integrating the CLSCs into the social affairs network and noted their innovative and experimental status. These were precisely the points the Federation planned to use in building its strategy to defend the model of community participation against the ministry's plans for integrating the CLSCs into the network. The minister then launched a direct attack on the aspirations for autonomy liable to be articulated in the new federation:

259

"This kind of anti-government dialectic used by some to insinuate that the ministry of social affairs is opposed to the development of the CLSCs seems to me to be patently ridiculous and wrong... I don't think you are expecting excuses from me for the government's control over CLSCs. This control is the normal and inseparable counterpart of our responsibilities, which are challenged much less frequently... The state defines the goals of a programme like the CLSCs and provides the means for carrying them out. The responsibility delegated by the state concerns the way these means are used to achieve the goals... Participation must be seen in this context. Let there be no confusion: participation does not mean that the state abdicates its role; it merely shares it... The proportion in which it is shared can of course be challenged, but not the basic idea."[42]

In the statement of principle adopted by the convention, the participants expressed their disagreement with the minister:

"We fear that CLSC programmes are now drawn up by planners... and no longer stem from the surrounding community, despite the fact that consultation with the public is the most important stage."[43]

The convention as a whole was characterized by a determination to "safeguard the CLSCs' original vision of participation and consultation." Right from the beginning the new federation was on the defensive with the ministry, which seemed to threaten the CLSCs' main strong points, namely their community orientation and especially their relative autonomy. Barely four years after the establishment of the first CLSCs, it was as if these new organizations had succeeded in achieving a partially autonomous status, thereby reproducing the detachment from the network that had characterized all the health and welfare institutions before the reform in social affairs. Yet their original role had been precisely to put an end to this institutional autonomy and include all the institutions in an integrated, functional system. Seen in this way, the ministry's renewed control of the CLSCs corresponded to similar previous moves to integrate more traditional institutions, and the Federation was put in the position of defending institutional acquired rights—making its battle seem curiously corporatist and defensive. But what the Federation was after—at least in its rhetoric—was something actually quite different; for despite the superficial similarities in the issues under attack conditions had in fact

260

changed radically. In the last four years the planned reform had basically met with a series of major failures. Not only had the physicians not been integrated into the new health care system, they had on the contrary managed to improve their bargaining position. The hospitals had done a good job of resisting any attempt to reduce their budgets. The Social Service Centres (CSSs) had by and large allowed the social workers and executives of the old "agencies" to retain and indeed often extend and consolidate their power. Faced with this generalized resistance, the ministry itself had been obliged to make major concessions, going so far (in the case of the general practitioners) as to officially ratify the existing balance of power that it had originally set out to change. The concessions had undeniably put the reform itself into question. The ministry had profoundly modified its strategy, with the result that the CLSCs were in danger of being reduced to a dependent and supplementary role. Proof of this could be seen in the ministry's inclination to assign them the administration of specific health and social programmes for social groups like the aged and the handicapped, where the government hoped to cut costs. Thus the Federation was indeed on the defensive, inasmuch as the CLSCs had achieved relative autonomy for the social vision of a class element that identified with demands for people's participation. But it took the offensive when it challenged the ministry's concentration of powers over the CLSCs, or what it considered to be the unacceptable concessions made to the FMOQ, or the ministry's refusal to let the CLSCs—the institutions primarily concerned—negotiate with the general practitioners.

In October 1975, the Federation held its first regular convention. The question of community organizing was the major theme in all the debates, reflecting its leading role in the strategy to defend the original orientation of the CLSCs. The convention recommended that community organizing be recognized as a distinct service sector within the CLSCs, comparable to the medical sector, enjoying similar resources and equally qualified personnel. The ministry, in contrast, wanted to have only three service sectors (health, social services and administrative support). Ultimately, the effect of the ministry's plan would be to disperse community organizers throughout the different programmes offered by the CLSCs, leading to the elimination of community work.

The convention also discussed the internal organization of work in the CLSCs and its interdisciplinary nature. This was the opportunity for CLSC employees to demand a share in authority and the co-management of the organizations. Unionization had not yet made a serious impact on CLSC employees, and the collaboration of the various parties involved was still taken for granted.

Community organizing, participation and an interdisciplinary approach were for the Federation the distinguishing characteristics of the methods and services offered by the CLSCs, characteristics that defined them differently from medical clinics and social service centres with their unique role and nature.

By early 1976, there was strong pressure on the CLSCs to integrate into the social affairs network. The development of CLSCs and service delivery had to be stepped up; the priority was to establish services where they were lacking, incomplete or poorly coordinated. Local autonomy, participation, prevention, community development and interdisciplinary approaches had been forgotten. Acceptance of the new orientation became a prerequisite for the creation of more CLSCs, and the existing centres were split on how to react: CLSCs more oriented towards the delivery of services were satisfied, while those that tended to favour community work were opposed.

During the same year, the organizing drive succeeded in unionizing the overwhelming majority of CLSC employees. The cohesion not only of the Federation but of the CLSCs themselves *vis-à-vis* the ministry was further undermined. This was also the year the collective agreements covering all public sector employees were renegotiated with the state. CLSC employees participated in these negotiations for the first time, and at the same time the government converted the Federation into a purely management body for negotiations.

The community organizers played such a decisive role in the unionization of CLSC employees that their job was commonly identified with that of union organizing. Above all,

262

they were seen as the leaders of the challenge to management's authority that had so far been exercised informally and with moderation. Implicit collaboration among the various partners in the CLSCs had come to an end.

The president's report to the Federation's second convention in October 1976 was a response to the unionization that had revealed the Federation for the employer it was, putting an end to its strategy of collaboration and of being a participatory model for the CLSCs. He held the community organizers basically responsible for this turn of events, declaring that the CLSCs now had two internal "enemies"— the doctors belonging to the FMOQ and the community organizers. "It isn't the professional corporations that will make the CLSCs a reality, and it won't be a handful of theoreticians that do it either."[44]

Referring to the former, the president pointed out that the FMOQ had signed a collective agreement with the ministry that could well hinder team work in the CLSCs by expanding the privileges of one professional group.[45]

As for the latter, he said:

"Nothing is easier than to sabotage the instrument for change that the CLSCs can be in the name of certain theories of social change ... The struggle for power or opposition to power should not be confused with sharing in power... Our very objectives compel us to work together to find ways of sharing power. At the risk of scandalizing many of you, I invite the unions to join us in this task of renewal: the extremists will exclude themselves."[46]

The president was appealing to the "moderates" to find a new form of collaboration. His speech fitted the logic of a community orientation: "together," ways of sharing power could be found. "It would be too stupid to confront the authorities divided among ourselves. That is what they are hoping for—that we will lock ourselves into the mould of traditional institutions.... If we are to continue to exist in the way we would like to, we have to present a common front."[47] This dual threat of the authorities and the traditional institutions was used to justify the appeal for solidarity.

The process of negotiating the collective agreements had pointed up the division of labour in the CLSCs. The effect was to shatter the community ideal that only a few years earlier had brought together the many different agents in a common project. The conduct of those who we described (in Chapter Four) as the technical petite bourgeoisie, whose functions are to carry out programmes, was hereafter determined by the working relations embedded in the organization rather than by professional ethics or a set of values related to a project. The administrators, the technocratic petite bourgeoisie, were in a structural position of domination which allowed them to pursue their community project. Henceforth, however, this project served to mask the new relations of domination that they administered; for the subordinate employees, it could only be seen as an ideological instrument for achieving new relations of social and political control in the organization.

Many of the general directors, however, and in particular those with a background in social sciences or religious studies rather than administration, were loath to accept their new roles as employers. This was such a serious problem that the director of labour relations for the Federation lectured them on their new role in a document sent out in 1976.[48] He reminded general directors uncertain about their identity and role that however sympathetic they might be to the social and political goals of the unions, they were nonetheless general directors with a responsibility for keeping their administrative role and their private opinions separate.

"Relations between management and the unions in the CLSCs are in a state of confusion... it is important to reach a consensus among the different establishments... During the negotiations we have seen... alliances between the two parties at the local level... ranging from sympathy for union demands to firm stands by boards of directors in favour of one or another of the union demands... However, these alliances were not concerned with working conditions in the establishment; rather, they were concerned with the political aspects of the union position."[49]

General political positions had to be distinguished from negotiations on local working conditions.

"Thus, although the two parties may have similar political or ideological orientations, they nonetheless have fundamentally different roles in terms of labour relations. Unions are interest groups concerned with their members' working conditions[and nothing more] and these interests can easily come into contradiction with the interests of the establishment that the administrator must defend."[50]

264

The Federation explained that the union was using the general directors' ambiguous position. "They are taking advantage of the general directors' confusion about their identity and role."[51] Consequently, it was necessary that "regardless of the general directors' individual management styles, they should all realize that they are inextricably caught up in power relations... the establishments must accept that they are interdependent."[52] If they did not, the result would be that union demands won locally in one place would become the basis for new demands elsewhere—an intolerable situation given that the organizations did not control their revenue. The centralized nature of the negotiations required consensus and absolute unity among the general directors.

Strikes began to occur in the CLSCs in early 1977. The Federation publicly condemned them as illegal, claiming that the union strategy was to "rely on the innovative spirit often manifested by local administrations and above all the 'favourable prejudice' towards unions... that these establishments have always had... to make breakthroughs on matters that in fact have provincial and not just local significance and repercussions."[53] The Federation, which had previously always seen itself as an opponent of the ministry, now supported and actively promoted the state's strategy in handling labour relations with its employees.

The official publication of the Federation observed that "unionization... changes the situation. The cooperative approach that characterized the development of the CLSCs has been replaced by conflicts and power struggles."[54] At the Federation's annual general meeting in June 1979, a resolution aimed at controlling conflicts within the CLSCs was passed: a working committee was set up to "study and suggest a policy on Federation intervention in conflictual situations in local CLSCs."[55] Training in labour relations for Federation members was stressed, along with improvements in the services of expert consultants in this field. The Federation publication now carried regular specialized columns for general directors.

This preoccupation with labour relations and maintaining order in the CLSCs grew in direct proportion to the ministry's continued lack of confidence in the CLSCs. The Federation had clearly become an association of establishments like the others that already existed in the social affairs network, concerned with carving out its margin of manoeuvre in relation to the ministry and preventing direct ministerial interference in individual CLSCs—during a conflict, for example.

The head of the Federation explained:

"Any conflict in one CLSC eventually affects all the CLSCs because of the impact it may have on the public, the network, the government or workers in other CLSCs. For this reason, the Federation cannot remain indifferent to such situations."[56]

The question of a "complementary role" for CLSCs

Despite the Federation's evident desire to fulfill ministerial expectations and integrate the CLSCs into the social affairs network, the latter nonetheless continued to be reproached in scarcely veiled terms by the ministry for their continued interest in autonomy. It was quite clear that the two sides did not agree on the question of the complementary nature of the services offered by the CLSCs and existing establishments.[57]

Ambiguity about the political will to maintain and develop CLSCs was so rampant that the Federation organized a convention in October 1977 to publicly assess the first five years of the CLSCs. Once again the convention was part of the battle to defend and justify the CLSCs. But this time, the ministry had gone one step further in challenging the original vision of the CLSCs. Not only was the dialectical tension between their community role and institutional role resolved once and for all in favour of the latter; but furthermore, all future expansion was compromised by two budget cuts in July 1976 and March 1977. For the Federation, the viability of the CLSCs was at stake. The CLSCs wondered whether they would survive at all.

The history of the CLSCs was basically presented as the history of organizations whose powers were gradually reduced in inverse proportion to their growing degree of integration into the social affairs network. Facilities characterized by social-democratic ideals of community roots, participation and an interdisciplinary approach had become local agencies for implementing the major priority programmes imposed by the central government. Most of the services they offered were simple, non-professional and inexpensive, designed basically either to compensate for the deficiencies of the big existing health care institutions or to contain the larger institutions' tendency towards unlimited spending. The "proper" clientele of the CLSCs was no longer identified on the basis of local needs. Instead, it was defined and identified through central planning, using general social indicators, and on the basis of the state's general economic strategy. These clients could be dealt with by employees who were relatively much less skilled than the certified professionals. These social work assistants, homemakers and community workers were very productive in terms of the services they provided for the amount they were paid.

As one of the Federation documents pointed out, the CLSCs were in the process of being "vulgarized."[58] The decisive structural causes were the importance of the issues and social conflicts involved in the reform of health care and social services, combined with the repercussions of the growing economic crisis in the field of health and welfare. This had led to attempts at more rational and cost-effective organization and stronger central authority over the weaker components of the network. All the Federation could do was ask the government, once again, to "repeat... in favour[of the CLSCs] the same political choice that had guided the reform."[59]

In his closing speech to the convention, the minister of social affairs emphasized his determination to "reaffirm the pre-eminence... of political institutions—including the state—in articulating... national objectives" and the absolute necessity for the CLSCs to "provide services as much as possible and as rapidly as possible, with a view to complementing those offered by other establishments."[60] It was straightforward, unambiguous; there was no more time for "useless debates."

There were numerous channels for a rapid integration of the CLSCs into the network of existing services. By 1977, responsibility for creating new CLSCs had been taken away from the local committees and given to the Regional Health and Social Service Councils (CRSSSs), acting as decentralized branches of the ministry. The CLSCs were also incorporated into the regional administrative committees set up under the authority of the CRSSSs to supervise regional administrative and financial coordination of services. The coordination of preventive health care for defined areas, a responsibility originally confined to the CLSCs, was ultimately placed in the hands of the hospitals' community health departments (DSCs). New CLSCs were to "give services" as rapidly as possible, particularly those belonging to the ministry's priority programmes of care designed to allow the aged and the handicapped to remain at home. In fact, some CLSCs were authorized to limit their services to this one kind of programme in their developing period. CLSC activities were to be quantified and statistics compiled, using certain indices of utilization, impact and performance. Clinical and community practices were coded and quantified for inclusion in the development of an integrated information bank, sponsored by the Federation.

On several occasions the minister reiterated that the CLSCs had to "reject their old dream of being the universal point of entry for all services"[61] and that consequently the CLSCs could only exist "in a perspective of complementary services."[62] For the ministry, this meant that duplication of existing services had to be avoided in establishing CLSC programmes or in setting up new CLSCs. Concretely, new CLSCs were to be established in outlying rural or semi-rural areas where "the lack of facilities and services is felt most seriously." In some cases, they would be combined with existing health facilities to form new "health centres." Furthermore, the CLSCs were to play a complementary role at all three levels of policy orientation in health and social services: "national priorities"; regional analyses of "needs to be met"; and at the local level in supporting and encouraging volunteer initiatives in particular. Defined in this way, their "complementary role" confined the CLSCs to filling in the holes and patching over the gaps in the rest of the network. It is easy to understand why the Federation resolved in May 1978:

"That the Federation oblige all those involved to define their role in terms of the CLSC's specific vocation and to take this vocation into account, so that the CLSCs are no longer seen as the network's stop-gap solution... that the complementary role not result in a loss

268

of identity for the CLSCs or the other agencies and institutions in the network."[63]

The CLSCs pursued their frantic quest for more solid ministerial recognition of their originality and very existence, as well as for greater credibility in the eyes of the public. Their strategy consisted of challenging what they saw as the ministry's eternal hesitation with regard to the CLSCs and their consequent marginalization. They also tried, unsuccessfully, to carve out a market for themselves—to win recognition of a specific role for CLSCs in the many new social policies developed by the government. The ministry used the fact that CLSCs did not cover the entire province to justify excluding them from any significant role in the legislation on occupation health and safety, preferring instead to work through the community health departments (DSCs) in the hospitals. It also excluded them from the field of youth protection, reproaching the CLSCs with "having failed to prove themselves."

There seem to be two complementary reasons why the CLSCs were persistently consigned to a second-class role. We have noted several times that the ministry was faced with the need for budget cuts, which explains its repeated insistence on the importance of reducing the costs of delivering health care and social services, and also of residential care. Two major ways of doing this were through home services for the aged and the handicapped and a renewed interest in volunteer work. Originally, the CLSCs were supposed to actively contribute to both these options, in particular with their comprehensive, preventive and community approach to health and social problems. But resistance from the professional groups, especially doctors (both general practitioners and specialists), as well as from institutional associations like the one representing the hospitals (which had constituted a powerful permanent lobby in the social affairs ministry) had successfully prevented any significant reduction in the cost of delivering services. As a result, the ministry had had to concentrate attempts at cost-cutting in the field of residential care. This was why the CLSCs had been given responsibility for home services—a job they got with no trouble at all because no one else wanted it. The same was true for providing health services in particular in outlying regions where hardly

269

any physicians—and certainly no group practice clinics— were interested in setting up shop.

This helps explain why the ministry was so interested in developing the CLSCs' "complementary role." The CLSCs were very useful facilities to have around for implementing policies designed to correct the consequences of abuses by other establishments. It also helps clarify the minister's public remarks on the CLSCs in October 1980:

> "The CLSCs have become the main pillars of the home services programmes... [they] must adapt to the changing needs of the population... in particular the problems of the aged, the handicapped, in short, the least fortunate members of society... the misfits... The CLSCs should promote volunteer work... readily and eagerly provide information and education to guide the conduct of individuals and groups and facilitate access to government services... encourage them to adopt healthy habits and lifestyles."[64]

Thus the ministry's familiar attitude towards the CLSCs was confirmed once more: they constituted facilities at the ministry's disposal to apply certain cost-cutting policies and play a "complementary role" to existing services, in particular with regard to the most disadvantaged social categories. It was certainly a far cry from the vision of comprehensive social medicine, preventive health programmes and community organizing to mobilize citizens to take charge collectively of the problems in their community. But it was all the ministry was interested in from the CLSCs.

Another part of the minister's speech highlighted his lack of confidence in the CLSCs:

> "The CLSCs have had some difficult years... We soon realized that the work of the CLSCs violated some well-established practices in the fields of health care and social services, ignored certain traditions—for example, concerning leadership in certain sectors of activities—and seemed to be headed towards the creation of a new élite full of zeal and very upsetting and bothersome for many other medical, social and political bodies. We have all matured, though, and in recent years, thanks in particular to the arrival of efficient and rigorous administrators, the CLSCs have been managed in a responsible way."[65]

The message was clear: thanks to good administrators, thanks also to the inclusion of many programmes of concrete services, as the minister added later, the CLSCs were no longer "upsetting" or "bothersome." They had become politically acceptable.

As long as they efficiently fulfill their "complementary role," the CLSCs are more than acceptable; they are a necessity for the ministry. The extension of the CLSCs to cover the entire province could thus be announced as part of a policy of "administrative decentralization" of social and health services in the context of the more general reorganization of the "regional municipalities" (MRC—municipalités régionales de comté).[66] The ministry proposed that Québec be divided into 160 health and social service districts revolving around as many CLSCs, to be established by the mid-1980s.

It is worth emphasizing here how significant a turning-point this is in the ministry's perception of "complementary roles." Previously, the ministry had sought to integrate a supposedly marginal kind of establishment into the social affairs network. Now, faced with a full-blown fiscal crisis, the state has no choice but to reduce the cost of health and social services, and it is this necessity that now defines the CLSCs' complementary role. The CLSCs have been given the heavy responsibility of implementing the new political orientations of services: the gradual disengagement of the state; increasingly structured forms of mutual aid and solidarity; deinstitutionalization and the use of home services to avoid residential care; decentralization of budgetary responsibilities; attempts to provide services by using cheaper sources of labour or even purely volunteer labour. The technocrats put it this way:

"...the completion of the CLSC network has the following objectives:
— to make basic health care and social services accessible to the entire population...
— to meet the most urgent outstanding needs of the social groups most likely... to use costly services like hospitalization, rehabilitation centres or residential care
— to allow needs... to be met more adequately with local resources... by encouraging the public to participate more actively in organizing the services it needs
— to help people remain at home as long as possible...

In terms of preventive care, these same goals signify the two following imperatives: ensuring that the lack of inexpensive services does not force people to resort to more expensive services...

271

[and ensuring that] their capacities do not deteriorate to such a degree that they become eligible for or require specialized services...

These are the orientations increasingly favoured by the ministry with a view to promoting health, 'de-institutionalizing' patients and allowing people to remain at home. They are increasingly shared and promoted by its partners in the social affairs network."[67]

Does this mean that the CLSCs have finally become the "cutting edge" of the reform begun in the early 1970s? Not at all! The concept of complementary roles has been used to reduce the CLSC model to an absurd caricature of its potential for transforming the organization of health and social services. Its "new" legitimacy is the result of a reformulation of the technocratic strategy for controlling services. The socio-political dynamic and interaction between the surrounding community and a bureaucratic system of services has almost completely disappeared; participation has basically been reduced to technical support for the organization. In this sense, it works "against democracy"[68] and this accounts for the users' definite loss of interest in it under these conditions. As well, the whole effort to reduce costs was at the outset of the reform to be the logical result of a complete rethinking and overhaul of the system on the basis of a new vision of health and social development; but the reorganization never really affected the power of the professionals and the traditional institutions that were most responsible for the cost of the system. The budget cuts spared the doctors. In 1982, at the very moment the government was decreeing drastic cuts in jobs and wages for all its employees in the paramedical and social sectors, the doctors were granted substantial raises in their fees. Similarly, budget cuts for the hospitals have been very moderate compared to those imposed on other establishments in the network, and the main result of the cuts has been a further rationalization of work and an increasingly precarious job situation for workers with little protection.

The Federation of CLSCs has condemned—in vain—the continuing predominance of medical and hospital power and the flagrant injustice of the government's budget cuts. In this context of authoritarian state intervention, the CLSCs, acting through their federation, undoubtedly seem to be the organizations in the network most likely to articulate a

272

political criticism of state measures and to protest against the economic and social impact of the cutbacks on the most vulnerable sectors of the population, in particular the aged and young people. But the CLSCs are obviously not radically challenging their own role in the social management of poverty. On the contrary, it seems that the lack of financial resources that lies behind the government strategy of decentralization is paradoxically what will guarantee the expansion and full development of the CLSCs.

Complementary roles, decentralization and reliance on community resources are now the three key concepts in the strategy of the Welfare State in crisis to rid itself of its obligations without challenging the predominant interests in the field of health and social services.[69]

Footnotes

1. Dion, Léon, "L'État, les groupes populaires et la profession médicale," *Le Médecin du Québec*, June 1974, p. 51.
2. Renaud, Marc, "Réforme ou illusion? Une analyse des interventions de l'État québécois dans le domaine de la santé," *Sociologie et Sociétés*, Vol. 9, No. 1, April 1977, p. 149.
3. *Ibid.*
4. Québec National Assembly, *Journal des Débats*, Commission permanente des affaires sociales, July 5, 1971, B—3047.
5. Léonard, J.F., and Hamel, P., "Les Groupes populaires dans la dynamique socio-politique québécoise," *Politique aujourd'hui*, No. 7-8, 1978, p. 156.
6. U.S. Office of Economic Opportunity, *Community Action: The Neighbourhood Center*, Washington, D.C., July 1965. Robert Perlman and David Jones, *Neighbourhood Service Centers*, U.S. Dept. of Health, Education and Welfare, Welfare Administration, Office of Juvenile Deliquency and Youth Development, Washington, D.C., 1967.
7. *Journal des Débats, op. cit.*, June 23, 1971, B—2879-2881.
8. *Ibid.*, October 5, 1971, B—4367ff.
9. *Ibid.*, November 25, 1971, B—5353ff.
10. *Ibid.*, B—5356.

11. *Ibid.*, May 23, 1972, B—1957.
12. *Ibid.*, B—1973.
13. Québec Government, Ministry of Social Affairs, "Le CLSC Hochelaga-Maisonneuve: au départ, la participation," *65 à l'heure*, Québec City, October 1972, p. 11.
14. *Ibid.*, p. 10.
15. *Journal des Débats, op. cit.*, November 15, 1971, B—5092.
16. *Ibid.*, December 2, 1971, B—5441.
17. *Ibid.*, October 5, 1971, B—4373.
18. *Ibid.*, December 17, 1971, B—5978.
19. *Journal des Débats, op. cit.*, Parliamentary debates, December 24, 1971, p. 5769.
20. Godbout, Jacques, et Martin, Nicole, *Participation et innovation: l'implantation des CLSC et les organismes communautaires autonomes*, INRS-Urbanisation, Université du Québec, Montréal, 1974.
21. Loureau, René, "Critique du concept de participation," *Utopie*, No. 2-3, March 1969, p. 89; quoted in Jacques Godbout *et al.*, *op. cit.*, p. 13.
22. Québec National Assembly Act No. 65, section 48, article 87, December 24, 1971.
23. *Journal des Débats, op. cit.*, Commission permanente des affaires sociales, May 14, 1974, B—1702; Claude Forget, minister.
24. *Ibid.*
25. Hamel, G., president of the FMOQ, in *ibid.*, October 5, 1971, B—4353.
26. *Ibid.*, October 5, 1971, B—4352.
27. FMOQ, *Le Médecin du Québec*, editorial in the February 1974 issue.
28. *Ibid.*
29. *La Presse*, February 19, 1974.
30. Beauchamp, Nicole, "Le boom des cliniques," *La Presse*, July 25, 1977, p. A8. See also the articles of July 23, 1977, p. A7; July 27, p. A11; July 28, p. A9; and July 29, p. A8.
31. *Journal des Débats, op. cit.*, May 14, 1974, B—1705-07.
32. *Ibid.*, May 24, 1974, B—1715.
33. Ministry of Social Affairs, Service de l'Action communautaire, *Comptes-rendus des réunions avec les chargés de projet;* unpublished, November 29, 1973.
34. *Ibid.*, March 29, 1974, J. Brunet, deputy minister.
35. *Ibid.*, February 5, 1974, C. Forget, minister.
36. *Ibid.*
37. *Ibid.*, April 8, 1974.

38. *Ibid.*
39. *Ibid.*, April 29, 1974.
40. Ministry of Social Affairs, Guy Dumas, *Conférence aux directeurs généraux des CLSC*, L'Esterel, Québec, February 8, 1975; unpublished.
41. Forget, Claude, minister, *Discours prononcé devant la Fédération des CLSC*, Montréal, May 3, 1975.
42. *Ibid.*, p. 7, 8, 9.
43. Fédération des CLSC du Québec, *Déclaration de principe adoptée au Congrès de fondation de la FCLSCQ*, Montréal, May 4, 1975.
44. FCLSCQ, *Congrès 1976*, President's Report, Montréal, October 1976, p. 8.
45. *Ibid.*, p. 6.
46. *Ibid.*, pp. 11-12.
47. *Ibid.*, pp. 12 and 14.
48. FCLSCQ, *Relations patronales-syndicales dans les CLSC*, Montréal, November 25, 1976.
49. *Ibid.*, pp. 2-3.
50. *Ibid.*, p. 4.
51. *Ibid.*, p. 7.
52. *Ibid.*
53. FCLSCQ., *Réponse aux communiqués de presses des syndicats*, Montréal, February 15, 1977, p. 2.
54. FCLSCQ, "Pour un bilan," *"L'information*, Vol. 1, No. 4, 1977, p. 8.
55. FCLSCQ, *Procès-verbal de l'Assemblée générale annuelle de la FCLSCQ*, June 1, 1979, p. 15.
56. *Ibid.*
57. This section draws on Dorais, Philippe, *L'élite dirigeante québécoise et le nouvel ordre technologique, le cas des CLSC (1976-1980)*, M.A. thesis, Ecole de service social, Université de Montréal, 1981.
58. FCLSCQ, "Les CLSC 5 ans après: pour un bilan," *L'information*, Vol. 1, No. 4, 1977, p. 30.
59. *Ibid.*, p. 32.
60. FCLSCQ, "Rapport du congrès: les CLSC 5 ans après," *L'information*, supplement to Vol. 1, No. 4, p. 23, speech by the minister, Denis Lazure.
61. See the speech by the minister of social affairs, Denis Lazure, at the convention of the FCLSCQ in Québec City in October 1977, and similar remarks by him at the October 1980 convention in Hull.
62. *Ibid.*

63. FCLSCQ, *Procès-verbal de l'Assemblée générale annuelle de la FCLSCQ*, May 1978, pp. 23-24.

64. Speech by the minister of social affairs at the FCLSCQ convention in Hull, October 26, 1980.

65. *Ibid.*

66. *Le réseau des CLSC au Québec: un parachèvement qui s'impose*, policy statement by the ministry of social affairs, Québec City, April 1981.

67. *Ibid.*, pp. 8-9.

68. Godbout, Jacques, *La participation contre la démocratie*, Éditions coopératives Albert Saint-Martin, Montréal, 1983.

69. This strategy is not confined to Québec. In most of the industrialized societies that reformed their systems of services in the 1960s, similar strategies are being developed. The United Kingdom is one example. The Barclay Report *(Social Workers: Their Roles and Tasks*, National Institute for Social Work, Bedford Square Press, 1982) takes stock of the reform in social services that followed the Seebohm Report in 1968 and identifies deprofessionalization, volunteer work, debureaucratization of services, the development of basic services and the integration of services into the local communities as the paths being developed for the future.

By Way of Conclusion

The study of health and welfare reform in Québec presented here has emphasized the role of technocratic ideology. In this sense, it is a study of *one* of the actors in the field. A similar analysis could be undertaken on the roles of the professionals or the unions, etc.. I have not attempted to evaluate the social effectiveness of the technocratic ideology, for example, by analyzing the practical problems which arose when this ideology was translated into daily operation.

Usually, a conclusion provides the reader with an evaluation of the hypotheses and perspectives involved in the study and suggests some general comments on the theoretical questions involved. If I was to conclude in this fashion, however, I would be guilty of generalizing on the basis of a particular viewpoint from which I have studied a *part* of the health and welfare reform. This would have the effect of making the limited and specific nature of state technocratic ideology appear to be universally applicable. In other words, I would be objectively reinforcing the ideological impact of the technocratic social philosophy (even if I have been largely critical of this approach). The end result would be to give credence to this view of the world.

To provide a conclusion to the analyses which seek to prove the internal coherency of the ideological system of the social affairs technocrats would give the impression that their actions *really are* coherent, whereas I have attempted to show how they are fundamentally irrational. In this respect, the CLSCs constitute an eloquent exemple.

To refuse to conclude, then, is, I believe, the best way to keep the terms of analysis open. It is, I hope, a way to emphasize that this study has sought to clarify *some* of the stakes involved in the reforms and to underline the importance of concrete applications and struggles.

WORK AND MADNESS
The Rise of Community Psychiatry

by Diana Ralph

In this meticulously researched and immensely readable book, Diana Ralph takes on the community mental health systems. In a penetrating analysis of the expansion and innovation of mental health practices since the second world war, she argues that these changes have not been simply quantitative but that a qualitative shift has taken place in the definition and treatment of so-called mental health disorders.

These changes cannot be explained by available social theories whether liberal, Marxist or the radical anti-psychiatry approaches. Ralph proposes an alternative "labour theory" which situates the ideological origins of contemporary psychiatric practices within the tradition of industrial psychology and the needs of industrial management for control and regulation of the work force.

Dr. Ralph teaches social work at the University of Regina. She has been involved in a range of progressive issues including trade union and unemployment issues, occupational and environmental health programmes, native people's rights, and women's issues. She has also worked in a large mental health hospital and at counselling and rehabilitation centres.

3981 boul. St-Laurent
Montréal, Québec
H2W 1Y5

Publication date: May 1983
Paperback ISBN: 0-919619-05-3 $12.95
Hardcover ISBN: 0-919619-07-x $22.95
BLACK ROSE BOOKS No. L75

FEMINISM IN CANADA

From Pressure to Politics

edited by
Angela Miles & Geraldine Finn

This collection brings together for the first time the works of Canada's leading feminist scholars. From their different backgrounds in psychology, philosophy, sociology, economics, social work, and the literary arts, the contributors launch a swingeing attack on scientific orthodoxy in research practices and the androcentric biases in Western social thought.

After over a decade and a half of uneasy compromise, women's participation in "male stream" institutions has only served to exaggerate their sense of alienation and the futility of piecemeal reforms. Western institutions, their value systems and their research practices are antithetical to the fundamental concerns of women and do not allow for their articulation. In the world of male competition, pseudo-rationality and aggression, the qualities of caring, trust, emotionality and cooperation are either devalued or ignored.

If feminists are to have any real impact on the world, the rules of the game must be changed. Female values must be prioritized and must become the base line in feminist research and in the wider women's movement.

This is a scholarly book which reaches beyond the academic walls and which seeks an integration of thought and experience, research and politics.

Contributors: Margaret Benston, Marjorie Cohen, Yolande Cohen, Geraldine Finn, Madeleine Gagnon, Patricia Hughes, Helen Levine, Jill McCalla Vickers, Angela Miles, Mary O'Brien, Ruth Pierson, Alison Prentice, Jeri Dawn Wine, Carole Yawney.

315 pages
Paperback ISBN 0-919619-02-9   **$12.95**
Hardcover ISBN 0-919619-00-2   **$22.95**
BLACK ROSE BOOKS No. L74

Closing the Iron Cage

The Scientific Management of Work and Leisure

by Ed Andrew

In a major contribution to the discussion of work and leisure, Prof. Andrew presents an original critique and a persuasive alternative to mainstream sociology. Not satisfied with analysing the limitations of "scientific management" and the contributions of F. W. Taylor on the one hand and technocratic socialism on the other, the author presents a well worked out economic and organisational alternative that could usher in a society based on democratic self-management in and out of the workplace.

"Andrew's dry and charming wit, his ease in mingling linguistic analysis with individual biography and sociological data, his thoughtful and cogent distinctions and his deep concern for his subject make this book well worth reading." — ETHICS

..."represents a refreshing and theoretically important contribution to leisure sociology by successfully challenging many of its basic assumptions." — CONTEMPORARY SOCIOLOGY

205 pages
Paperback ISBN: 0-919619-58-9 $ 9.95
Hardcover ISBN: 0-919619-59-7 $19.95
Sociology / Political Economy

Printed by
the workers of
Editions Marquis, Montmagny, Que.
for
Black Rose Books Ltd.